A Guide
to
Teaching Strings

A Guide to Teaching Strings

Norman Lamb
Sacramento State College

WM. C. BROWN COMPANY PUBLISHERS
Dubuque, Iowa

MUSIC SERIES

Consulting Editor
Frederick W. Westphal
Sacramento State College

Copyright © 1971 by
Wm. C. Brown Company Publishers

ISBN 0–697–03506–9

Library of Congress Catalog Card Number: 75-129532

Fourth Printing, 1974

Printed in the United States of America

Contents

Preface

Essential to the preparation of every instrumental music teacher is an adequate knowledge of and experience with the string instruments. The prospective teacher should, first of all, take a course which covers the pedagogical aspects of string instruction. He should then have some experience playing each of the string instruments and should attempt to become proficient on at least one of them. If possible, he should do extensive work on either the violin or the viola and on either the cello or the bass.

Some time spent playing one of the string instruments in an orchestra will be of great value. This experience will give the "feel" of playing in a string section, and, at the same time, will reveal some of the orchestra techniques which are commonly found in string music. The importance of bowing styles, bow placement, and skill in the use of the positions will become apparent; and the director-to-be will become aware and appreciative of the difficulties involved in playing one of these instruments.

Guide to Teaching Strings is unique in that it includes under one cover practical information which, heretofore, if it was available at all, could be found only by consulting a number of sources. In addition to providing specific and detailed information about each of the string instruments and how to teach them, this book discusses ways to teach these instruments in classes, how to recruit students, how to organize and schedule classes, how to motivate and evaluate pupils. Beginning with a brief history of and introduction to the string instruments, the book then discusses each of the instruments from a general point of view. Then the teaching of each instrument is dealt with separately. These sections include photographs and detailed instructions for the important basic steps of establishing good playing position. Valuable suggestions are made regarding the selection, care, and repair of instruments. And of great importance to the non-string player and string player alike are the chapters on strings and other accessories, information which is generally left to chance.

The contents of *Guide to Teaching Strings* are the product of many years of study, teaching, and performance at the artist level, coupled with a long career as head of the instrumental music program of a city school system. The book is designed to provide the practical knowledge needed by the teacher to be successful. When used in conjunction with a good string method, it should accomplish this aim to a degree not previously possible. *Guide to Teaching Strings* will serve as an excellent text for string methods and instrumental methods courses at the college level and should be on every string teacher's desk as a reference.

In regard to the matter of body, hand, and arm positions in holding the various instruments and bows, the author is very aware that there are many varitions which may be espoused. He is firmly convinced that to think there is "only one correct position" in regard to any of these instruments is to evidence blindness. The manner of holding the instruments and bows suggested in this book has been proven satisfactory. They are not the only way, but they will be found to be practical and should be acceptable.

Assistance in preparing this book has come from many sources. I should like to express my appreciation to Dr. Frederick Westphal for his advice and encouragement; to my teachers, over the years, from whom I have learned what I know; to Robert Comer, musician and photographer, who understood what needed to be done photographically, and achieved such excellent results, and also served as the model with the bass; to Wallace Rushkin who served as the model with the cello, and Tommy Peron, the little boy with the violin; to Leland Long for advice on the cello and Loren Douglas for advice on the bass; to Curt Minard for excellent line drawings; and last, but by no means least, to my wife, Jane, and our children, Karen, Kent, and Susan, for their patience and understanding during the preparation of this book. A special word of appreciation must go to the firm of Scherl and Roth for so graciously making their photographs available to me. Others have helped, and I hereby acknowledge my appreciation to them.

Prologue

The four instruments which will be discussed in this book are the violin, the viola, the cello, and the bass. These four instruments make up the string section of the orchestra. Collectively they are referred to in any of the following ways:

The String Family   The String Quartet
The String Section   The String Instruments
The String Orchestra   The Strings
The String Choir

In the orchestra, as in the string quartet, the violins are divided into two sections—firsts and seconds. Since the full string section of a symphony orchestra comprises nearly two-thirds of the total membership of the orchestra—and hopefully the school orchestra aspires to these proportions—it is extremely important that anyone who contemplates the possibility of directing an orchestra become as knowledgeable as possible of the problems and possibilities of these instruments.

Part I

The simplicity of the design and function of the string instruments tends to be somewhat misleading. The absence of keys, corks, springs, valves, and pads creates the impression that there is little that one needs to know about the workings of these simple wooden boxes with the strings stretched across them.

While it is true that a well constructed, correctly outfitted and adjusted string instrument can give months or even years of relatively carefree service, the details that go into putting an instrument in this condition originally are of the utmost significance and importance.

One of the major deterrents to a string program is poor equipment or good equipment which is in poor condition. Frequently the reason poor equipment is tolerated is that the teacher is not aware of the problems. The aim of chapters 1 through 5 is to provide an understanding and appreciation of the details which must be considered in equipping and adjusting a string instrument properly. If the teacher is aware of what is required for string instruments to function well, and is diligent about keeping them in prime condition, he will have eliminated a prevalent cause of frustration and failure. Chapter 12, Care and Maintenance of the String Instruments, will be very helpful also in indicating the kind of a maintenance program needed to keep equipment in good order.

CHAPTER 1

Introduction
to the String Instruments

Before beginning the study of the practical aspects of string instruction, the student will benefit from this brief history and over-view of the instruments of the string family.[1]

History

Early Ancestors

The string instruments, as we know them, date back to the 16th century. Immediate forerunners were the viols. Still earlier ancestors were the Arabian rebab and rebec (14th-16th centuries). There were two types of viols. The viola da gamba was played on the knee; the viola da braccia was played on the shoulder.

1. This history is not intended to be complete or exhaustive. Any student who is especially interested in this aspect of study need only consult the standard reference books and books on the history of music.

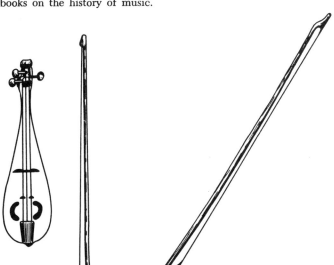
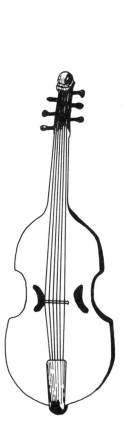
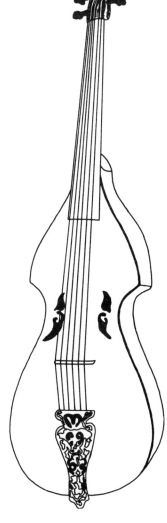

FIGURE 1.1. Left to right: Rebec (14th-16th centuries); Viol (1632); Viola da Gamba (1550).

FIGURE 1.2. A fine old Italian violin.

The various members of the viol family were the bass viol, tenor viol, treble or descant viol, and the double bass viol. Each of the viols had six strings. Another strain which developed concurrently was the viola d'amore and the viola bastarda. These latter instruments had two sets of strings. One set was played with the bow while the other set vibrated in sympathy. The tone of these early instruments was soft and sweet in contrast to the power and brilliance of the string instruments of today. It is likely that the treble viola da braccia became the violin, the alto the viola, and the tenor viola da gamba the cello.

16th Century Italian Violin Makers

The present form of the violin family was developed in Italy in the 16th century by an Italian maker named Gasparo da Salo. Gasparo da Salo and later the Amati family are credited with establishing the design which has been duplicated with only very minor modifications by hundreds of makers since that time. Stradivarius, Guanerius, and Guadagnini, successors to Amati, brought the art of violin making to a point which has never been excelled. Instruments made by these famous and unparalleled craftsmen are in use today and often are valued at many thousands of dollars.

The fine old instruments by such makers as Stradivarius, Guanerius, Guadagnini, and others are regarded as masterpieces. They are breathtaking to look at and to hear. The design of these instruments is a thing of beauty in itself. The curve of the ribs, the slope of the top and back, the elegance of the scroll—each is beautiful in form and shape. Add to this the natural beauty of the woods used, enhanced by varnish of unsurpassed lustre, and one can understand one of the compelling reasons people of wealth seek to acquire the instruments of the masters as they do fine paintings and precious jewels. For from the standpoint of intrinsic value, these instruments are works of art comparable to a painting by da Vinci or a statue by Michelangelo.

These instruments inspire a cult of near worship. The worshipers divide themselves into three groups—the players, the dealers, and the collectors. The players know the instruments in terms of their playing quality; the dealers and the collectors are conversant with the physical characteristics such as model, grain of wood, color of varnish, blemishes, if any, and last but not least value.

The large majority of these fine instruments are catalogued, their location and ownership is known, and their condition, value, and line of ownership is a matter of record.[2] Many of these fine instruments have taken on as nicknames the name of an early prominent owner. A few examples of the names given to certain strads are: "The Hellier," "Betts," "Sarasate," "Rode," to name a few.

Modern Instruments

Fine handmade instruments are produced today in Italy, Germany, France, England, the United States, and some other countries. Some of these instruments are exquisitely made and rival the old masters in tone quality.

Mass Production of Violins

Burgeoning string programs in the public schools in the last thirty years have placed heavy demands upon string instrument suppliers. The need for large numbers of instruments of various sizes at minimal cost has brought about mass production techniques in the manufacture of string instruments—particularly violins.

In mass production techniques much of the work is done by machine. Parts are stamped out or sawed out in quantity; care is not given to graduation or consideration of the grain of the wood. In the factory-made instruments the wood is not always carefully selected or matched; parts do not always fit as they should; and symmetry is often lacking.

These remarks are not meant to imply that all quantity-produced instruments are cheap and tawdry. To the contrary, many production-line instruments are carefully made; good wood is used, and many of the finish details are done by hand by competent craftsmen.

Labels

The maker(s) or manufacturers of a string instrument identify themselves by means of a label which is glued inside the instrument. The label is glued to the back and is visible through the "f" holes.

In the case of a handmade instrument the label usually contains the following information:

The maker's name
The year the instrument was made
The city or town in which the instrument was made
In the case of modern instruments a serial number is not uncommon

Labels in mass-produced instruments generally show the following information:

The name of the shop or firm for which the instrument was made

The name of the maker whose instruments were used as a model
The year the instrument was made
A serial number or model number

The name Stradivarius is placed on the label of many factory or production-line instruments. These labels simply indicate that the instrument is a copy of a model made by Stradivarius. People often become excited when they discover that a violin which has been in their house for many years, (It was passed along to them by a relative, or brought from Europe by some one who used to play), has a label bearing the name Stradivarius. If it were a true "Strad," they would surely have an instrument of considerable value. But there is little likelihood that the instrument is a Stradivarius; since no unaccounted-for Strads have shown up for many years.

Principle of Tone Production

Modern string instruments have four strings. These strings are stretched between the tailpiece and the tuning pegs, and each string is tightened to the tension which produces a given pitch. The hairs of the bow are drawn across the string setting the string into motion. The vibration of the string is carried through the bridge to the top of the instrument and to the back via the sound post. These two members in vibration cause the air contained within and without the instrument to vibrate.

In order for the various parts of the instrument to react and respond as needed to produce an even quality throughout its more than four octave possible range, these parts must be measured and carved to exact proportions. Careful attention must be given to the graduation of the thickness of the wood from side to center and from top and bottom to the center. Careful selection of wood is also important.

Maple is usually used for the back and ribs and pine or spruce for the top. The wood must be properly aged and have the kind of grain needed for the various parts. The varnish must give a lustre to the wood and must be able to withstand the effects of constant handling, perspiration, and rosin.

When the bow is drawn across a string or strings which the fingers of the left hand are not touching, the result is known as playing on the "open string" or "open strings." When a finger is pressed down on

2. Hill and Sons of London, one of the largest dealers in string instruments in the world, claim that Stradivarius made 1116 instruments between 1666 and 1737. Of these, 540 violins, 12 violas, and 50 cellos are known and catalogued. (*Grove's Dictionary of Music and Muscians*, Volume V, p. 154, *Third Edition, The Macmillan Company, 1942*.)

a string, it is said to be "stopping" the string. This process raises the pitch of the string by reducing the length of the string. When one string is played in this manner, the term "single stop" is used to describe the effect. When two strings are played simultaneously, the effect is described as a "double stop."

Use of Strings In the Orchestra

The string choir has an enormous range. Extending from the lowest notes on the bass to the highest notes on the violin, this range spans more than six octaves.

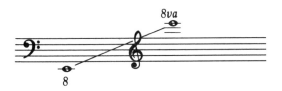

This extensive range, plus the great variety of tonal effects of which the strings are capable, and the nearly limitless number of ways in which they can be divided and combined, has interested and intrigued composers through the centuries. There are many beautful and varied works for string orchestra. In the full orchestra context the strings form the basic foundation of sound to which the woodwinds, brasses, and percussion add color and reinforcement.

In the symphonies of Haydn and Mozart the strings were treated much as if they were a quartet.

Their technical limitations were determined by the extent of musical and technical exploration of that period. The romanticists extended the playing range of each of the instruments and suited the treatment of the string choir and its members to the more advanced demands made by the richer, more opulent texture of their kind of music. Wagner, Strauss, Berlioz, and later Ravel and Debussy, expanded and extended the technical demands made upon the strings. These composers discovered new vistas of color and required the ultimate in technical dexterity from each section of the string choir.

In string writing the violin plays the dominant role to a great extent. It carries the lead, the soprano, the melody. An examination of the symphonies and quartets of Haydn, and Mozart will bear this out. Beethoven and Brahms gave increased importance to the viola and cello, and the more recent composers have placed increasing demands on all of the strings. But it still remains that heaviest demands and greatest musical responsibility lies with the violins. These demands include speed, variety of techniques, and range.

Ranges

In writing for strings the high range limits must be used with care, knowledge, and skill. The extremes should only be used in music intended for performance by accomplished players. For school musicians ranges must be somewhat limited. Beginning, intermediate, and advanced ranges are shown below.

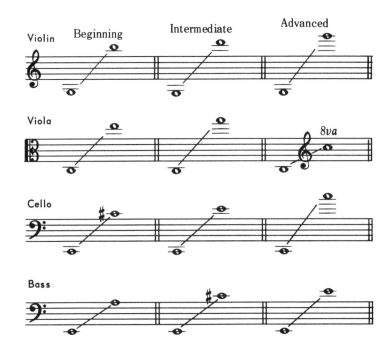

FIGURE 1.3. Bass, Cello, Viola, Violin.

Parts of the String Instruments

The violin, viola, cello, and bass are much alike except for size and a few minor details such as tuning mechanisms and end pins. Each is made of wood, is played with a bow, and employs four strings.

Of the four instruments, the bass differs most in that it retains the sloped shoulders of the viol family. In addition, the back of some basses has an angular rather than a curved construction. It is literally the bass viol.

On the other hand, the violin, viola, and cello look like small and large versions of one another. If seen from a distance, without the benefit of perspective or relationship, they can be mistaken for each other in appearance. This is particularly true of full-size violins and small violas, which are nearly identical in size.

The most important parts of the instruments are described below. The parts are identified in Figures 1.4, 1.5, and 1.6.

Body

The body consists of the top, back, and ribs. Note the points at which body length is measured. The body is the resonating chamber of the instrument. It is this resonating chamber which receives and amplifies the vibrations set up by the strings. Each part of the body vibrates in the tone producing process. It is for this reason that the selection of wood, the manner in which it is graduated, the final design

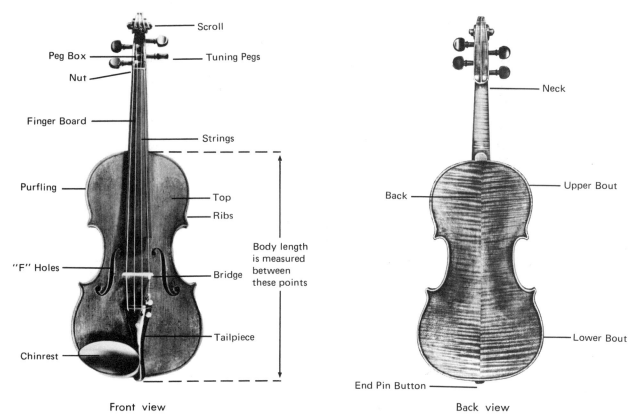

FIGURE 1.4.   Parts of the violin and viola. (Courtesy Roth Violins, Cleveland, Ohio.)

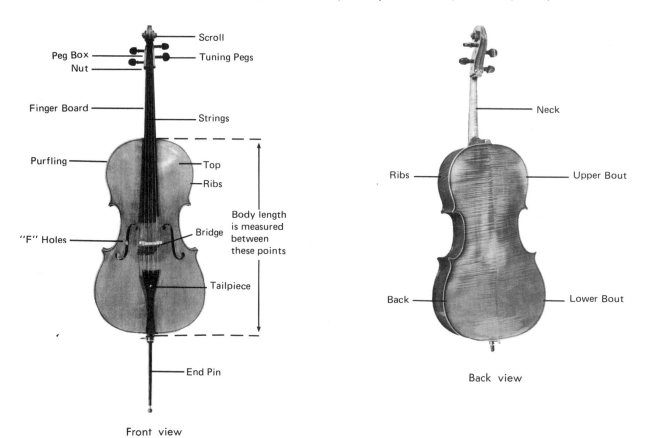

FIGURE 1.5.   Parts of the cello. (Courtesy Roth Violins, Cleveland, Ohio.)

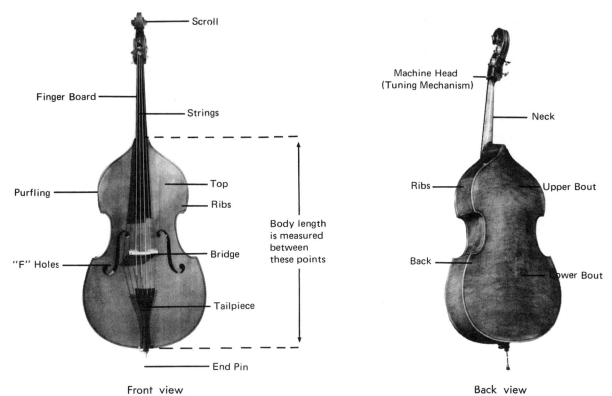

Front view

Back view

FIGURE 1.6. Parts of the bass. (Courtesy Roth Violins, Cleveland, Ohio.)

FIGURE 1.7. Violins: 1/16, 1/8, 1/4 sizes. (Courtesy Roth Violins, Cleveland, Ohio.)

FIGURE 1.8. Violins: 4/4, 3/4, 1/2 sizes. (Courtesy Roth Violins, Cleveland, Ohio.)

Standard   Intermediate   Junior

FIGURE 1.9. Standard, intermediate and junior violas. (Courtesy Roth Violins, Cleveland, Ohio.)

of the instrument, and the varnish which is used to preserve the wood and give it beauty are so important.

It should be pointed out here that with the exception of some basses and cellos which are made of plywood, the wood used in the making of the string instruments is generally maple and spruce. These woods are carefully selected for their grain, strength, and beauty.

Top (Belly, Table)

The top is made of a soft wood such as spruce. It is usually made of two pieces joined in the center. The center of the top is its highest point. It then dips to the outer edges at the top, bottom, and sides.

Just below the center and to each side of the middle, "f" holes are cut. These holes permit the flow of the vibrations from the instrument. The design of the "f" holes has undergone some modification up until the period of the great Italian masters, at which time it became fairly stereotyped. The "f" holes are both beautiful and practical. In addition to acting as air vents, they give access to the interior of the instrument. It is through the "f" holes that the sound post is inserted and set, and the bass bar and other parts of the interior may be examined.

Bass Bar

The bass bar is a long, narrow piece of spruce cut to conform to the curve of the top. It is glued length-wise to the top, left of center, in line with the left foot of the bridge. Its purpose is to reinforce the top of the instrument. It strongly influences the tone quality of the instrument.

Back

The back is made of a hardwood such as maple. Most often two pieces of wood are glued together to form a two-piece back. When the two pieces have been joined, they are then treated like one piece of wood as it is shaped into the back. Occasionally a back is made of one piece of wood.

Purfling

The purfling is a decorative line of inlaid wood which runs around the outline of the violin, close to the edge, on the top and the back. It is made of three very narrow strips of wood, the two outer strips being dyed black. The purfling is laid in a channel. In addition to adding beauty to the instrument, the purfling will prevent cracks from reaching the outer edge of the top or back. In some inexpensive instruments a painted line replaces the inlaid purfling.

Ribs

The ribs are also made of hardwood, usually matching the grain of the back. The ribs are made in six pieces, each about 3/64 inch thick, in the case of the violin.

Blocks and Linings

The top, back, and ribs are glued together with the help of blocks at the four corners of the middle bouts and at the center of the top and bottom of the body. The linings are long, wedge-shaped pieces of soft wood which are glued to the top and bottom edges of the ribs. They provide added gluing surface for the joint between the ribs and the top and back.

Sound Post

The sound post is a dowel made of soft wood which fits vertically between the top and the back of the instrument. It is generally positioned just to the rear of the right foot of the bridge; although the exact location is determined by trial and error. The position of the post has a great deal to do with the tone quality and playing properties of the instrument. The ultimate objective of "adjusting" the sound post is to find the exact spot which produces the optimum tone and response from the instrument. This process requires skill, patience, and a discerning ear.

Neck

The neck is made of maple. It is fastened into the top of the body with the help of a gluing block. Its shape and smoothness are important to the player; for it is the neck upon which the important thumb of the left hand moves about.

Fingerboard

The fingerboard is made of ebony, an extremely hard wood. The fingerboard is fitted and glued to the top of the neck. It provides the surface upon which the strings are pressed down by the fingers of the left hand in the process described as "stopping" the strings.

Nut or Saddle

This is a small piece of ebony which fits across the top end of the fingerboard. It is slightly higher than the fingerboard and is notched for the strings. Its purpose is to position the strings at the correct height above the fingerboard and provide the correct spacing of the strings.

Pegs and Peg Box

The pegs are fitted into holes in the peg box. They are made of ebony or box wood. The strings are inserted into holes in the pegs and are tuned by turning the pegs.

Machine Head

This is the metal, screw-type tuning mechanism which is used almost exclusively on the bass. At one time this type of tuning mechanism was used on the other instruments, but it is unusual to find such instances today.

Scroll

This is the only part of the instrument which is almost completely ornamental. The only practical use which can be attributed to it is that it balances the instrument. The scroll adds to the artistic appearance of the instrument and is a point of great interest and importance to the dealer in fine old instruments. Each maker carves the scroll in his own, personal style; so the scroll becomes a source of valuable information when attempting to identify the maker of an instrument which has no label and has, perhaps, undergone some transformations.

Bridge

The bridge is maple and is cut with a traditionally elaborate design. The feet of the bridge are carved to conform to the top of the instrument. The top is cut to match the curvature of the fingerboard and to position the strings at the desired height above the fingerboard. Notches are made in the top of the bridge to space the strings at the desired distance.

The bridge serves the very important function of carrying the vibrations from the strings to the top of the instrument.

Tailpiece

The tailpiece is made of ebony. The lower ends of the strings are held in the slotted holes in the tailpiece. The tailpiece is fastened to the end pin by a strong loop of gut, nylon, or wire. This anchors the strings to the bottom of the instrument.

End Pin

Violin and Viola

The end pin is a small peg which is inserted into a hole at the base of the instrument. The loop from the tailpiece goes over the end pin, thus anchoring the strings to the bottom of the instrument.

Cello and Bass

The cello and bass end pin serve the same purpose as described above, and, in addition they contain a slot for an adjustable peg. This peg has the capability of regulating the height of the instrument from the floor.

Chinrest

The chinrest is, in the truest sense, an accessory to the violin and viola since it is not an integral part of the instrument's construction. But it is as important to the player as the neck and fingerboard. The chinrest can be made in many shapes and sizes. Its function is to provide a surface which the player can grasp firmly with his chin and jaw. The chinrest is fastened to the bottom of the instrument to the left of the tailpiece by means of a screw-type clamp.

Violin

Violino (Italian)   *Violon* (French)

Geige (German)

The violin is the smallest member of the string family. Being the highest pitched of the four string instruments, it is referred to as the soprano. The violin has four strings which are tuned as follows:

The violin is made in 4/4, 3/4, 1/2, 1/4, 1/8, and 1/16 sizes. The 1/4, 1/8, and 1/16 sizes are less common than the others and are rarely found in schools. The body lengths of each of these sizes is shown below as well as the age span when each size is most commonly used. It should be understood that the age indications are approximations only, since children grow at different rates.[3]

The small instruments have been developed in order that children can begin instruction when they are young. In the case of the child who starts his instruction on one of the smaller instruments, the teacher and parents should be aware of the need

---

3. A method of determining the right size instrument for a child is explained in Chapter Seven.

for successive changes to progressively larger instruments until the full size is reached.

The tone quality of the small size instruments is sometimes disappointing; since the quantity, and usually the quality, of tone diminishes proportionately as the size of the violin becomes smaller. This is attributable to the fact that the resonating chamber is smaller in the smaller instruments.

TABLE 1.1

Violin Measurements

Size	Over-all Length	Body Length	String Length	Typical Age
4/4	23 1/4″	14″	12 3/4″	9-10 adult
3/4	21 2/3″	13 1/8″	11 7/8″-12″	8-11
1/2	20 1/2″	12 3/8″	11 1/8″-11 1/2″	6-10
1/4	18 1/8″	11″	9 1/2″-10″	4-7
1/8	16 1/2″	10″+	9″+	3-5
1/16	15″	10″−	8 1/4″	3-5

String length is measured from the nut to the bridge. The bridge should be centered on the inside notches of the "f" holes. The bridge setting and degree of tilt of the bridge are variables in determining string length.

The small-size instruments are not always carefully fitted and adjusted. This is less true of the 1/2 and 3/4 sizes than it is of the smaller models; since the 1/2 and 3/4 sizes are made and sold in such large numbers and have, therefore, become more standardized. Furthermore the Music Educators National Conference has been influential in establishing minimum specifications for material and workmanship for the 4/4, 3/4, and 1/2 size instruments because it is these sizes which are purchased most frequently by schools.

For the player, the length of the string between the nut and bridge is an extremely important factor; since it is this distance which determines where the fingers must be placed on the strings to produce desired pitches. A string length 1/4 inch longer than normal means the fingers will have to be placed proportionately farther apart to produce accurate intervals.

String length becomes a factor of paramount importance if a player uses two instruments interchangeably. If circumstances compel one to use different instruments on occasion, then it is incumbent upon the player to see that the string length of the instruments is identical; for only then can he expect to be able to execute acceptable intonation. This is important for the experienced player who can compensate for slight differences in instrument size and string length. For the young student it is absolutely vital. For him, satisfactory intonation is enough of a problem without the presence of added obstacles.

Viola

Viola (Italian)   *Alto* (French)

Bratsche (German)

The viola is the alto of the string family. It is pitched a fifth lower than the violin. The basic construction of the viola is identical to that of the violin. The viola is larger than the violin, which accounts for its deeper, richer, more somber tone quality. The viola has four strings which are tuned as follows:

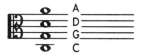

For school purposes violas can be considered to be made in three basic sizes. These are Junior, Intermediate, and Standard. Junior size has a body length of 13 1/4-14 inches, which is about the size of a 4/4 violin. Intermediate size is 14 inches. Standard sizes range from 15 to 16 1/2 inches and larger.[4]

TABLE 1.2

Viola Measurements

Size	Over-all Length	Body Length	String Length	Age When Used
Standard	26 1/4″+	15″-16 1/2″+	14 1/2″±	12-Adult
Intermediate	25 1/4″+	14″	13 3/4″+	11-13
Junior	25″	13 1/4″	13 1/2″	9-11 (or under)

In the artist-model line the design of violas has been subjected to considerable experimentation. The object of this experimentation has been to develop an instrument with the much desired "big" viola sound but which is not uncomfortably large for the player to hold and play. Lionel Tertis, the famous English violist, has been a prime-mover on this front. He was responsible for a viola model which was named after him. With the collaboration of an English maker, Richardson, Tertis designed a viola with narrow shoulders to facilitate playing in the high register, and with greater width in the lower bouts to compensate for the loss of internal air space in the upper section. To gain yet greater inside volume, the ribs were made wider than normal, creating a "thick" appearance.

---

4. Violas are made as large as 17½ inches, but the larger sizes are not recommended for public school use.

FIGURE 1.10.   Cellos: 4/4, 3/4, 1/2 sizes. (Courtesy Roth Violins, Cleveland, Ohio.)

Figure 1.11.   Bass.
(Courtesy Roth Violins, Cleveland, Ohio.)

Figure 1.12.   Bass
mechanical extension.

Violoncello (cello)

Violoncello (Italian)   *Violoncelle* (French)

Violoncell (German)

The cello is the tenor of the string family. Its basic construction is identical to that of the violin and the viola except that the cello has an adjustable end pin. The end pin is a rod which may be extended to a desired length from the bottom end of the cello. It is usually made of steel and has a sharp point. It is adjusted to place the cello at the correct height for the player. The end pin is held in place by a thumb-screw. The pointed end then is placed in a hole in the floor, or in a cello board, or some other device that will prevent the cello from slipping forward.[5]

Cellos are made in several sizes ranging from 4/4 to 1/8. Sizes found most frequently in schools are 4/4, 3/4 and 1/2. Dimensions of these three sizes are given below.

TABLE 1.3

Cello Measurements

Size	Over-all Length	Body Length	String Length	Age When Used
4/4	48 3/4″	30″ + or −	27″ + or −	12-adult
3/4	44 1/2″	27″ +	24 1/2″	10-13
1/2	41 3/4″	25 1/2″	23″	9-11

The cello has four strings which are tuned as follows:

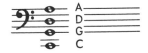

String Bass, Double Bass, Bass

Contrabasso (Italian)   *Contre basse* (French)

Kontrabass (German)

The bass is, as its name implies, the bass of the string family. Its design is different from the other string instruments, but its basic construction and component parts are comparable to those of the cello.

The unique features of the bass are its size and its machine-screw tuning mechanism. This mechanical tuning system makes raising and lowering the pitch of the weighty and large-diameter bass strings a relatively easy matter. Furthermore, when this device is in good condition it virtually guarantees against string slippage.

The bass, like the cello, has an end pin. The purpose of the end pin is to elevate the instrument above the floor to suit the height of the player. The bass is held in a nearly vertical position, but it is still necessary for the end pin to rest securely in a hole in the floor or in a holding device of some kind to prevent slippage.

TABLE 1.4

Bass Measurements

Size	Over-all Length	Body Length	String Length	Age When Used
3/4	71 3/4″	43 3/4″	41 5/16″	11-adult
1/2	65 3/4″	40 1/8″	38″	9-13

The bass has four strings which are tuned as follows:

Note: These strings sound one octave lower than where they are written.

At one time the bass had only three strings. Around the start of the 19th century the three string bass was discarded for the four string bass. Five string basses are to be found occasionally, the fifth string allowing the player to reach notes lower than the bottom "E" which is normally the lowest note on the bass. A more common method of accomplishing this is to install a mechanical device on the "E" string which elongates that string and makes it possible to reach the extra low notes via mechanical fingers. With the mechanical device shown in Figure 1.12 the levers make it possible to play E♭, D, D♭, and C.

---

5. See Figure 4.25 for cello end pins. See Figures 4.26-4.28, for devices to hold end pins in place.

CHAPTER 2

The Bow

Bow

Arco (Italian)   *Archet* (French)

Bogen (German)

Early Bows

The bow, like the instruments it is used with, has undergone a number of changes in reaching its present shape. The bow used with the early viols had an outward curvature in contrast to the inward curvature of the modern bow. These early bows resembled the hunting bow after which they were probably designed.

Because of the straight or outward curvature of the stick, the hair of the viol bow was under less tension than the hair in the modern bow. Being under less tension, it was not able to withstand a great amount of downward pressure upon the string, and consequently was not capable of producing a loud or brilliant tone. In fact, the dynamic range of the viol was limited quite as much by the shape of the bow as by the design of the instrument itself.

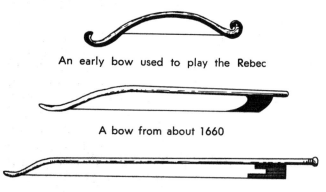

An early bow used to play the Rebec

A bow from about 1660

A bow from 1700

FIGURE 2.1.

The Modern Bow

As the instruments changed and the demands placed upon them changed, the design of the bow had to change too. In its present design the bow has much more strength and spring than its forerunner. It is capable of producing more tone and a wider range of dynamics; although the ability to sustain tone on more than two strings simultaneously has been sacrificed. The present design of the bow was perfected by the French bow maker, Francois Tourte, toward the end of the 18th century.

Violin, viola, and cello bows are similar in appearance. The viola bow is slightly larger in diameter and is slightly longer than the violin bow. The cello bow is larger in diameter and shorter in length than the violin and viola bows.

Bass bows are made in two models—the Butler or German model, and the French model. Each of these models is shown below. The German model bow is held differently than the other bows in that the third and fourth fingers actually extend through the open-

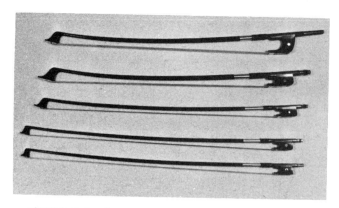

FIGURE 2.2. From top to bottom: German model bass bow, French model bass bow, cello bow, viola bow, violin bow.

ing in the frog, and the first and second fingers are placed along the side of the stick. The French model is similar in appearance to the violin, viola, and cello bows and is held in much the same way as the cello bow. The French model is presently used more extensively than the German model.

Bow Sizes

Bows come in various lengths to match the size of the instrument they are to be used with. A 3/4 violin bow should be used with a 3/4 violin; a 1/2 size cello bow should be used with a 1/2 size cello; other sizes should match accordingly. The lengths of the various bows are shown below. Measurements are from the tip to the end of the screw button. Measurements may vary slightly from those given.

TABLE 2.1

Bow Length

Violin	Inches
4/4	29 1/4
3/4	27
1/2	24 9/16
Viola	
Standard	29 5/8
Intermediate	29 3/16
Junior	27 1/4
Cello	
4/4	28 1/8
3/4	26 7/16
1/2	24 1/4
Bass	
French Model	28 1/16
German Model	30 3/8

Parts of the Bow

The main parts of the bow are pointed out below. These are the parts which are referred to in everyday use.

The Stick

Fine bows are made of pernambuco, a very hard, dense wood which comes from South America. Lesser quality bows are made of rosewood and brazilwood, as it is called. A few years ago a number of student bows were made of metal. These bows produced a very unpleasant tone quality. Fortunately they have nearly completely disappeared from use. Very recently experiments have resulted in a promising bow constructed of fiberglass. This bow has many of the qualities of a conventional wooden bow and is less susceptible to breakage. The fiberglass bow is said to return to its original curvature even after being subjected to exaggerated tension over a long period of time.

The Hair

The best bow hair comes from Siberian horses. Some say the hair is taken from the mane; others say it is taken from the tail. The hair is cut to the correct length and is fitted into the tip and the frog. It can then be tightened and loosened by turning the screw in the frog.

Rosin is applied to the bow hair so that the hair will cause the strings to vibrate when it is drawn across them. Microscopic barbs on the hair hold the rosin and activate the string. The quality of the hair is measured by the smoothness and steadiness with which it functions on the string, and how long it continues to function effectively, that is, before it loses its ability to "grip" the string.

As in the case of the attempt to find substitutes for wood for the stick, recent experiments have been made to find a suitable substitute for horse hair, which is becoming hard to acquire and very costly. Some synthetics have been tried and have been discarded as unsatisfactory. Others are on the market and appear to be comparable to horse hair in their performance.

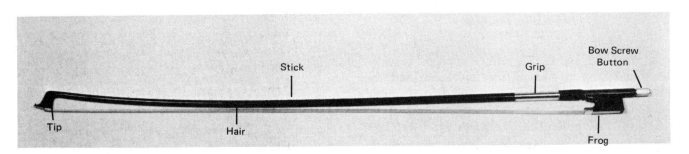

FIGURE 2.3. Parts of the bow. (Courtesy Roth Violins, Cleveland, Ohio.)

18

The Frog

Frogs are made of ebony or other hardwoods; ivory, or tortoise shell. The function of the frog is to hold the hair and, with the help of the screw, tighten and loosen the hair. It also serves as a point against which to brace the thumb of the right hand. The frog must fit snugly onto the bow and must slide freely as the hair is tightened or loosened.

The Grip

The grip provides a slightly raised surface upon which to place the first and second fingers when holding the bow. Some grips are made only of leather which is wrapped around the stick. Other grips begin at the frog with a leather wrapping and then continue with a silver wire or herring bone winding. The thickly wrapped part of the grip provides a secure place for the thumb and second finger to hold the bow. The wire wrapping which extends toward the middle of the bow provides a surface for the first finger to rest upon and protects the wood from wear.

The Screw Button

The screw button is made of metal and ebony, or other matching wood, in better bows, and of wood or plastic in cheaper bows. Turning the screw button tightens and loosens the hair.

Other Parts

Other parts which are essential to the bow, but which are not necessarily part of the vocabulary of the player are:

The slide on which the frog moves
The eyelet into which the screw fits
The wedges which hold the hair in at the tip and frog
The ivory tip which covers the plug, or wedge, and protects the point
The metal sleeve (ferrule) which holds the wedge in at the frog

Tightening the Bow

To tighten the hair (or to tighten the bow, as is more frequently said), the frog is grasped between the thumb and fingers of the left hand, and the screw is turned with the thumb and first finger of the right hand.

There is no prescribed tension to which the bow should be tightened. Each bow has its own peculiarities. The tension of the bow must be suited to the

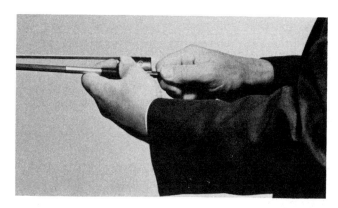

FIGURE 2.4. Correct way to hold the bow when tightening the hair.

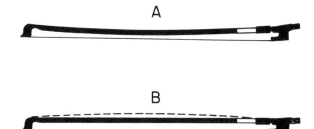

FIGURE 2.5. A. bow correctly tightened: B. bow which has been over-tightened.

player and the instrument. For young players, the general rule may be applied that the bow should be tightened until the hair is about one half inch from the wood at its closest point. This may require from three to five turns of the screw, depending upon the bow. Unless guided, young students will often over-tighten the bow to the point that the stick is straight or even attains an outward curvature.

If the bow is in satisfactory condition—that is, if the stick has its initial curvature—it is never necessary to tighten it to the extent shown in (B) above. In fact, doing so completely removes any semblance of flexibility from the bow and produces what is slurringly referred to as a "club." The hair should always be loosened when the bow is returned to the case. Failure to do this can result in the bow becoming warped or losing its curve.

Rosining the Bow

Rosining the bow properly is a technique which is usually learned by trial and error. Some guidelines for the beginner are quite in order. Profes-

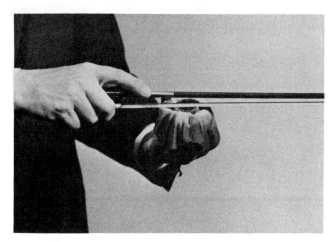

FIGURE 2.6. Correct way to hold the bow when applying rosin.

sionals know that rosin must be applied carefully and in the right amount. Children frequently apply too much rosin, none at all, or apply it too infrequently.

In rosining the bow, the rosin should be held in the left hand, the bow in the right. The first finger of the right hand rests on top of the stick; the remaining fingers grasp the frog. The hair is placed on top of the rosin cake, and the bow is drawn across the rosin from frog to tip and back.

A few back and forth strokes at both the frog and the point produce a small quantity of rosin dust which is distributed the length of the hair as the bow is drawn across the cake. The bow should not be pressed down on the rosin too heavily; this causes excessive friction and will result in too much rosin or in the rosin melting and forming a glaze on the hair. Care should be taken to avoid touching the hair with the fingers; since oil from the skin removes the rosin and leaves a smooth spot on the hair which will not grip the string. The violin, viola, and cello bows are moved in both directions on the rosin, but because the bass rosin is so sticky, the bass bow is drawn across the rosin from the frog to the point only.

How often the bow should be rosined is a question which cannot be answered specifically because of the variables which apply. These variables are: the type of rosin used, the condition of the hair, the way the person plays, and the amount of use the bow is given. A general rule which is fairly reliable is that one rosining is good for approximately an hour of playing.

CHAPTER 3

Selecting Instruments, Bows, and Cases

Quality Categories

String instruments can be grouped roughly into two quality categories—artist and student. It must be understood that these terms are broad and overlapping. Student instruments are available in several grades, and artist instruments range from poor to magnificent.

In overly simplified terms, a student instrument is one intended for use by a person in the beginning stages of development. This could be interpreted to mean students between the ages of nine and fifteen years of age. For the talented student who makes rapid advancement this may mean moving into the artist quality bracket at a relatively early age.

An artist instrument is any instrument which can be rated superior to those instruments generally considered to be of student quality. It will surely be a hand-made instrument. It will have carefully selected wood throughout, and will reflect the artistry of the maker. Grain of the wood and appearance of the varnish will be distinctive.

Selecting An Artist Caliber Instrument

When an accomplished string player sets out to find an instrument for his personal use, he looks for one with the following qualities:

The potential to produce a variety of tone qualities
Even tone quality from string to string
Even tone quality throughout the range of each individual string
Carrying power
Responsiveness to the bow; ease of playing
Freedom from flaws such as wolfs (distortions of tone), loud spots, soft spots

In addition to the above named playing features of the instrument, the physical features looked for are:

Good choice of wood, with good grain
Fine varnish, which brings out the grain of the wood
Fine workmanship, which is apparent from the way the wood is carved and assembled
Correct proportions, and a "right feel" in the hands

Cost is not mentioned here because it is only important in relation to the individual. Good instruments can be purchased for prices ranging from $200.00 to $20,000.00 and more. Therefore, when shopping for an instrument, it is only practical and reasonable to inform the dealer of the price bracket you have established. On this point, if you are inexperienced, it is advisable to discuss with the dealer how you intend to use the instrument—orchestra, chamber music, solo, etc., and whether you are a professional or amateur. The dealer can then advise you as to the quality instrument you should have, what he may have that is suitable, and the price range you should consider.

The artist or collector looks for all of the qualities mentioned and then brings in the added dimension of the instrument's pedigree. Of first importance is the maker. Every maker of any reputation is known and his instruments are a matter of record. The name of the maker is not an absolute indication of quality or price; since every maker passes through various stages of development. But it is a consideration of utmost importance. Then comes the question of whether the instrument has undergone any major repairs such as replaced parts, large cracks, or severe damage. In the case of the extremely rare and valuable instruments, the line of ownership will play an important part; for the reputation and importance of the people who have possessed the instrument is in large measure a determiner of its value.

Selecting An Artist Caliber Bow

To a fine player, the bow is equal in importance to the instrument. It must suit his manner of playing and be satisfactorily matched to his instrument. Bows vary in weight, strength, and balance. When an accomplished string player sets out to find a bow for his personal use, he looks for one with the following qualities:

Weight and balance suited to his manner of playing and to his instrument

Weight distributed so that the bow "clings" to the string in the upper half

The bow bounces easily and produces a satisfactory spiccato

The stick is strong enough to produce a big tone and supple enough for sensitive shadings of tone and volume

In addition to the above named playing features of the bow, the physical features looked for are:

Good choice of wood with good grain

An artistically carved tip

A frog that fits securely on the bow and moves easily in the tightening process

A suitable grip

Absence of splits or breaks [The tip should be examined particularly. This is the delicate part of the bow. If it should become cracked, the value of the bow is severely impaired. In repairing cracks at the tip, repairmen sometimes insert metal pins which alter the balance of the bow.]

Selecting Student Caliber Instruments

For many years there was a wide and very discernible gap between even the best student-grade instrument and a medium quality hand-made instrument. Student (school) instruments were made of poor materials, and workmanship left much to be desired. Student instruments of that era were abominable. They could scarcely be tuned, and would not stay in tune. They were frequently out of alignment, with crooked necks and warped fingerboards. Their tone was something less than poor.

Fortunately this situation has been almost completely corrected as a result of the self-imposed standards of some of the string instrument dealers and

the impetus toward improvement brought about by the "Minimum Standards" adopted some years ago by the Music Educators National Conference.

String instruments are made of wood and glue, and wood cannot be standardized. Consequently it is not possible to make two instruments which will be exactly alike in tone quality. All other things being equal, then, the final selection of an instrument must be based upon its individual tone quality, its response to the bow, its evenness from string to string, and the volume of sound it is capable of producing.

This very individuality of tone quality of each string instrument contributes to the beauty of sound of the string section, blending many different timbres into the several voices of the string choir in the way a choir blends the voices of its members into a unified whole.

Because of the improvements in standards of construction, school orchestra directors and their students no longer need to be frustrated by poorly made, poorly equipped, and poorly adjusted instruments. By dealing with a reputable supplier and insisting upon a satisfactory product, it is possible to obtain quality instruments and avoid the problems of former years.

Instruments furnished by suppliers who conform to the MENC standards quoted on pages 24-26 will be quite satisfactory. If some oversight has produced a flaw in the instrument, these dealers, being reputable, will remedy the complaint.

In spite of quality controls and good intentions on the supplier's part, you, the purchaser, should put every instrument to some kind of a test. If you are in a small system and only a few instruments are purchased, you can probably accomplish this inspection yourself. If a number of schools are involved, and a large number of instruments, ask some experienced teachers to assist.

A systematic approach, with the use of a checklist, will help to assure thoroughness. The instrument, bow, and case should be completely checked. The primary objective, of course, is to make certain that the instrument you put into the student's hands will not present problems over which he has no control. Tuning pegs that slip or cannot be turned, end pins that will not hold where they are set, or bows that cannot be tightened are things to watch for. These faults, and others, can discourage a student, retard progress, interrupt class procedures, and generally cause frustration. Many of these problems develop as instruments are used. Preventing problems from developing is a matter of maintenance. To avoid starting out with such problems is a matter of checking new equipment carefully.

Use of check-lists such as those on pages 27-28 will provide a way to make a careful and thorough examination of instrument, bow, and case. It is recommended that this procedure be followed whether it be for one or one hundred instruments.

Every item on the check-lists can be evaluated objectively. Unfortunately tone and playing qualities cannot be. It follows, then, that instruments must be evaluated and accepted on the basis of objective criteria unless arrangements are made whereby they are hand-picked from the dealer's stock. Even if this latter procedure is followed, the equipment should be scrutinized to determine the degree of compliance with the items on the checklists. For, although it is not common, it is possible for an instrument to produce a beautiful sound but have so many problems that a student cannot handle it readily.

Another point that should be kept in mind on this matter is that young children, generally, find a shiny, new instrument much more attractive than an older one, even though the older one may be superior tonally. This is mentioned because the string teacher frequently finds his program in a competitive situation. With many children the decision to begin (or continue) a string instrument is weighed against one or any combination of the following: band; grades in mathematics, English, social studies; choir; recess; sports; television, and other attractions, ad infinitum. So the appearance of the instrument and the case take on importance out of proportion to what they should. But if a shiny, new violin or cello is what it takes to win a convert, then shiny and new they should be.

All of this is said with full realization that new violins do not stay that way very long and budgets do not allow for replacement as often as it is needed. The alternative is to enforce strict rules in regard to the use of instruments and have them checked, cleaned, and polished by a competent repairman on a regular schedule. This kind of maintenance will extend the youth and life of the instrument as well as its attractiveness.

Purchasing Instruments for Schools

Determining what instruments to buy for school programs, and in what quantity, depends upon several factors. The first is the basic philosophy of the administration regarding the kind of equipment the school should furnish, to whom it should be loaned, for what purpose, and for how long. In regard to this matter there are two extremes.

One point of view is that the school should furnish only the instruments that parents normally would not purchase. The school that follows this line of thinking would limit its inventory to basses in the elementary and junior high schools, the conclusion being that every student should be able to furnish his own instrument by the time he is in senior high school. It is obvious that the success of such a program is completely dependent upon the ability and willingness of parents to spend their money for instruments for their children.

The other point of view is that the school should furnish some instruments. These instruments are for beginners who need a period of experimentation to help them decide what instrument they will stay with. For this purpose, instruments are loaned for a period of six months or one year. At the end of this time the child is expected to make a decision and buy his own instrument.

Schools should furnish string basses at all levels since the purchase of a string bass imposes a hardship upon a family, and furthermore regularly transporting a bass to and from school is a great deal to expect.

Junior and senior high schools should own some instruments in order that students can try instruments in addition to their "main" instrument. Violinists should have the opportunity to become acquainted with the viola, cellists with the bass, etc. The school's basic inventory of instruments also makes it possible for the teacher, with the above mentioned "switching" process, to achieve a complete string section. Violinists can be asked to play viola for a set amount of time. This gives them the experience of playing the viola and, at the same time, fills out the section. Pianists or cellists may be given a stint on the bass for the same reasons.

If a school, or a school system, adopts the policy that it should furnish a basic inventory of instruments, the degree of affluence and the nature of the community must be considered when determining what to purchase. Recommendations in Table 3.1 are for new schools in an average community.

Shop Adjustments

Many school-quality instruments arrive in this country unfinished. They are in a rough, incomplete condition. Putting the finishing touches on these instruments is called "shop adjusting." A "shop adjusted" instrument has had the following things done to it:

1. *Bridge*—precisely fitted, feet graduated, top arched

2. *Soundpost*—scientifically measured as to diameter, height, arch
3. *Pegs*—properly set for string clearance and ease of tuning
4. *Fingerboard*—dressed for correct dip, accurate measurements
5. *Fingerboard nut*—proper height and string spacing
6. *Edges*—checked and glued where necessary
7. *New Strings*—good quality and matched for gauge, correct length
8. *String adjusters*—where needed for metal strings
9. *Tailpiece gut*—correct length, efficiently secured
10. *Chinrest*—new, correctly placed
11. *Instrument*—cleaned and polished
12. *Bow inspected*—stick straight, screw and screw-eye operational, suitable bow grip
13. *End pin*—properly aligned, operational
14. *Machine head*—operational
15. *Case*—good quality and correct fit.

When string instruments are ordered for schools, they are usually ordered as "outfits." An outfit includes the instrument, a bow, and a case. Criteria for instruments have been pointed out. In examining bows the following should be checked:

> The stick
>> Is it straight?
>> Does it have sufficient curve?
>> Is it strong enough?
> The frog
>> Does it conform to the shape of the stick, and does it move easily?
> Does the screw turn easily?
> The hair
>> Is there enough of it?
>> Is it straight?
>> Are there loose hairs at the frog or tip?
>> Can it be tightened and loosened sufficiently?

Cases should be sturdily made of tough material. Hinges and clasps should work easily and be durable. The case should have a carrying strap. The interior should be lined with a soft, durable material, and should contain dependable bow holders and accessory compartments.

On pages 27 and 28 are check lists which can be used in examining new equipment. These lists may also be used for periodic maintenance examinations.

TABLE 3.1

Minimum Number of String Instruments
to Buy for New Schools

Elementary (Enrollment 400)	*Junior High* (Enrollment 1000)	*Senior High* (Enrollment 2000)
Violins	Violins	Violins
4 1/2	6 3/4	10-12 4/4
4 3/4	6 4/4	
Viola	Viola	Viola
2 Junior	4 Intermediate	2 Intermediate
		4 Standard
Cello	Cello	Cello
1 1/2	2 3/4	6 4/4
1 3/4	2 4/4	
Bass	Bass	Bass
1 1/2	2 1/2	4-6 3/4
	2 3/4	

MINIMUM STANDARDS FOR STRINGED INSTRUMENTS IN SCHOOLS

THE String Instruction Committee of the Music Educators National Conference, in cooperation with committee representation from the Music Teachers National Association, the National Association of Schools of Music and the American String Teachers Association, believe that by encouraging the purchase of string instruments and string instrument supplies, which at least meet with the following minimum standards, string instruction and the development of orchestras in the schools can be materially advanced.

Because the "playability" of string instruments depends so much upon proper construction, correct adjustment and alignment, it is hoped these "Minimum Standards for Stringed Instruments in the Schools" will be followed by consumers and teachers and met with by merchants, irrespective of the price bracket in which the instruments happen to fall.

MEASUREMENTS AND TERMINOLOGY OF SIZES

Note: Measurements are given with a "plus or minus (+ or −) sign because instruments of different well-established makers (or even those of the same maker) will vary slightly. It is not the wish of the committee to rule out the many fine instruments that will vary somewhat from the accepted "standards."

A. INSTRUMENT MEASUREMENTS

VIOLIN

Standard (full)	(4/4)	body length 14″	+ or −	(35.56 cm. + or −)
Intermediate	(3/4)	body length 13¼″	+ or −	(33.65 cm. + or −)
Junior	(1/2)	body length 12-7/16″	+ or −	(31.52 cm. + or −)

VIOLA

Standard	(4/4) (large)	body length 16½″ and up	(41.9 cm. and up)
(full)	(4/4)	body length 15¾″ to 16½″	(40.9 cm. to 41.9)
	(4/4) (small)	body length 15″ to 15¾″	(38.1 cm. to 40.9)
Intermediate		body length 14″ + or −	(35.56 cm. + or −)
Junior		body length 13¼″ + or −	(33.65 cm. + or −)

CELLO

Standard (full)	(4/4)	body length 29⅝″	+ or −	(75.3 cm. + or −)
Intermediate	(3/4)	body length 27-5/16″	+ or −	(69.4 cm. + or −)
Junior	(1/2)	body length 25½″	+ or −	(64.77 cm. + or −)

BASS

Standard	(3/4)	body length 43¼″ to 44½″	+ or −	(109.85 cm. to 113 + or −)
String length from fingerboard nut to bridge		41½″ to 43½″	+ or −	(105.4 cm. to 109.85 + or −)
Intermediate	(1/2)	body length 41¼″	+ or −	(104.8 cm. + or −)
String length from fingerboard nut to bridge		38¾″	+ or −	(98.45 cm. + or −)
Junior	(3/8)	body length 36⅝″	+ or −	(93. cm. + or −)
String length from fingerboard nut to bridge		35″	+ or −	(88.9 cm. + or −)

B. BOW LENGTH (from tip to end of screw button)

Note: Bows for use with a particular instrument should be the same proportionate size as the instrument, as follows:

Violin	(4/4)	29¼″	+ or −	(74.3 cm. + or −)
	(3/4)	27″	+ or −	(68.6 cm. + or −)
	(1/2)	24-9/16″	+ or −	(62.4 cm. + or −)
Viola	Standard	29⅝″	+ or −	(75.2 cm. + or −)
	Intermediate	29-3/16″	+ or −	(74.1 cm. + or −)
	Junior	27¼″	+ or −	(69.2 cm. + or −)
Cello	Standard	28⅛″	+ or −	(71.4 cm. + or −)
	Hair length	23¾″	+ or −	(60.3 cm. + or −)
	Intermediate	26-7/16″	+ or −	(67.1 cm. + or −)
	Hair length	22-1/6″	+ or −	(56.2 cm. + or −)
	Junior	24½″	+ or −	(61.6 cm. + or −)
	Hair length	20⅜″	+ or −	(51.8 cm. + or −)
*Bass	French Model	28-1/16″	+ or −	(71.5 cm. + or −)
	Hair length	21-9/16″	+ or −	(57 cm. + or −)
	German (Butler) Model	30⅜″	+ or −	(77.2 cm. + or −)
	Hair length	22-1/16″	+ or −	(56 cm. + or −)

MATERIALS AND CONSTRUCTION

A. INSTRUMENTS

1. Back, sides, scroll and top. Wood preferably seasoned seven years before use for instrument construction.

   a. Back sides and scroll—hard maple preferred. (carved).

   b. Top—spruce preferred (carved).

   c. Plywood approved for cellos and basses, thickness to be approved by committee.

2. Construction

   a. All joints glued tightly and reinforced with four full corner blocks and solid upper and lower blocks, full lining inside of top and back. Inlaid purfling preferred.

   b. All edges glued securely.

   c. All cracks, if any, properly repaired (reinforced and glued).

   d. Inlaid purfling strongly preferred over painted purfling.

   e. Bass bar should be of harder spruce than wood used for top itself. Bass bar must be glued in and not carved out from top wood.

3. Trimmings

   a. Pegs—ebony, rosewood, boxwood or cocobola.

   b. Fingerboard:
      (1) First choice—ebony.
      (2) Second choice—rosewood treated to resist absorption (bass and cello only).

   c. Nut and saddle—ebony preferred.

   d. Tailpiece (copper wire loop accepted for elementary school instruments):
      (1) First choice—ebony.
      (2) Second choice—boxwood.
      (3) Third choice—rosewood (cello and bass only).

   e. Cello and Bass end pin:
      (1) Sturdy, metal adjustable, extra long.
      (2) Set screw, extra large "thumb — first finger" grip area.

4. Varnish

   a. Type—good quality of soft texture (oil type varnish preferred; thick hard glossy finish discouraged).

   b. The neck should not be coated with any finish which will prevent the hand from sliding smoothly.

   Recommended process: Wood surfaced with 00 sandpaper and 00 steel wool. Wood wiped with water-moistened cloth to cause loose fibers to "burr," then again rubbed with 00 steel wool; surfaced again with 00 steel wool and, after a second application of linseed oil, polished with a chamois or wool cloth. (Other processes producing this result acceptable.)

5. Attachments

   a. Chinrest—ebony, boxwood or plastic, suitable size, without sharp edges. Player to have choice to suit his own needs.

   b. Strings—should be good quality fresh strings, properly matched.
      Note: The following are recommended for the majority of instruments in most school situations. Climatic conditions and differences in instruments may suggest some deviation.
      (1) Gauges for gut strings (medium):
      Violin - E steel, with adjuster. (See Item 4 "Tuners" below.)
      single strand .010 (.25 mm.) aluminum wound on steel .011 (.27 mm.)

   A .029 (.73 mm.) gut
   D .034 (.85 mm.) aluminum on gut
   G .032 (.80 mm.) silver on gut

   Viola - A .029 (.73 mm) gut
   D .035 (.87 mm.) gut or aluminum on gut
   G .033 (.82 mm.) silver on gut
   C .045 (.112 mm.) silver on gut

   Cello - A .044 (1.1 mm.) gut(metal smaller)
   D .051 (1.126 mm.) gut (metal smaller)
   .056 (1.35 mm.) aluminum on gut
   G .054 (1.36 mm.) silverplated wire on gut
   .053 (1.4 mm.) silver on gut
   C .074 (1.75 mm.) silverplated wire on gut or silver on gut

   Bass - G .088 (2.20 mm.) gut
   D .114 (2.85 mm.) gut
   A .110 (2.75 mm.) copper or silver (or plated copper) on gut
   E .138 (3.45 mm.) copper or silver (or plated copper) on gut

   Note: Standardization of large gear box in bass is hoped for.

   (2) Metal strings are supplied by manufacturer in balanced sets.

   (3) For general school use, metal strings with tuners (see Item 4 "Tuners" below) approved as follows:

   Violin - E single strand .010 (.25 mm.)
   E aluminum wound on steel .011 (.27 mm.)
   A steel core with chromium or aluminum winding over silk or plastic underlay .017 (.43 mm.)

   Viola - A (same as Violin A) .017 (.43 mm.)
   D (same as Violin A) .024 (.60 mm.)

   Cello - A (same as Violin A) .025 (.625 mm.)
   D (same as Violin A) .036 (.90 mm.)

   (4) Tuners (adjusters):
   Violin-Viola — type which will not tilt tailpiece or mar top of instrument.
   Cello — extra sturdy.

B. BOWS

1. Bow stick.

   a. First choice — Pernambuco, seasoned at least 10 years.

   b. Second choice — metal (aluminum).

   c. Third choice — brazilwood, seasoned at least 10 years.

2. Frogs and tip.

   a. Ebony frog preferred.

   b. Ivory tip preferred; plastic tip acceptable (metal tip acceptable on bass bows).
   Note: Importers and dealers are urged to standardize eyelet threads on all bows.

3. The bow grip.

   Sterling silver wire with thumb leather at lower end and leather ring at upper end preferred. The leather at both ends should be securely glued or shellacked to stick, and wire should be held together by two runs of solder or other appropriate adhesive. In wrapped bow grips, the winding should not be loose. Thumb leather should be of proper length and thickness at upper end.

C. CASES

1. Type — shaped or oblong type. Hard shell ply-

wood with Keratol, leather or other durable covering preferred. Cases must fit the instrument as well as being of proportionate body area. Special attention should be given to viola cases since there are varied sizes within the 4/4 or standard group.

2. Interior.
   a. Lining soft and attractive (plush material preferred).
   b. Bottom and sides well padded.
   c. At least one accessory pocket and two bow holders.
   d. Zipper instrument cover highly desirable.
3. Zipper cover for case desirable, especially in colder climate.
4. Cello and Bass bags—zipper openings preferred. (Cloth or leather between zipper and bouts.)

ADJUSTMENT

A. PEGS
1. Must be properly fitted to give snug fit at both sides of peg box.
2. Must be lubricated with fresh yellow laundry soap, commercial peg soap, or ordinary chalk.

B. FINGERBOARD
1. Must be straight but slightly concave.
2. Must have medium curvature.

C. NUT
1. Height must be that to give small clearance below strings.
2. Over-all spacing of nut (full or standard size) center of string to string:
   Violin E to G 5/8″   (15.6 mm.)
   Viola   A to C 11/16″ (16.9 mm.)
   Cello   A to C 7/8″   (21.5 mm.)
   Bass   G to E 1-3/16″ (29.6 mm.)

D. BRIDGE
1. Curvature.
   a. Same as the curvature of the fingerboard, but slightly higher on the G string side (E string side for bass).
   b. Material — hard maple preferred.
2. Grooves.
   a. Should be made just deep enough to hold the strings in place.
   b. Should be half round in shape and just large enough to accept the string which it is to accommodate.
   c. Ebony or equivalent inlay desirable under metal strings.
3. Height.
   a. Should be high enough to give the following clearance between strings and end of fingerboard (standard or full-sized instruments; smaller instruments slightly less):
   Violin - E 1/8″   (3.12 mm.)
   Violin - G 3/16″ (4.6 mm.)
   Viola - A 3/16″ (4.6 mm.)
   Viola - C 4/16″ (6.25 mm.)
   Cello - A 1/4″   (6.25 mm.)
   Cello - C 5/16″ (6.80 mm.)
   Bass   - G 7/16″ (10.9 mm.)
   Bass   - E 11/16″ (17.17 mm.)
4. Feet must be shaped to fit the instrument top, bridge tilted backward to form right angle between back side of bridge and top of instrument.
5. Unfitted bridge must be cut to medium thickness and tapered to the top thickness as listed below:

Violin - 1/16″ (1.55 mm.)
Viola - 1/16″ (1.55 mm.)
Cello - 3/32″ (2.32 mm.)
Bass   - 3/16″ (4.67 mm.)

6. Proper string spacing at bridge (center of string to center of string), full size (smaller instruments slightly less):
   Violin - 7/16″ (10.9 mm.)
   Viola - 1/2″ (12.5 mm.)
   Cello - 5/8″ (15.6 mm.)
   Bass   - 1-1/8″ (28.1 mm.)
7. Bridge should center on the inner F hole notches.

E. TAILPIECE
1. Gut should be just long enough so that the end of the tailpiece is even with the center of the saddle.
2. Saddle should be high enough so that the tailpiece and ends of tailpiece gut are well in the clear over the top plate. Violin, at least 1/16″ proportionately more for other instruments.

F. SOUND POST
1. Location immediately behind the right foot (1st string side) of the bridge. The distance between the back of the bridge and the front of the sound post should be approximately one-half the thickness of the post (a little more for some instruments).
2. Size:
   Violin - 1/4″ (6.1 mm.) diameter
   Viola - 1/4″ (6.1 mm.) diameter
   Cello - 7/16″ (10.9 mm.) diameter
   Bass   - 11/16″ (17.1 mm.) diameter
3. Fitting — must fit snugly (but never glued), ends beveled to fit flush with top and back.

G. BOW
1. When the frog is in full forward position, the hair should be relaxed (not loose) and the opposite test should also apply in tightening the bow screw.
2. The hair should be "sighted down" to make sure there are no crossed hairs.
3. The stick (tightened 1½ or 2 rounds for playing) should be "sighted down" to see that it is straight.
4. The frog should seat firmly on the bow, not rock from side to side.
5. The bow screw should work smoothly.
6. The bow grip should be properly attached. (See Item 3 under "Bow Materials").

MISCELLANEOUS

(Direction sheet for Care of Instruments)

A. Keep bow and instrument in case when not in use.
B. Keep bow hair always under slight tension. To use, tighten bow screw only about two (+ or −) rounds.
C. Leave strings always tuned up to pitch.
D. Wipe rosin dust from instrument top and bow stick after playing.
E. Never leave an instrument near a radiator or in a cold room.
F. Do not allow anyone except your teacher to handle your instrument.
G. Have your teacher check frequently for cracks, bridge adjustment, buzzes, etc.
H. Keep case latched (but not locked with the key) when instrument is not in use.
   (Excellent literature on the care of the instrument has been published by leading stringed instrument dealers.)

CHECK SHEET FOR NEW STRING INSTRUMENTS
Note: If an item is checked as satisfactory, none of the
discrepancies listed is found to be present.

Instrument

Strings
_____ Satisfactory
_____ Poor quality (   )
_____ Wrong length (   )
_____ Loose wrapping (   )
_____ False (   )

Fingerboard
_____ Satisfactory
_____ Uneven
_____ Warped
_____ Too low
_____ Too high

Bridge
_____ Satisfactory
_____ Too low
_____ Too high
_____ Notches too shallow
_____ Notches too deep
_____ Notches incorrectly spaced
_____ Feet too thick
_____ Feet do not conform to top
_____ Warped

Pegs
_____ Satisfactory
_____ Too tight
_____ Slip
_____ Too long
_____ Too short
_____ Do not conform to holes in peg box
_____ String hole too far to left or right

Tuners
_____ Satisfactory
_____ Wrong size
_____ Thumb screw hard to turn

Tail Gut (Wire on Bass)
_____ Satisfactory
_____ Too long
_____ Too short

Neck
_____ Satisfactory
_____ Improper alignment
_____ Rough or sticky

Glue Joints
_____ Satisfactory
_____ Seams open (   )
_____ Neck loose
_____ Fingerboard loose

End Pin (Cello and Bass)
_____ Satisfactory
_____ Improper fit
_____ Set screw hard to turn
_____ Set screw does not hold
_____ No device on peg to prevent it from slipping
_____ into instrument

Machine Head (Bass)
_____ Satisfactory
_____ Not screwed tightly to scroll

Bow

Wood
_____ Satisfactory
_____ Insufficient arc
_____ Lacks strength

Hair
_____ Satisfactory
_____ Too sparse
_____ Too long
_____ Too short
_____ Large number of hairs crossed or broken
_____ Hair loose at frog or tip

Frog
_____ Satisfactory
_____ Does not conform to stick
_____ Too large
_____ Too small
_____ Loose, wobbles
_____ Eyelet improperly adjusted
_____ Frog movement stiff
_____ Gap between frog and stick

Screw (Button)
_____ Satisfactory
_____ Hard to turn
_____ Threads stripped
_____ Threads do not match eyelet
_____ Head loose or off center

Tip
_____ Satisfactory
_____ Loose
_____ Incorrect fit

Violin and Viola Cases

Fit
_____ Satisfactory
_____ Too small for instrument
_____ Too large for instrument

Hinges, Snaps, Lock, etc.
_____ Satisfactory
_____ Poor quality
_____ Too light
_____ Snaps do not hold tight
_____ Top does not close properly

Outer Cover
_____ Satisfactory
_____ Not durable
_____ Not well glued

Lining
_____ Satisfactory
_____ Not durable
_____ Not well glued

Fittings
_____ Satisfactory
_____ Compartments not securely glued
_____ Bow-holders weak

Cello and Bass Bags

Fit
_____ Satisfactory
_____ Too large
_____ Too small

Material
_____ Satisfactory
_____ Too light-weight
_____ Not well sewn
_____ Seams not bound

Snaps or Zipper
_____ Satisfactory
_____ Hard to work
_____ Snaps do not hold

Bow and Music Compartments
_____ Satisfactory
_____ Poorly stitched
_____ No fasteners

CHAPTER 4

Accessories

The string instruments are, by their nature, rather awkward to play, particularly the violin and viola which call for a highly unnatural position of the left arm. Also, the cello demands exaggerated movement of the left arm, and the bass is ungainly and cumbersome, to say the least. To compensate for the physical problems which these instruments present, players, over the years, have invented numerous devices whose aim is to help the player. In time many of these accessories have become accepted as necessities. Included in this category are such items as shoulder pads, tuners, bow grips, and cello end pins. There are few players today who do not regard some of these accessories, in one form or another, as essential.

Of the accessories which will be discussed, only one, the mute, was designed deliberately to affect the tone of the instrument. All other accessories have to do with the mechanics of holding or playing the instrument, or with some aspect of the physical make-up of the instrument itself.

Some players argue that the type of shoulder pad used affects the tone of the violin and that the kind of end pin used influences the tone of the cello. The point made in regard to the shoulder pad is that if the shoulder or the pad is allowed to come into contact with the back of the violin or viola, the vibration of the back of the instrument may be somewhat reduced. For this reason a number of shoulder pads have been invented which keep the back of the violin completely clear of any contact, the feet of the pad, or rest, bearing only on the extreme edges of the instrument. The point made in the case of the end pin is that some of the vibrations set up by the instrument are carried through the end pin to the floor, or stand, upon which the player is seated, thus enhancing the quality and quantity of sound produced by the instrument.

It must be kept in mind that accessories come and go, and that new devices are continually appearing. Many are an improvement over their predecessor and may offer increased playing ease to the player, but each must be examined with an eye to utility, quality, and cost.

Chinrests

Purpose

Chinrests are used on violins and violas. The purpose of the chinrest is to provide an elevated, concave area which the player can grasp firmly with his chin and/or jaw. Chinrests are made in a great variety of shapes and sizes to accommodate the many shapes and sizes of chins.

Before the invention of the chinrest, players simply grasped the violin between the shoulder and the chin, without the aid of a chinrest. This was unsatisfactory for two reasons. First, there is only the slightest rise at the outer edge of the violin and viola; thus providing very little for the player to get ahold of with his chin. Secondly, without a chinrest, the top of the instrument was subjected to extreme wear from the constant rubbing of the male player's whiskers. Some fine old instruments were worn through in the chinrest area as a result of excessive use without the protection of a chinrest.

Types of Chinrests

The cheaper chinrests are made of plastic. Better ones are made of wood. Some go across the tail-piece. Others are positioned in the middle of the instrument. But the majority of chinrests are positioned to the left of the tail-piece. An assortment of chinrests is pictured below.

Selection of a Chinrest

The comfort and security of the player are the first things to consider when selecting a chinrest. A person with a long neck may find one of the higher chinrests desirable and vice versa. A square-jawed person may find the flatter type chinrest more comfortable than the deep-cupped type. Color of wood used in the chinrest can be another factor in selection. The best way to find a satisfactory chinrest is to go to a dealer or repairman who has a variety of chinrests to choose from. By trying one after another one will find the one best suited to his physical make-up and way of holding the instrument.

The Problem of Skin Irritation

There is constant friction between the chinrest, the base of the violin or viola, and the player's neck and chin. Many players, particularly men, have extreme difficulty with irritation of the skin in this area. The degree of the problem depends upon the nature of the individual's skin, the amount of pressure used to hold the instrument, temperature, and climate. To counteract this skin problem, some players have experimented with sponge-rubber pads glued to the chinrest. Others have experimented with chamois covers. Both of these latter devices are intended to protect the skin on the neck. A clean cloth, such as a handkerchief, placed between the neck and the instrument, can also do much to reduce the cause of skin irritation.

Clamping the Chinrest on the Instrument

The chinrest is clamped onto the instrument by two threaded sleeves which fit over two oppositely threaded projections, one from the chinrest itself, and one from the foot, or clamp. This portion of the chinrest is shown in Figure 4.2. To secure the chin-

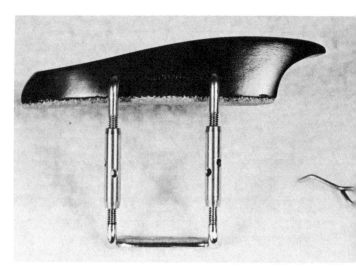

FIGURE 4.2. Back view of chinrest.

rest to the instrument, a small nail or a chinrest key is inserted into the hole in one of the chinrest sleeves. By tightening one and then the other of these sleeves, the chinrest can be secured firmly to the instrument. Caution should be used when inserting the chinrest key or any other metal tightening device to avoid damaging the wood.

Care

The chinrest requires little care. It should be cleaned occasionally with soap and water, and the screw sleeves should be checked occasionally to see that they are tight.

Shoulder Pads

Purpose

The purpose of the shoulder pad is to fill the space between the top of the left shoulder and the back of the violin or viola. Its effect is to reduce or eliminate the need to elevate the left shoulder. It provides a non-slippery surface against which the shoulder can press in the holding process. (It is the upward pressure of the shoulder and the downward pressure of the chin which hold the instrument, with the help of the left hand.)

Types of Shoulder Pads

Shoulder pads range from the simplicity of the turned back lapel, as used by the late Fritz Kreisler, to the relatively more complex "Resonans" and "Menuhin" types. There are probably a dozen different shoulder pads available. Four are shown below.

FIGURE 4.1. A variety of chinrests. (Courtesy Roth Violins, Cleveland, Ohio.)

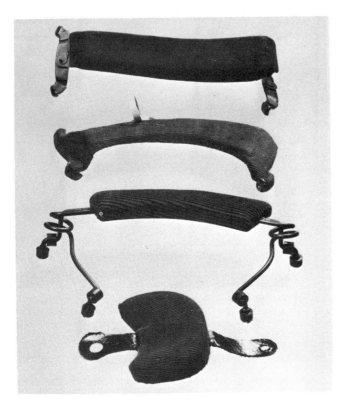

FIGURE 4.3. Shoulder pads: from top to bottom, Resonans, Kolitsch, Menuhin, Poehland model C. (Courtesy Roth Violins, Cleveland, Ohio.)

RESONANS

This pad has a metal cross-bar covered with velvet. Rubber covered feet clamp onto the edges of the instrument. These feet fold flat for easier storage of the pad in the case. The feet may be bent inward or outward to fit instruments of different widths. Position of the pad on the instrument can be adjusted. The pad is made in three sizes—low, medium, and high. The viola model can be adjusted for width.

KOLITSCH

This pad has a metal or plastic form covered with corduroy. Rubber covered feet fit over the edges of the instrument. A rubber band stretches over the corner of the bout to hold the pad on the instrument. The position of the pad on the instrument can be adjusted.

MENUHIN

This is a corduroy covered pad mounted on spring steel. The legs can be bent to fit instruments of different widths. The feet are covered with rubber tips to protect the instrument.

POEHLAND MODEL C

This pad is crescent shaped and concave. It is made of sponge rubber covered with velveteen or corduroy. It attaches to the end pin and the rubber band loops over the corner of the bout. The position of the pad can be adjusted by sliding it along the strap.

There are other pads, but they are variations of those described above. Pads listed range in price from $1.00 to $5.00.

Care

About the only care required by shoulder pads is that the rubber which covers the feet be replaced occasionally. This rubber deteriorates and rots off leaving the metal feet bare. In this condition they can mar the varnish on the ribs and back of the instrument. Also the rubber bands will have to be replaced occasionally.

Rosin

Rosin is hardened pitch from which the turpentine has been distilled. It is available in several qualities and at least two shapes—round and oblong.

Purpose

Rosin is rubbed onto the bow hair to make the hair sticky enough to grip the string and set it into vibration. The hair does not have sufficient gripping power to do this by itself, a fact which is immediately evident if one draws a newly rehaired bow, which has not been rosined, over the string. Little or no sound will be produced, and until the bow has been well rosined, it will not produce a steady tone. After rehairing a bow, repairmen usually apply a liberal amount of powdered rosin to the hair. If powdered rosin is not used, extensive use of cake rosin will be needed to make the bow grip the string consistently. Rosin has been brought out recently in liquid form. It is used in this form by some repairmen in place of powdered rosin. No evaluation of this product is available.

Shapes of Rosin Cakes

Rosin is generally made in either round or oblong cakes. The round cake usually has a protective cloth cover which keeps the fingers out of contact with the rosin and protects the cake. The oblong cake usually has a wood or cork outer cover which keeps the fingers off the rosin and also helps to prevent the cake from being completely demolished if it is dropped to the floor.

FIGURE 4.4. Rosin in oblong and round cakes and powdered rosin. (Courtesy Roth Violins, Cleveland, Ohio.)

FIGURE 4.5. Tuning pegs. (Courtesy Roth Violins, Cleveland, Ohio.)

Qualities of Rosin

The variation in rosins lies in the coarseness of the grit which they dispel to the bow hair. A good rosin gives the bow the ability to "grab" the string without being rough or coarse.

Cello rosin is softer and more coarse than violin rosin. Bass rosin is gummy in consistency. It is made in several degrees of hardness.

Rosin will melt or become soft if subjected to too much heat. And since rosins come in varying degrees of hardness, it follows that a soft rosin may be used in cool climates but may not be satisfactory in warm climates.

The choice of rosin finally rests with the player. He must experiment until he finds a type which suits him, his bow, and his instrument.

Tuning Pegs

The tuning pegs are the four wooden pegs which are located in the peg box at the top of the instrument.

Purpose

Tuning pegs, as the name implies, are used by the performer to tune the strings. Except for the bass, which uses a machine head, standard tuning pegs for the string instruments are made of hardwood such as ebony, rosewood, or boxwood. The string is inserted through a hole in the peg, and then by turning the peg one way or the other, the string is raised or lowered in pitch.

FIGURE 4.6. Pegs and peg box. (Courtesy Roth Violins, Cleveland, Ohio.)

The primary requirements of the peg are that it turn easily and smoothly, that it may be "set" at any of the infinitesimal number of points in its circle, and that it will stay, or hold, wherever it is set.

For a peg to meet the demands listed, it must be perfectly matched to the holes in the peg box, a condition not always found in instruments after a period of use. Pegs are tapered and peg holes are bored conically to match the taper of the peg. The taper is what makes it possible to set the peg so that it will not turn. By forcing the peg inward as it is turned, it is possible to set the peg very tightly.

Care

If pegs are in good condition, there is no need to do anything to them between string changes. By applying a small amount of peg compound to a peg when a string is changed, it should continue to function well indefinitely.

Poor quality pegs, or pegs that are not properly fitted to the instrument, will cause trouble until the basic problem is corrected by a competent repairman. No amount of peg compound, chalk, or rosin will make them work smoothly and hold.

Peg Compound, Peg Soap, Peg Dope

Peg Compound is also called Peg Soap or Peg Dope. The individual products may appear to be different, but they are all basically the same. They consist of an abrasive substance mixed with jewelers rouge. A light coating on the peg lubricates the peg at the same time that it provides a gritty, holding quality.

Pegs can become worn or peg holes enlarged to the point that the peg no longer fits the peg hole. The result is that the peg no longer turns smoothly and it becomes difficult to set the peg so that it will not slip. In many cases an application of Peg Compound will solve the problem. More severe problems of slipping or sticking require the attention of the repairman, who may find it necessary to ream the holes and reshape or replace the pegs. This is not a job for the layman.

Patent Pegs

Any peg which incorporates a screw or other mechanical device is classified under the heading "Patent Peg." There are a number of patent pegs on the market, some of which are described below.

Purpose

All of the patent pegs have a common aim and purpose—to make it easier to tune the instrument.

The two main reasons patent pegs have been developed are (1) young players have difficulty setting pegs so that they will not slip; (2) good peg action is a quality which is not invariably present in school-grade instruments.

The beauty of the patent peg is that it can function perfectly despite the condition of the peg box; for patent pegs are designed to act independently of the peg hole into which they are inserted. They supply their own bushings and their own holding tension. They should be installed by a skilled repairman. Breakage and mechanical defects can occur, but they are infrequent.

Types

ROTH-CASPARI PEGS[1]

The Roth-Caspari pegs look from a distance like ordinary pegs. They are distinguished by a screw which is located in the center of the knob. The ease with which the peg turns is regulated by this screw. The action of the peg is tightened by turning the screw to the right and eased by turning the screw to the left.

These pegs are available for 1/2, 3/4, and 4/4 sized violins, for viola, and for 1/2 and 3/4 sized cellos. They can be purchased from music dealers or repairmen. They should be fitted to the instrument by a repairman.

FIGURE 4.7. Roth-Caspari pegs. (Courtesy Roth Violins, Cleveland, Ohio.)

1. (The name Roth-Caspari is registered at the U.S. patent office, all rights reserved.)

SCHALLER PEGS

"S" (Schaller) Pegs are available for violin, viola, and cello. This peg is made of plastic and has a tension regulating device similar to the Roth-Caspari. They are available for 1/2, 3/4, and 4/4 sized violins, for viola, and 3/4 and 4/4 sized cellos.

ROTH-DE JACQUES PEGS

The Roth-De Jacques peg is made of plastic and has screw-type tension regulators. This peg is made for violin, viola, and cello and in various sizes.

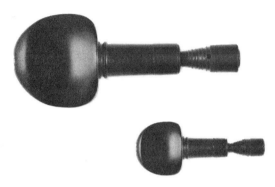

FIGURE 4.8. Roth-De Jacques pegs. (Courtesy Roth Violins, Cleveland, Ohio.)

Recommendations

Patent pegs are strongly recommended for the intermediate grade instrument which is equipped with gut and gut-wound strings. The fingers of the student at this stage of development are usually not yet strong enough or well enough coordinated to turn and firmly set an ordinary peg. The slipping which results is a cause of great frustration to both student and teacher. Patent pegs can remove this source of frustration.

Tuners or Adjusters

A tuner is a small metal device consisting of a thumb screw and a hook over which the end of the string is looped. Tuners are fastened to the tailpiece by inserting the threaded sleeve through the appropriate hole at the wide end of the tailpiece and securing it with the round nut which is part of the tuner. Tuners are used on violins, violas, and cellos. By turning the thumb screw to the right the pitch of the string is raised. By turning it to the left the pitch is lowered.

Purpose

Tuners are used with metal strings to enable the player to tune these strings more easily and accu-

rately than can be done with the tuning peg. For this reason the device is sometimes referred to as a "fine tuner."

When to Use Tuners

As stated in the section, *Strings,* tuners should always be used with metal-core strings; since the pitch of these strings is altered considerably with the slightest change of tension, and the tuner makes possible the most minute adjustment in tension. Tuners should not be used with gut or gut-core strings; since these strings must be moved one way or the other across the nut, or saddle, in order to effect a change in pitch. This movement across the saddle cannot be accomplished readily by increasing or decreasing tension on the tailpiece side of the bridge through the use of the tuner. Hence, the tuner is of no practical value in the case of gut strings.

It is recommended that string instruments for young beginners be equipped with steel strings and tuners. Steel strings stretch very little and are affected by temperature changes far less than gut strings; and if the pegs are in good condition, the child will probably be able to make all necessary tuning adjustments with the tuners. This removes the danger of having the peg slip and completely release the tension of the string or strings. The latter is an annoying experience. One string slipping usually leads to another. On cellos this can be a test of strength. You may win eventually, but you will very likely lose your patience in the process.

Types of Tuners

Tuners are made in a variety of types. In principal a threaded sleeve fits through the hole in the tailpiece that corresponds to the string the tuner is to be used with. A round nut is screwed down over this sleeve, holding the tuner firmly on the tailpiece. A prong, or hook, projects up through the slot ahead of the hole, or out beyond the front of the tailpiece. The loop-end of the string is placed over this prong.

A rather special tailpiece with fixed tuners is made by "Thomastik." This consists of a molded plastic tailpiece of which the tuners are a permanent, integrated part. On this tailpiece the conventional gut tailpiece loop is replaced with wire. The "Thomastik" is made for violin, viola, and cello.

Tuners are not made for bass since the bass is already equipped with a mechanical screw-type tuning device. With the exception of the "Thomastik," tuners may be installed and removed from the tailpiece at will. Not every tuner works satisfactorily

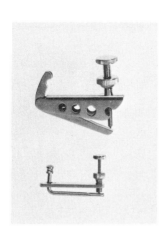

FIGURE 4.9. A. An assortment of tuners. B. View of a full set of tuners on a violin. (Courtesy Roth Violins, Cleveland, Ohio.)

with the small size violins. Because of the small amount of clearance between the top of the violin and the bottom of the tailpiece, some tuners, when turned too far, will press down into the top and cause ugly scars.

Care

It is possible for the threaded screw of the tuner to become gritty with rosin dust. As a result it may become hard to turn. If this should happen, the tuner should be removed and washed in warm soapy water. A small drop of light oil should be placed on the screw. If the threads become stripped, the tuner should be replaced.

The Bridge

Purpose

The bridge is an extremely important part of the string instrument, for it is through the bridge that the vibrations of the strings are carried to the instrument itself where the tone generation and resonance takes place.

Bridges are made of seasoned maple. Violin and viola bridges are designed somewhat differently from cello and bass bridges, and, of course, the size of the bridge is in proportion to the instrument. The design of the bridge is both practical and aesthetic.

Fitting the Bridge

Essential to the optimum function of the bridge is the exactitude with which it is fitted to the top of the instrument. "Fitting" a bridge is a job for a professional repairman. It involves thinning the feet of the bridge and carving them to match the contour of the top of the instrument. Next the top of the bridge is curved to match the contour of the fingerboard and to bring the strings to the correct height above the fingerboard. Notches are made carefully in the top of the bridge to space the strings at the correct distance from each other.

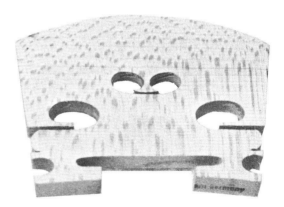

FIGURE 4.10. Violin bridges. (Courtesy Roth Violins, Cleveland, Ohio.)

FIGURE 4.12. Bass bridge. (Courtesy Roth Violins, Cleveland, Ohio.)

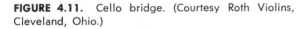

FIGURE 4.11. Cello bridge. (Courtesy Roth Violins, Cleveland, Ohio.)

FIGURE 4.13. Repairman fitting bridge. (Courtesy Roth Violins, Cleveland, Ohio.)

Most repairmen have personal idiosyncrasies about cutting wood away from one part of the bridge or another. This process amounts to a ritual in most shops and is predicated upon the repairman's intuitive sense of what is right for a given instrument. The placement of the bridge in relation to the "f" holes is also very important.

To recapitulate, the four most obviously important factors in fitting a bridge are:

1. Shaping the feet to the contour of the top of the instrument
2. Achieving the correct distance between the strings and the fingerboard
3. Spacing the strings correctly
4. Finding the most desirable position for the bridge in relation to the "f" holes. Generally this is in line with the inner notches in the "f" holes.

Bridge Height

The bridge should be high enough to allow the following clearances between strings and the top of the fingerboard at the bridge end. These distances are for standard or full-sized instruments; smaller instruments are slightly less.[2]

Gut Strings

Violin	E	1/8″	G	3/16″
Viola	A	3/16″	C	4/16″
Cello	A	1/4″	C	5/16″
Bass	G	7/16″	E	5/8″

All Steel Strings

Violin	E	3/32″	G	5/32″
Viola	A	9/64″	C	3/16″
Cello	A	11/64″	C	1/4″
Bass	G	21/64″	E	7/16″

Author's Note: Authorities differ on these measurements. Climate and personal preference must also be considered.

Bridge Curvatures

Obviously, the bridge curvature must conform to the curvature of the fingerboard. However, in the last few years two distinctive curvatures have been developed:[3]

French Curvature

Possesses less curve—(not as round)—and is slightly lower at the A and D (Violin) strings. It enables the player to perform more rapidly and to develop better and faster technique. Another advantage is the reducing of fatigue since the actual distance between two strings is shorter and less motion of the arm is required. The French curvature of the bridge requires perfect alignment of the fingerboard; otherwise, the player is apt to touch two strings simultaneously.

Viennese Curvature

Slightly rounder and a trifle higher at the A and D (Violin) strings. It is usually necessitated because the fingerboard has not been "dressed" perfectly. The advantage is the elimination of the problem of playing two strings simultaneously. The disadvantages are the wider travel of the bow and greater fatigue of the bow arm.

Special Bridges

The coming of metal strings brought with it some problems. The metal string acts as a blade or a saw-tooth as it moves back and forth across the bridge in the tuning process, causing it to cut more deeply into the top of the bridge. This brings the string closer and closer to the fingerboard, which eventually causes buzzes and rattles.

Bridges With Ebony Inserts

One solution to this problem was the construction of a bridge with an ebony insert, or inserts (see fig. 4.14), which withstands the wearing affect of the string better than maple. Another solution has been to place a small piece of chamois or skin under the string, or a thread winding around the string, to act as a buffer. This second technique also serves to reduce some of the metallic sound of the wire string. Some metal strings are supplied with a small rubber "Tone Filter" which is intended for this purpose.

Roth-de Jacques Bridge

This bridge is a recent development. It has adjustable feet which are joined to the bridge by an

2. "You Fix Them" (Second Edition), Scherl and Roth, Inc. Reprinted with permission.
3. *Ibid.*

BRIDGE DIAGRAMS

These illustrations are drawn to exact measurements for all string instruments. In addition to proper curvature for each model, the small indentations in the curve indicate the correct string spacings.

In the center of each diagram the vertical lines crossing the horizontal bar indicate the correct string spacings at the fingerboard nut of the various instruments.

The measurement on the lower left corner of each diagram is the correct height between the end of the fingerboard and the fourth gut wound string on each instrument.

The measurement on the lower right corner of each diagram is the correct height between the end of the fingerboard and the first string of each instrument.

(Note: refer to previous section, "Bridge Height" for proper measurement when using steel strings in place of gut.)

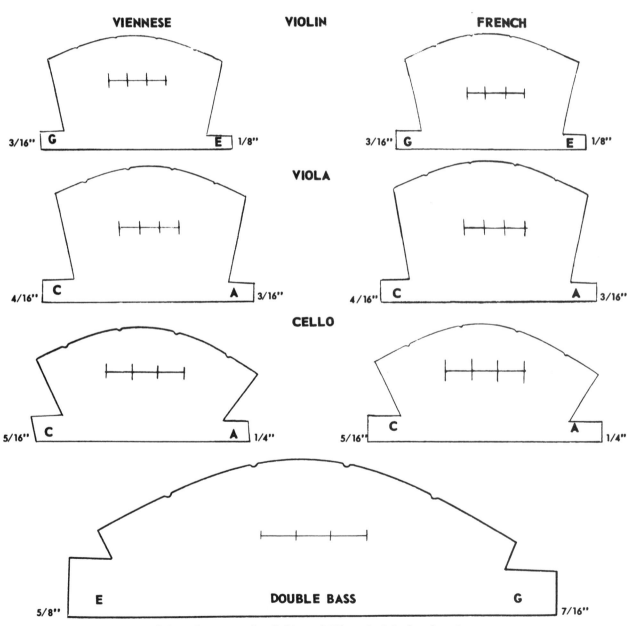

Reprinted from "You Fix Them" (Second Edition), Scherl and Roth, Inc.

FIGURE 4.14. Bridges with ebony inserts.

interlocking swivel joint. Under tension the feet adjust automatically to the curvature of the top.

Starker Bridge

Janos Starker, the famous cellist, has taken an ordinary bridge and bored a conical hole in the bottom of each foot. This process is supposed to increase the power and resonance of the instrument.

Care of the Bridge

The bridge is a relatively delicate part of the instrument. Its narrow width and small feet support the combined tension of the four strings. Each time the strings are tuned, the tendency is for the bridge to move minutely toward the fingerboard. In time this will cause the bridge to tilt forward until it falls or cracks; or the bottom part of the bridge may remain in position and the top portion above the weak mid-section will tilt forward, causing the bridge to warp.

These problems can be avoided if the position of the bridge is observed periodically and corrected if needed. Exerting pressure on the top of the bridge in the direction of the tailpiece will return it to its upright position. But this must be done carefully to avoid pushing the bridge backward so far that it falls over. To avoid this, the fingers of one hand should grasp the string directly behind the bridge while the fingers of the other hand gently push the bridge to an upright position. This technique, as well as the correct position of the bridge are shown in Figures 4.17 and 4.18.

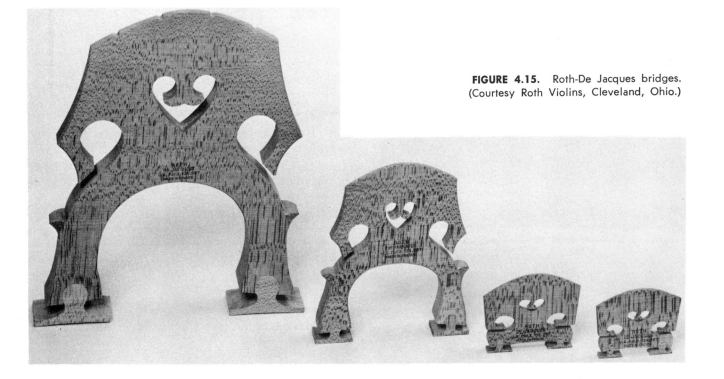

FIGURE 4.15. Roth-De Jacques bridges. (Courtesy Roth Violins, Cleveland, Ohio.)

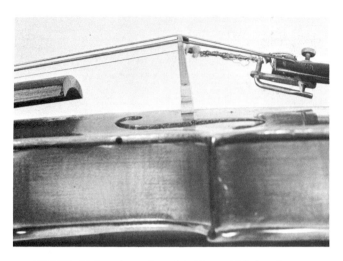

FIGURE 4.16. A neglected bridge which has become warped.

FIGURE 4.17. Correct way to return the bridge to an upright position.

EXACT BACK TIP ANGLE

FIGURE 4.18. Correct position of the bridge. (Courtesy Roth Violins, Cleveland, Ohio.)

Mutes

Purpose

The mute is a device which, when placed upon the bridge, deadens, dampens, or reduces the amount of tone produced by the instrument. It also changes the quality of the sound. Muted passages are used by composers to achieve contrast and special effects.

Physically the mute acts as a clamp on the bridge and reduces the free passage of vibrations through the bridge to the top of the instrument. For many years the design of mutes was limited to two types. One was three pronged; the other five pronged. They were made of hard wood (ebony), metal, or leather with wire reinforcing. They clamped onto the top of the bridge. Each affected the tone of the instrument in its own special way.

Beginning with the music of Debussy and Ravel, composers have made increasing demands upon orchestra players in regard to speed and frequency in the use of the mute. Split-second application and removal is not uncommon, and a composer may ask for the mute to be used a dozen or more times in a movement or section of music.

Foreign Terms for Mute

One needs to be acquainted with some of the foreign terms for the mute, its application, and its removal. Italian, German, and French are the most important, and Italian is used most frequently.

	Word for Mute	*To Apply*	*To Remove*
Italian	Sordino(i) Sord.	Con sordino	Senza sordino
German	Dämpfer	Mit Dämpfer	Ohne Dämpfer or Dämpfer weg. or ab.
French	Sourdine(s)	Avec les sourdines	Otez les sourdines

Mute Problems

The mute has always presented a series of problems to the orchestra musician. First, it was an easy piece of equipment to forget. It could be left in the instrument case backstage, or at home in the suit worn at the last concert. Second, if the player was well disciplined and remembered to take the mute onto the stage, finding the best place to keep it was a problem. If he put it on the music stand, it was usually knocked off when a page was turned. If he put it in a coat pocket, he might have difficulty retrieving it in a hurry when it was needed. In full dress the player usually put the mute in the pocket of his vest. But what to do with it in

FIGURE 4.19. An ebony mute. (Courtesy Roth Violins, Cleveland, Ohio.)

FIGURE 4.20. Roth-Sihon mutes. (Courtesy Roth Violins, Cleveland, Ohio.)

rehearsal when vest and coats were not worn? And last, but by no means least, in the process of frantically fumbling for a mute—in the coat or vest or on the stand or chair—it was not unheard of to drop it onto the floor. Mutes are most often called for in quiet moments, and the clatter of a mute as it strikes the floor is not conducive to a harmonious relationship between the conductor and the offender. Orchestra players long ago learned the technique of maintaining a steely and eyes-averted detachment during this kind of episode, giving the conductor and the audience no help in identifying the culprit.

Attached Mutes

The kind of trauma described above and the simple need to find a better way, led practical and inventive minds to discover a mute which could be attached to the instrument. This solution meant that the mute would always be with the instrument; it simplified the process of application and removal; and it eliminated the chance of the mute falling to the floor.

The new mutes fit securely over the strings just behind the bridge. To mute the instrument, the device is pushed toward the bridge. The "Off" position is achieved by returning the mute toward the tailpiece.

The Roth-Sihon mutes, shown in Figure 4.20, are available for violin, viola, cello, and bass. It is recommended that all school instruments used on the secondary level be equipped with a mute of this or some other style which can be attached to the instrument.

Other Special Mutes

HEIFETZ MUTE

The Heifetz mute is an invention of the famous violin virtuoso of the same name. It is made of rubber with wire reinforcing and can be used with the violin or viola. It produces a pleasant and resonant tone.

HALL MUTE

The Hall mute is a two pronged mute made of aluminum. It also produces a pleasant and resonant tone.

PRACTICE MUTE OR TON WOLF

Practice mutes are heavy metal devices which, when placed upon the bridge, reduce the volume of the instrument to nearly zero. Using a practice mute, it is possible to practice in an apartment or rooming house without disturbing occupants of adjacent quarters.

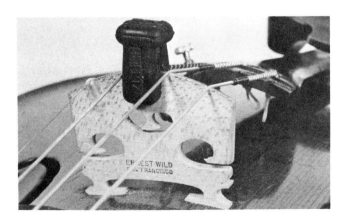

FIGURE 4.21. Heifetz mute.

FIGURE 4.22. Ton wolf.

Wolf Suppressor or Eliminator

The term "wolf," when used in regard to a string instrument, denotes a note or notes which produce an undesirable resonance pattern, causing that note(s) to have a different tone quality than the other notes on the instrument. The wolf tone can be described by such words as super-resonant, boomy, or hollow. Wolfs are undesirable, not only because they produce unevenness in the scale of the instrument, but because the note on which the wolf occurs does not respond to the bow as the other notes do. The wolf is balky and undependable, and requires special treatment; it must be favored.

A wolf frequently occurs on C or C♯ on the violin, and on F or F♯ on the viola and cello. It is most evident on the bottom string; however it will usually be present in the upper octaves of the same note. Wolfs are to be found in very fine instruments, and are attributed to some idiosyncracy in the design of the instrument. Most repairmen are reluctant to attempt structural changes to cure the wolf.

Pressure just behind the bridge or under the tailpiece will suppress the wolf. A device has been contrived to accomplish this. It consists of a piece of cork and a screw mechanism which makes it possible to press the cork onto the top behind the bridge. Another device which suppresses the wolf consists of a metal sleeve which is screwed onto the G string just behind the bridge.

Tailpiece Gut

The term "tailpiece gut" is becoming less and less literally descriptive with the passing of time. The term refers to the material (gut, nylon, or wire) which is attached to the tailpiece and then looped over the end pin, thus anchoring the tailpiece to the instrument.

The tailpiece gut must be strong enough to resist the combined pull of the four strings without stretching. Traditionally a short piece of gut string has been used, for the violin a piece about the diameter of a cello "A" string, and proportionately larger sizes for the larger instruments. The two ends of the piece of gut are inserted into holes on the underneath side of the tailpiece. These two ends are heated and flaired and thread is wrapped tightly up against the flaired end to prevent the ends from slipping back through the holes in the tailpiece. The loop, thus formed, is placed over the end pin. If the tailpiece gut is cut to the correct length, the end of the tailpiece will be directly over the saddle.

Gut has been used for this purpose because it is extremely strong and durable. But it does become weak with age, and damp weather softens it, increasing its tendency to break.

Importance of Tailpiece Gut

The tailpiece gut is a true life-line. Without it all is lost. Four strings hanging from the scroll, limp and useless, is a sad but ludicrous sight. Truthfully, the breaking of a tailpiece gut is calamitous. In addition to totally immobilizing the instrument, the sudden and complete release of tension can cause the bridge to snap, the sound post to fall; and the flailing tailpiece can seriously scratch or gouge the top of the instrument. The only sure way to prevent this kind of occurrence is to check the condition of this part as you would strings, bow hair, etc. If it begins to fray, have it replaced. If gut is used, this usually means a trip to the repair shop, for the majority of players do not have the skill to make this kind of repair.

Because the breaking of the tailpiece gut is an unpleasant thing to have happen, substitutes for gut have been sought. Wire has been substituted for gut on the bass. And another recent development is described below.

Sacconi Tailpiece Adjuster

Inventive genius applied itself to the solution of the tailpiece gut problem for the violin, viola, and cello. The Sacconi Tailpiece Adjuster is the result. This ingenious device is made of an extremely strong synthetic which is claimed to be ten times stronger than gut. The ends, which are threaded, are inserted into the tailpiece in the conventional manner. Nuts are screwed down until the tailpiece is in the correct position. The loop is placed over the end pin and the job is done. It is clean, simple, quick, and easy. No tools are required. In addition to being many times stronger than gut, the material is said to be weather and water proof.

Bow Grips

Most of the information regarding bow grips is covered in the chapter on the bow; however there are two items in this category which, because of their "do it yourself" aspect, may logically be dealt with here. The first of these is the Rolland Bow Grip; the second is the Thermal Grip.

Rolland Bow Grip

This is a small, soft rubber device which is slid over the existing bow grip. It is shaped with a depression into which the right thumb fits while playing. Its purpose is to provide a positive place for the thumb and thus prevent the thumb from wandering toward the middle of the bow or into the hollow of the frog. It can prevent the "roving thumb" problem and lend security to the student who is so afflicted.

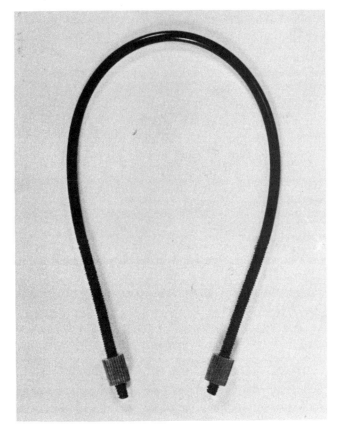

FIGURE 4.23. Sacconi tailpiece adjuster.

Thermal Grip

This is a general term used to describe a bow grip which consists of two pieces of thin plastic tubing which are shrunk onto the stick by heat. The longer of the two pieces is placed on the stick in position and heated. It shrinks tightly onto the stick. The short one is placed over the long one at the end near the frog. This is shrunk onto the stick and a grip is formed. The plastic is very tough and durable. Anyone can make this installation with the help of a match, candle, or lighter.

Cello End Pins

Purpose

The cello end pin is as much an integral part of the cello as is the bridge or the tailpiece. And although it is not proven to be directly related to the

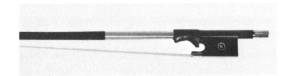

FIGURE 4.24. Rolland Bow Grip. (Courtesy Roth Violins, Cleveland, Ohio.)

playing properties of the instrument, it has a great deal to do with the player's comfort and security. The end pin is to the cellist what the shoulder pad is to the violinist and violist. It puts the instrument at the correct height and makes it possible for the player to hold it firmly. An indication of the importance of this part of the instrument is the fact that the first thing a cellist does after sitting down to play is to look for a hole for the end pin.[4]

Parts of the End Pin

The end pin consists of the following parts:

1. A wooden (usually ebony) sleeve or socket which fits into a hole at the base of the cello.
2. A metal rod which is inserted into the hole in the sleeve. This rod has either a sharp point or a rubber tip and a restraining band which prevents the rod from slipping into the sleeve. The rod sometimes has grooves or notches to receive the point of the thumb screw.
3. A metal sleeve which fits around the socket and contains a thumb screw. The thumb screw is used to set the rod at the desired position.

Function and Problems of the End Pin

The rod, or peg, is adjusted by the player according to his needs and is secured by the thumb screw. It is important that the thumb screw hold the rod firmly. And it is important that one of the following conditions be met:

1. The tip of the end pin rod be sharp,
2. The tip be of soft rubber which will not slip,
3. An end pin holder be provided.

Unless one of these conditions is complied with, the cellist is confronted with a difficult, frustrating, and nearly impossible situation. In order to meet

---

4. There is a good deal of experimentation going on at the present time with cello end pins of various designs. The Tortellier is one which has gained some acceptance. The objective of these new end pins is to elevate the bottom of the cello so that it comes closer to being horizontal. This reduces the cello's contact with the body, and, according to proponents of these devices, elevates the finger board and thus places the hand in a more advantageous position to function.

the first requirement, the point of the end pin will need to be sharpened periodically with a steel file.

The restraining sleeve which was mentioned above deserves a special bit of discussion. It seems inconceivable that an end pin could be made without some means to prevent it from slipping completely inside the instrument. Probably no end pin is made without such a device, but with repeated use, and sometimes mistreatment, it is broken or dislodged. Sometimes this restrainer is a pin through the rod; sometimes it is a sleeve around the rod; sometimes the end of the rod is flaired. It appears that time and use can destroy the effectiveness of any of these methods, and the result is that there is nothing to prevent the pin from slipping completely inside the cello, or becoming stuck in the socket with the point recessed in the socket so that it cannot be grasped by fingers or pliers. The latter is worse than the former. When the rod slips into the instrument, it can usually be retrieved by turning the instrument belly-down and rolling it back and forth until the rod can be grasped through one of the "f" holes. When the rod becomes stuck in the socket, it usually means that the entire end pin assembly must be removed in order that the pin can be driven out. This means releasing the tension on all the strings and freeing the tailpiece gut from the end pin.

An additional common problem with the less expensive end pins is that the sleeve into which the thumb screw is threaded is not thick enough to provide a firm purchase for the thumb screw. Unless it is given careful use, the sleeve threads become worn and the sleeve must be replaced.

Bass End Pins

Bass end pin assemblies are heavier and larger than the cello's. The rod is larger in diameter and shorter. The purpose of the end pin is to raise the instrument to the correct height for the player and to anchor the instrument in the desired spot.

Everything which is said about cello end pins applies to bass end pins.

Cello and Bass End Pin Rests

Purpose

The purpose of all of the gadgets in this category is to give the player the security of knowing that his instrument is going to stay where he puts it. Since a player may encounter hardwood, tile, concrete, or carpet as floor material, he should be ready to cope with any situation. A sharp steel point may embed itself satisfactorily in wood, but it will be less successful on concrete, and some people are sensitive about their carpet or rugs.

Several different methods of coping with this problem have been developed. They are listed and described below.

Rubber End Pin Holders

In this category there are several styles on the market. The Waller End Pin Rest consists of a piece of sponge rubber with a metal cover plate. The cover is made with a depression in the center into which the end pin is placed. The sponge rubber is supposed to prevent the rest from sliding about, but it is not completely satisfactory on all surfaces.

Another type is made of rubber. A hollow throat receives the end pin and a flat base makes contact with the floor. The throat forms a flexible joint with the base.

Cello Boards

Cello boards are used in schools as much as any other device. They are inexpensive to produce, foolproof, and virtually indestructible if made of relatively hard wood.

A piece of wood 1/2 inch to 3/4 inches thick is cut 3 inches wide and about 28 inches long. A hole large enough for a chair leg (about 2 inches in diameter) is drilled at one end and a series of 3/8 inch diameter holes are drilled at an angle half-way through the board at varying distances from the large hole.

The left leg of the cellist's chair is inserted into the large hole and the end pin is placed in the hole which puts the cello at the most comfortable angle for the player.

Cello boards are not the most convenient device if they must be moved about frequently. But they serve admirably in the orchestra rehearsal room where they can be left in place.

There are also contrivances made of leather or web belting which function on the same principal as the cello board. Loops are secured to the legs of the chair and a cup like device receives the end pin.

Bass Stools

The bass player has the option of standing or sitting while he plays. If the rehearsal or performance is extended, or if there are long waiting periods, he will probably choose to sit. Most professionals

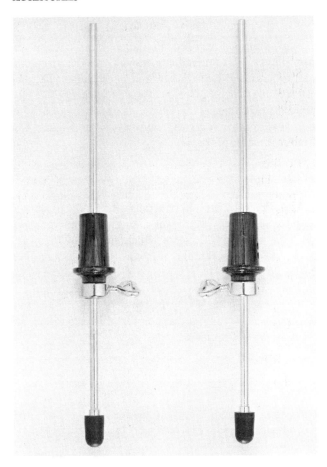

FIGURE 4.25. Cello end pins. (Courtesy Roth Violins, Cleveland, Ohio.)

FIGURE 4.26. Roth-Waller end pin rest.

FIGURE 4.27. Rubber end pin rests. (Courtesy Roth Violins, Cleveland, Ohio.)

FIGURE 4.28. Cello board.

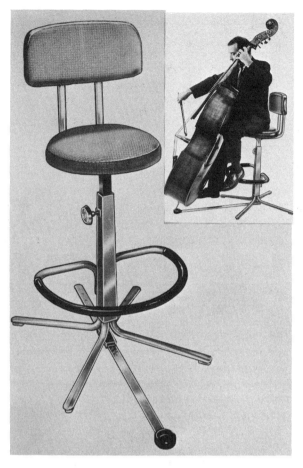

FIGURE 4.29. Wenger bass chair. (Courtesy Wenger Corporation, Owatonna, Minnesota.)

sit. They use a stool which has been adjusted to their height.

Teenage bass players tire quickly. They should have a suitable stool. Too often this is not provided, and the results are not conducive to a good rehearsal situation. Since these students feel that they must sit, and they should not be denied this comfort, they place chairs behind them into which they noisily collapse each time the director stops the orchestra, or they have a thirty-two bar rest. This kind of activity is disruptive and interferes with the concentration level of the entire orchestra.

Any stool which is suited to the height of the player is satisfactory. The player sits on the edge of the stool with the right leg on the floor and the left leg supported on a rung of the stool.

The *Wenger Bass Chair* is designed strictly for the bass player. It is made of metal. The height of the seat is adjustable. It has a back support. And it has its own end pin holder which is adjustable.

Bass Stands

Bass stands are used in dance bands when the bass player is required to move quickly from the bass to another instrument and vice versa. In such a situation there is often no time to pick up the bass from a position on the floor; it must be ready to play. A stand such as the one shown in Figure 4.30 is used for this purpose.

Cello Chairs

The desirability of a straight-backed, unslanted chair for cellists is important enough to warrant mention here. Chairs with seats which slope down toward the back are extremely uncomfortable for cellists. The cellist needs to sit forward on the chair, with his back away from the back of the chair, and a sloping seat makes this difficult. With a flat seat the cellist can assume a comfortable position and retain it without effort.

FIGURE 4.30. String bass stand.

Most metal folding chairs have a sloped, contoured seat which is designed to throw some of the person's weight against the back of the chair. For this reason they are unsuitable for cellists. A flat seated, wooden desk chair is much better suited to the cellist's special needs.

Cases

Violin and Viola Cases

Violin and viola cases are generally of the shaped type, that is the outline of the case conforms roughly to the shape of the instrument.

Oblong cases are also available. They have the advantage of providing more inside room for storage of shoulder pads, strings and rosin. Some people advocate the oblong case for boys since it looks less like a violin case than does the shaped variety. This is prompted by the still present onus of "sissy" in regard to the study of the violin by boys.

Cases today are either of plywood construction covered with plastic or leather, or of a new molded plastic process. The main requirement of a case is

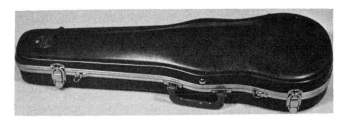

FIGURE 4.31. Shaped case. (Courtesy Roth Violins, Cleveland, Ohio.)

FIGURE 4.32. Oblong case. (Courtesy Roth Violins, Cleveland, Ohio.)

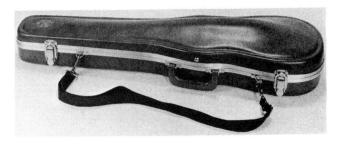

FIGURE 4.33. Violin case with strap. (Courtesy Roth Violins, Cleveland, Ohio.)

that it be functional. It should be sturdy so that it can stand abuse. The hardware should be made of sufficiently heavy metal that hinges and clasps do not wear out. The metal should be rust and corrosion proof. The exterior should be of tough, durable material.

The interior of the case should be lined with soft material and provide a snug fit for the instrument for maximum protection against shock. Pockets, or compartments, should be big enough to accomodate rosin, strings, and perhaps a shoulder pad. They should be glued and hinged strongly enough to prevent them from coming apart. The bow holder at the narrow end of the case should be nailed and glued so it will not come loose, and the bow clamps should be of a good quality spring steel so that they do not lose their shape and their usefulness.

Many student cases are made with two rings affixed to the handle side of the case. A carrying strap may be snapped into these rings. By slinging the strap over his shoulder, a child can free his hands for carrying books or riding a bicycle.

A canvas cover is highly recommended for the protection of good quality cases. A cover will double the life of a case. It is generally not practical to equip school cases with covers because of the cost of covers.

Cello and Bass Bags

Cello and bass bags are made of canvas or duck. The better bags have a fleece lining or inner coating. A recently introduced bag of excellent quality is lined with foam rubber and is reinforced in the neck area.

The bag keeps the instrument dry and prevents nicks and scratches, but it does not protect against hard blows by heavy objects. A sleeve for the bow is located in the front of the bag and a music pouch in the rear. The quality of the bag depends upon the weight of the canvas, the thread used, the kind

FIGURE 4.34. Cello bag. (Courtesy Roth Violins, Cleveland, Ohio.)

FIGURE 4.35. Hard cello case. (Courtesy Roth Violins, Cleveland, Ohio.)

of material used to bind the seams, and the quality of the zippers or snaps.

Hard Cello Cases

Every artist-quality cello should be furnished with a hard case to protect it against damage. The same criteria which apply to violin and viola cases apply to the hard cello cases. In the cello case the end pin is held in a slotted retainer at the base of the case, and a strap holds the neck at the top. The combined weight of the instrument and this type case can come to eighteen pounds and more. The size and weight make it prohibitive for a young child.

Trunks for Cellos and Basses

Professional cello and bass players who must travel and send their instrument as baggage often make use of trunk type cases. These are heavily reinforced pieces of luggage and require several men or a mechanical lift to handle them. They are fitted inside so that the instrument is held tightly in padding with the use of straps.

Pitch Pipes

Pitch pipes with four pipes (one pipe for each string) are available for violin, viola, and cello. The pitch pipe can be helpful in teaching students to tune their instruments and to make them conscious of the importance of checking their strings each time they practice. It is particularly important that students without a piano in their home be supplied with a pitch pipe.

CHAPTER 5

Strings

Strings

Corda (Italian)   *Corde* (French)

Saite (German)

Strings are to the violin, viola, cello, and bass what the reed is to the oboe. They must be well made of good materials, properly matched, and suited to the instrument if the instrument is to function at its best. Strings are made of several different kinds of material—gut, synthetics, and metal.

Players develop preferences for certain types of strings. Some prefer metal; others prefer gut and gut wound with silver or aluminum. Still others prefer to intermix these types. Some recommendations and options regarding types of strings and their use are made following the descriptions of the various types of strings.

Qualifications of a Good String

The first requirement of a string is that it produce a pure fundamental tone, undistorted by pitch fluctuations or faulty overtones. The second is that it is responsive throughout its playing range to the great variety of demands placed upon it—a broad range of dynamics, quick spiccato notes, heavy chords and accents, etc. The third is that it stretch completely in no more than three days. The fourth requirement is that it give a reasonable length of service. Under most circumstances this should be at least one year. Of course, a heavy schedule of playing can reduce this span to six months or even less.

Historical Development of Strings

Strings, like most products, have gone through a process of change. And, like the early resistance to the automobile, changes in the materials used and the design of strings has met with occasional re-

sistance. For instance, fifty years ago the wire "E" string for the violin was relatively new. Violinists were reluctant to accept this metal substitute for the thin-guage gut they had been using, even though the gut string was extremely undependable. Players were sure that the wire string would not have the "sweet" quality of the gut string, and there was widespread doubt about the advisability of subjecting a fine old instrument to the added tension created by a wire string.

But the wire "E" had more power and brilliance than the gut string, and it did reduce the probability of the "E" string breaking in the middle of a recital or concerto, which was a common experience with the gut "E." So, of course, the wire "E" was finally accepted, and today the gut "E" is rarely used. Later, in addition to the "E", other strings were made of metal and various alloys. These strings, too, were accepted slowly. Today there is little real antipathy toward the metal strings.

Selection of Strings

Many very fine players use metal strings. Others are convinced that gut-core strings are superior. Still others continue to use those gut strings which are available. Most personal preferences for particular strings or string combinations are developed through a trial and error method. The player tries various strings until he finds what works best for him and is best suited to his instrument.

The instrument itself can dictate the types of strings which should be used. For instance, the stronger new instruments are better able to withstand the added tension produced by the metal strings than are the old instruments. But it must be re-stated that in the case of advanced players personal preference, rather than scientific evidence, is most frequently the determining factor in selecting string types.

For optimum results in the areas of intonation and equalization of tone from string to string, strings should be matched according to gauge, a matter which the player should take up with a competent string dealer or repairman. Problems of a thin tone or lack of responsiveness can sometimes be cured by changing the guage of the string.

Advantages of Metal Strings for Students

Where students are concerned, some practical considerations are more important than aesthetic considerations when selecting the types of strings to be used. Metal strings are preferred for young players because they hold their pitch better than gut-core strings. Furthermore, an instrument equipped with metal strings and tuners is far easier to tune than one with gut-core strings.

By the time a student reaches junior high school, has graduated to a full-size instrument, and is tuning his instrument with a minimum of assistance, he is ready for a change from metal to gut-core strings. This type of string frequently improves the tone quality of student instruments.

Types of Strings

Type 1, Gut

Not of the cat, as is so often said, but nonetheless fabricated from an animal intestine, most often sheep. Gut strings are available as follows:

Violin E, A*, D	Cello A*, D*
Viola A, D	Bass G*, D*

Note: Only the gut strings marked (*) are recommended, and then only when they sound well on the instrument.

Type 2, Aluminum wire wound on a gut core

This combination of materials produces excellent results. Strings of this type are made and used as follows:

Violin A, D
Viola A, D
Cello A, D

The ends of these strings are tied with colored thread. The color indicates the pitch and the quality bracket of the string. This type string usually has a tied loop at the end which is intended for insertion into the appropriate slot in the tailpiece. At the opposite end, the wire winding stops and is tied off about two inches short of the end of the violin

string (correspondingly further on others). This leaves the gut core exposed. Better quality strings are now being made with thread or wire wrapping at this end to prevent the string from slipping on the peg.

Type 3, Silver wire wound on a gut core

This combination provides excellent results and is made and used as follows:

Violin G	Cello D, G, C
Viola G, C	Bass A*, E*

Note: The two strings marked (*) are also made with bronze wire wrapping.

Type 4, Single strand wire

Violin E only. It is used almost universally in place of the gut E.

Type 5, Metal alloy or combinations of synthetics and plastics wound on single strand or multiple strand wire core

This type of string is available in full sets for all string instruments. This type string causes more tension on the instrument than the gut core. Because of the added tension which they create, they are not advisable in all cases for fine old instruments.

An important factor is that these strings are made in 1/2, 3/4, and 4/4 sizes for violin and viola. "Super Sensitive" and "Ultra Sensitive" strings are available in three degrees of loudness—soft, medium, and orchestra (loud). Some other brands are available in the same assortment.

The string with the "cable" type core is more flexible than the string with the solid wire core. In addition to greater flexibility, this type string has a somewhat softer tone than the solid core string.

Type 6, Aluminum wound on steel core

Available as follows:
Violin A, D
Viola A, D
Cello A, D

Recommended Combinations of String Types

As stated earlier, advanced players will discover their string preferences over a period of time, and through a trial and error method. There are, however, some suggested "do's" and "don't's" which will help the prospective teacher. Experience has proven that certain types of strings are preferable to others in certain circumstances, and that there are some combinations of strings which are undesirable. First of all, then, some general comments:

1. The gut E and gut D are not recommended for violin or viola. The gut G and D are acceptable for the bass. Some violins and some cellos sound better with a gut A than with a metal A.

2. Using the wire E on the violin, and the wire core A on the viola or cello in combination with aluminum and silver wound strings is acceptable. Further mixing of these two types is not recommended.

3. The use of all Type 5 strings on 1/2, and 3/4 violins, violas, and cellos is strongly recommended. Use of this type string on 4/4 instruments is a matter of personal taste. These strings are strongly recommended for students in the beginning to intermediate categories since they stay in tune for a much longer period of time than gut core strings. Their fluctuation from temperature changes and use is minimal.

4. Metal core strings can be recommended for the bass. They are responsive, and their smaller diameter is less bulky under the fingers than the gut and gut-wound strings. The dance bass player will find this type of string hard on the fingers of the right hand, which may be reason not to use them for this kind of work. These strings are also available in solo tunings for the bass.

Specific Recommendations

For Beginners

Violin, viola, cello—All Type 5 with tuners

		Type
Bass—G	. . .	1
D	. . .	1
A	. . .	3
E	. . .	3

or all Type 5

For Advanced Players

		Type
Violin — E	. . .	4, 5
A	. . .	1, 2
D	. . .	2
G	. . .	3
Viola — A	. . .	1, 2, 5
D	. . .	2
G	. . .	3
C	. . .	3
Cello — A	. . .	1, 2, 5
D	. . .	1, 2
G	. . .	3
C	. . .	3

		Type
Bass — G	. . .	1
D	. . .	1
A	. . .	3
E	. . .	3

Note: If Type 5 strings are used, it is recommended that they be used in complete sets. The exception is when one of these strings is used as the top string in combination with gut-wound strings.

Use of Tuners

Tuners should always be used with metal core strings; since metal core strings are under considerable tension, and the pitch is altered by the most minute change in tension. The tuning peg should be used to bring the string to the approximate pitch when the string is first installed. The tuner is used for fine-tuning thereafter. With tuners these strings can be brought to the desired pitch easily. Without tuners, getting them in tune is a frustrating and time consuming task.

There is no advantage in using tuners with gut core strings. This type of string requires more change in tension to effect a pitch change than can be practically accomplished with a tuner. In brief, with gut strings the tuner is more bother than it is worth, and is best avoided.

Tone Filters

A "Tone Filter" is a piece of rubber or plastic shaped like a miniature doughnut. Small pieces of leather or thread windings serve the same purpose. This device is placed between the string and the bridge to cushion the contact of the string on the bridge. It also helps prevent rattles and buzzes which can occur from the contact of the string and the bridge, and helps prevent the metal string from cutting too deeply into the bridge.

Bridge and Nut Adjustment for Metal Strings

When metal strings are used on any of the stringed instruments, the bridge should be cut down and the notches in the nut cut somewhat more deeply than is normal so that the height of the string above the fingerboard will be reduced. Without this adjustment, the player must use an excessive amount of force to press the string to the fingerboard.

Putting Strings On the Instrument

The order in which the strings are placed on the pegs is the same for all four of the instruments, with the single exception that the G and C are sometimes interchanged on the viola in order to reduce the acuteness of the angle of the C string between the nut and the peg. The standard and accepted order of matching strings to pegs is shown in Figure 5.1.

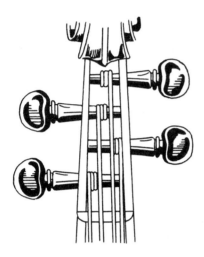

FIGURE 5.1. Strings and pegs.

"Stringing Up" is a string player's colloquialism. It refers to the function of putting a string or strings on a string instrument. There are two basic steps involved in this process. (1) The loop end of the string is secured in the correct hole in the tailpiece, or on the correct tuner. (2) The other end of the string is fed through the hole in the correct peg, secured on the peg, and tightened to the desired pitch. This two-step process is not difficult, but it is extremely important that it be executed carefully. Neglect of any of the details can result in a false string or in slippage of the string on the peg, causing the string to go flat.

Because strings break, and because the teacher will find it necessary to replace broken strings for most elementary pupils, it is of primary importance that he learn well the steps involved in changing a string. This process is now described in detail:

1. Remove any pieces of the broken string from the tailpiece and the peg.
2. Check to see if the peg concerned is working smoothly. If it is not, apply a small amount of peg dope.
3. Select a good quality string of the correct gauge and size.[1] Be sure strings are matched for type.
4. Remove the string from the envelope or string tube carefully. Do not twist, bend, or kink the string.

Note: It is desirable to keep wound strings **straight**, either in a tube or string case.
5. If the string is metal, place the string on the tuner, as shown in Figure 5.2.

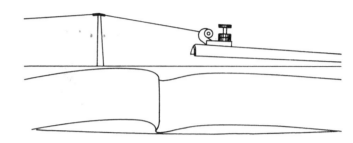

FIGURE 5.2. Metal string looped over tuner.

If it is a gut core string, insert the knotted end of the string through the hole in the tailpiece and pull the string toward the bridge. See Figure 5.3.

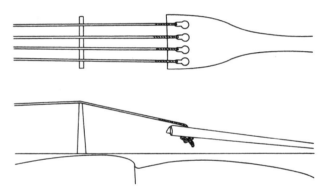

FIGURE 5.3. Gut string inserted into tail piece.

Make sure that the knot is well forward in the slot by tugging firmly on the string.
6. If the peg end of the string has a twisted or rough winding designed to prevent slippage, it is enough to insert the end of the string through the hole in the peg. The length of string allowed to protrude through the peg increases proportionately with the size of the instrument. About 5/8 inch is sufficient for the violin with only slightly more for the viola. For the cello 3/4 to 1 inch should be allowed, and for the bass 1 1/2 to 2 inches.

If the peg end of the string has no coating or winding, more of the string must be inserted through the peg in order that the end of the

1. It should be kept in mind that $\frac{1}{2}$ and $\frac{3}{4}$ size strings are available for violin and viola in Type 5.

string can be looped back under the main body of the string. When tightened, the end of the string will be cinched against the peg. See Figure 5.4.

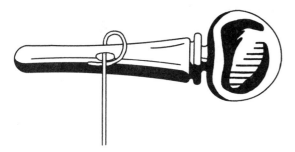

FIGURE 5.4.   String inserted through peg.

Difficulty is sometimes incurred in feeding the string through the peg—the top, right peg in particular. A pair of tweezers, or small pliers, should be carried in the case for these occasions. With tweezers the string can be pulled through the peg even if only a quarter of an inch of the end is all that can be fed through with the fingers.

7. Wind the string onto the peg carefully in order that it will have a straight or an inward pull on the peg. The importance of winding the string properly cannot be overstated since it has a significant bearing upon the ease with which the peg may be set in tuning. It can be seen in Figure 5.5A that the pull of the string is outward, tending to loosen the peg.

Winding the string as shown in Figure 5.5B, on the other hand, results in assistance from the natural pull of the string in keeping the peg tight.

8. Bring the string up to pitch slowly. Do not tune it higher than the desired pitch; this may damage the string. The strings should now appear as shown in Figure 5.1.

9. To be grasped and turned easily, the pegs must be in the positions shown in Figure 5.6. If, after a string is fully stretched, the peg is in an awkward position, it is possible to alter the position by pulling more or less of the string through the peg. By pulling more of the string through the peg, the peg will not have to be turned so far to produce the desired pitch, and vice versa.

10. After the string is completely stretched, it should not be allowed to slip to a loose condition. When re-tightened, it will again do some stretching, and this can be an annoyance.

FIGURE 5.6.   Pegs in right position to turn.

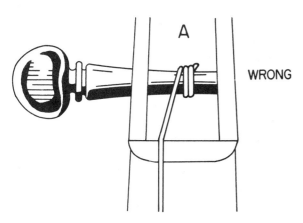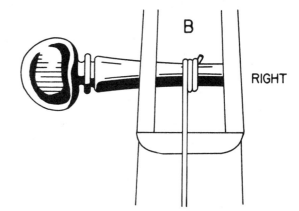

FIGURE 5.5.   A. Wrong way to wind string. B. Right way to wind string.

Care of Strings

If the rosin dust is wiped from the strings after each extended playing, nothing else will need to be done to keep the strings in good playing order. If the string is in good condition when put on the instrument, and if it is kept clean, it will not present problems until age and wear begin to affect it.

It has already been stated that the life of a string normally depends upon the way it is used and how much it is played. The age-at-purchase of the strings which contain gut is an important predictor of their life span. String envelopes are not dated, and gut-wound strings frequently are stored in plastic tubes with no more than a brand label. The only way to be assured of buying fresh strings is to buy from a dealer whose rate of stock turnover is known to you.

Some String Problems and Their Solutions

Strings can and do cause problems, and some strings may have inherent problems. A number of these problems are discussed below. Causes and solutions are given when known.

Problem: Strings break at bridge when first tightened.

Cause: Bridge notch is too narrow, or bridge has been planed so thin it cuts the string instead of providing a bearing surface.

Solution: Have bridge re-cut if this is possible, if not, replace.

Problem: Strings break at nut when first tightened.

Cause: Notch is too narrow and string is pinched or a rough or sharp surface has developed.

Solution: Have repairman widen or smooth the notch.

Problem: Gut and wound strings are difficult to tune. They can be tuned just above or just below the correct pitch, but not to it, precisely.

Cause: The string may not be sliding along the notch in the nut.

Solution: Loosen the string and remove it from the notch. Run a lead pencil (graphite) in the notch several times. If this does not correct the problem, see your repairman.

When to Replace a String

Some strings let you know clearly when they are ready to be replaced. But in some cases the time for replacement comes and goes before the need is obvious, unless the player is aware of the subtle signs that develop. The consequence is that the player uses a false or faulty string without knowing it. Described below are a few of the obvious signs of impending trouble and suggested action.

Gut Strings

Problem: Fraying, particularly where the fingers contact the string most frequently. Dark discoloration in the same area.

Cause: String absorbs oil and moisture from the fingers, darkens, and unravels.

Solution: Snip off loose ends as close to the string as possible, as long as the string still performs satisfactorily. Learn to judge the point of no return, and replace the string when that point occurs.

Wound Strings

Problem: Winding separates. Winding breaks and unravels.

Cause: Flaw in string. Sharp edge on nut. Finger nails too long.

Solution: Correct problems and replace string.

Problem: String wears flat on side next to fingerboard. String becomes false.

Cause: Age and use.

Solution: Replace it before it breaks.

Single Strand Wire Strings

Problem: String wears flat on side next to fingerboard.

Cause: Age and use.

Solution: Replace it before it breaks.

Nearly any of the problems listed above can cause the string to buzz, rattle, produce poor tone quality, or become "false."

Repairing a Broken String

If a string breaks close to the peg or the tailpiece, it may be temporarily repaired in an emergency by tying the broken ends together. A knot which will not slip, such as a square knot, should be used. This kind of repair should be considered temporary and the repaired string should be replaced with a new one as soon as possible.

Falseness

A string is false when it fails to produce a pure representation of the desired pitch. That is to say, the open string sounds impure, does not ring true, and other notes on the string produce a distorted pitch. This condition makes itself most evident in the case of open strings, harmonics, and double stops.

When a string is false, it sets up an irregular vibration pattern which gives off overtones other than those normal to the fundamental pitch. The result is a pitch which sounds sharp or flat regardless of where the finger is placed to stop the string. *Immediate replacement of the string is the only solution to this problem.* Do not delay in replacing a false string. The fingers will adjust to compensate for the "out-of-tuneness" of the string. In compensating, they are learning incorrect placement, which, if prolonged, will take valuable time to correct.

Testing for False Strings

One way to check strings for "falseness" is to play the interval of a minor sixth in a high register, using the three pairs of strings, and keeping the hand in the same relative position as you cross from one pair of strings to the next. The example shown is for the violin. Corresponding intervals and positions can be applied to the viola and cello.

The hand remains in the same position as the fingers move across to the next pair of strings. If the distance between the fingers remains the same

on the three pairs of strings, and a true minor sixth is produced, the strings are not false. If an adjustment is necessary in the spacing of the fingers, the string upon which the adjustment must be made is false.

Another method of checking for false strings is by playing 5ths. Begin in first position, using the questionable string as one of the pair. Move the hand upward, using the same finger to play the 5th. If a noticeable adjustment becomes necessary to keep the 5th true, one of the strings is false. By doing the same thing with the next pair of strings, the false string can be identified.

A Few Final Remarks about Strings

1. Always keep a complete set of extra strings on hand.
2. Buy only good quality strings. **Do not mix types** other than as recommended. Correct gauge is important.
3. Wipe the rosin from the strings after each playing.
4. Through experience try to determine the useful life of a string and change it before it goes false, unravels, or breaks.

Part II

There are many aspects of string playing which are common to the four string instruments. For example, shifting is a process of moving the hand from one place to another on the fingerboard, and even though it may be accomplished in a slightly different manner on each instrument, the basic movement is the same. Spiccato means to bounce the bow against the string, whether it is on the violin or the cello. Intonation is a problem of finger placement on the string which is common to players of all string instruments, and a trill is a trill regardless of the instrument involved. Some techniques, such as vibrato, are treated generally here and are given more specialized consideration in the chapters dealing with the individual instruments.

These functions and the terms which denote them form a common core of technique and language for the strings. Therefore, for ease of reference, as well as to avoid needless repetition, these techniques are dealt with in the single chapter which follows.

CHAPTER 6

Techniques Which Apply
to All of the String Instruments

The four string instruments have much in common. Each is made of wood; each has four strings; each is played with a bow. Tone is produced by drawing the bow on the strings or by plucking them. Pitch changes are produced by placing the fingers of the left hand at various points along the string.

The violin and viola may be played in either a standing or seated position. The cello is always played in a seated position. The bass player may stand or use a stool.

Because of the many basic similarities in the way these four instruments are played, techniques, as they apply to all of the instruments, will be discussed in general terms in this chapter. In the chapters devoted to the individual instruments, these same techniques may be discussed in more specific terms with application to the instrument in question.

Holding the Instrument

Many students have great difficulty attaining an acceptable playing position. Holding the violin and the viola is difficult and awkward. The cello and bass are somewhat easier to hold since the floor helps support them. A quick perusal of some of the miserable positions which can be found among intermediate and some advanced players is ample evidence of the need to maintain constant vigilance during the early stages of the learning process. Constant attention and prodding by the teacher will be needed during the first year of instruction if acceptable results are to be achieved in this all important area of instrument and bow position.

The way in which the instruments should be held is covered in considerable detail in the chapters on the respective instruments. This has been considered to be necessary because of the brief, and sometimes incomplete, manner in which the matter is handled in some method books. Some books have very good pictures or drawings which show how to hold the instruments. Others contain poor illustrations or none at all. At least one method takes care of the matter with the statement: "Your teacher will show you how to hold the instrument." The difficulty some students have in learning to hold the instrument, and the shortage of help in some of the instruction books is pointed out here simply to bring the problem into perspective.

Tuning

Sources of Pitch

In an experienced orchestra the oboe provides the "A." All instruments in the orchestra tune to this source of pitch. In school groups an electronic "A" or a tuning bar is frequently used as the pitch source. At home the student may use a piano, organ, or pitch pipe. The latter comes in two types. One type is the "A" alone; another is a group of four tubes which correspond to the four strings. Pitch pipes or tuners, as they are sometimes called, are not always reliable. Even those that are accurately in tune must be blown gently to avoid distortion of the pitch. Even so, they are better than having nothing to tune to.

Steps In Tuning

In tuning it is important that the tuning tone be established clearly and steadily. Only then will it be possible to match it.

On the violin, viola, and cello the "A" is invariably tuned first; then the other strings are tuned to the "A." The top two strings are usually tuned first, then the two middle strings, followed by the two lower strings. This order is not sacred and can be varied if desirable. For instance, in a string class, there may be an advantage in tuning all "A's" and "D's" together first, etc.

Because the pitch of the bass strings is so low, and because the bass is tuned in fourths instead of fifths, it is not practical to tune the bass by sounding two open strings simultaneously. Instead, students may tune one string at a time to the piano or along with the other instruments. More advanced players may tune using natural harmonics, which puts the pitch in a more easily discernible register.

Following is a list of points to be kept in mind in learning to tune the violin, viola, and cello:

1. Listen carefully for at least five seconds to the tuning note.
2. Tune the "A" string carefully and quietly.
3. Use a steady, light bow. This will avoid pitch fluctuations and distortions.
4. Tune the two top strings together until the interval of the fifth is perfect. (When "perfect," no vibration nodes will be apparent.)
5. With metal strings use tuners or adjusters. Avoid turning pegs unless absolutely necessary.
6. When turning peg, always grasp the scroll between the fingers and squeeze the peg in toward the peg-box as it is turned. This keeps the peg seated and prevents slippage.
7. Minute pitch adjustments of gut-wound strings can be made by pushing on the string just above the nut to raise the pitch, and by rubbing the finger along the length of the string or pulling it slightly to lower the pitch.
8. Avoid any exaggerated or rapid increase or decrease in tension through extreme tightening or loosening of the string. To bring a string to the desired pitch, it should first be lowered slightly and then raised to the correct pitch.

Tuning a string instrument is not easy. It calls for a well developed sense of pitch and a good deal of strength in the fingers which turn the pegs. More often than not the young beginner does not have either of these requirements in sufficient degree to do the job. The teacher must accept the fact that he is going to have to tune the beginner's instrument for a considerable time. When the teacher feels that the student has developed to the point that he can begin to tune his instrument himself, he should begin to provide the motivation and instruction that will lead to the student's ability to tune independently at the earliest moment.

Techniques of the Left Hand

Intonation

Intonation is the word used to describe the degree of in-tune-ness or out-of-tune-ness of a player's or a group's performance. Acceptable intonation is a prime objective of every instrumentalist and vocalist. It surpasses every other musical goal in importance; for without acceptable intonation, all other aspects of performance—rhythm, tone, expression—are wasted.

Without going into a long and involved discussion of intonation expectations, it should be stated here that a first year student is not expected to perform with the same intonation standards as a third year student. During the early months of instruction you will be pleased if the student puts the finger on the right string for the right note. If, at first, the notes produced are recognizable as what they are supposed to be, intonation is regarded as satisfactory. As the student progresses, the accuracy of his intonation should progress with him to the point that high school students' intonation should be judged quite strictly.

Achieving acceptable intonation on a string instrument is at once easier and more difficult than on the woodwinds and brasses. These latter instruments have natural limitations in the form of the keys which are pressed down to produce various pitches. No woodwind or brass instrument is acoustically perfect; so just pressing down the correct key does not automatically produce the exact pitch desired. It is necessary, therefore, for players to "favor" certain notes on their instrument in order to play in tune. Needless to say, this matter is not given serious consideration in the early stages. But it becomes a matter of real importance and concern as the woodwind and brass players move into the advanced stages of instruction. This "favoring" of a note is done on a string instrument by moving the finger forward or backward on the string; it may amount to nothing more than an infinitesimal rolling of the finger when the finer shades of intonation are at stake. The string instruments do not have the advantage the woodwinds and brasses have of a specific key or combination of keys to produce a specific note; but neither do the strings have any limit on their ability to produce *perfect* intonation. The trumpet and clarinet players may find beginning intonation less of a problem than the violinist, but later the clarinetist will be fighting certain notes on his instrument in the middle and upper registers, and the trumpeter may find problems with notes that utilize the third valve. At this stage the string player can blame no one and nothing but himself.

In the early stages of string instruction it is imperative that the instrument be properly adjusted, the strings in good condition, and the instrument carefully tuned by the instructor for each lesson. Neglect of any one of these matters can impair the young student's attempts to play in tune. (The value of tuners and metal strings from the standpoint of easy tuning and staying in tune has already been discussed.)

When the fingers of the left hand are first placed on the string, the problem is to get the child to place them at the point on the string which produces the correct pitch. There are approximations which can be used, such as: the first finger should be placed on the string "so far from the nut" in terms of inches.

Finger Placement Aids

Various devices have been tried in an attempt to assist young students to orient their fingers correctly to the strings. A few of these devices, or techniques, are listed below:

1. Pieces of adhesive tape are placed under and perpendicular to the strings to mark the places where the fingers are placed.
2. A piece of string is stretched across the fingerboard and fastened with cellophane tape. This provides an elevated strip which is easy for the finger to feel.

3. Finger positions are marked on the fingerboard with chalk or crayon.
4. A patented device called "Gay Instant Pitch Finder" after the inventor. This aid is a piece of heavy paper shaped like the fingerboard with holes cut out at the places where the fingers are placed. These holes act as "inverted frets." Fastened onto the fingerboard, it can help the young beginner come closer to the notes he is in search of.

There is a continuing pedagogical argument about the use of aids, or crutches, such as those described above. One side of the argument abhors the use of anything but the ear in the note-finding process, and claims that the child will remain dependent upon the aid long after its period of usefulness. The other side is willing to accept anything which can assist the young student over some of the early hurdles on the premise that success is thus more easily achieved, and success breeds success. As far as the author knows, no research has been done with a control group to prove or disprove either of these arguments. Sheer desperation will drive the teacher to try anything to help students who show little or no aptitude for pitch discrimination, in the hope that they will one day see the light.

FIGURE 6.1. Tape marking the place for the first and second finger on the violin.

FIGURE 6.2. Instant pitch finder.

Vibrato

Among the functions of the left hand, vibrato is second only to intonation in importance; for when the vibrato begins to develop, the player begins to move out of the beginning student category onto the path which leads to artistry. It is the vibrato which imbues the tone with warmth, vitality, and lustre.

The vibrato is produced by a back and forth rolling motion of the finger on the string. This motion alternately raises and lowers the pitch, but it does it in such a way that the listener is not aware of pitch fluctuation but rather of the beauty which vibrato adds to the tone.

It is the flexibility in the width and speed of the vibrato which is largely responsible for the tremendous range of expression of which the string instruments are capable. It is the variety and expressiveness of the vibrato which has led to the contention that the strings have the closest kinship to the human voice of all of the instruments.

The vibrato should never be purely mechanical. To be truly effective it must respond to the emotional stimulus of the music. It depicts calmness and serenity through its own lack of agitation. It heightens the drama and intensity of the music by becoming more rapid, more violent, more agitated. Those vibratos which are too slow or too fast, too wide or too narrow, which function at a constant speed, or which impair intonation are detrimental to the ultimate in performance in the same way that a wobble or a quiver can make a voice unpleasant.

The actual movement of fingers, hand, and arm in producing vibrato will be discussed in relationship to each instrument. The preparation of these movements can be assisted through various kinds of exercise and practice. Joints can be flexed and the hand and arm can be put through motions which will condition them to produce a vibrato. But a degree of physical coordination and emotional compulsion that verges upon a mystique seem to be needed before the vibrato will function freely. For some it comes as naturally as eating. For others it remains elusive, defying long and arduous effort to acquire it. To repeat, exercises may condition the mechanism but they will not "cause" a vibrato to function.

Students should not be encouraged to use vibrato too early in their development. It should wait until intonation is reliable; since the movement of the fingers and the fluctuation of pitch in the vibrato can cover up poor intonation. If poor intonation persists, the vibrato should be avoided and the student should practice with a "dead" hand.[1] As stated earlier, the vibrato should not be mechanical. With some players a constant vibrato becomes a habit, and curbing the vibrato when desirable or requested is hard for them.

Shifting and Positions

Shifting positions on a string instrument is the process of moving the hand closer to or farther from the nut. The positions available to the string player begin with half position and progress up the string to seventh, eighth, or even ninth position.

The availability of numerous positions expands the capability of the string instruments in the following ways:

It extends the over-all range of the instruments by extending the high range
It extends the playing range on each string
It facilitates the playing of certain note combinations or sequences which otherwise would be awkward
It makes the portamento possible.

If the string instruments could play only in first position, two limitations would be imposed upon them. First, the number of notes that could be played on each string would be those which can be reached in first position. Second, the high range would be limited to the notes that can be reached with the little finger while playing in first position on the top string.

By utilizing the higher positions it is possible to play many more notes on each string and the over-all range of each instrument is expanded by more than two octaves. In the examples below the range of notes played on each string, using first position, is compared with the expanded range using the higher positions. Over-all ranges using first and fifth positions are also shown.

In the following chart, beginning, intermediate, and advanced ranges are shown for each instrument. The beginning range does not exceed first position. At the Intermediate stage the violin and viola are in third position, the cello in fourth position, and the bass in third position. The advanced stage makes use of fifth through seventh positions. It should be understood that standard solo and orchestral literature require the player to exceed the top limit shown in this chart.

---

1. This term describes a manner of playing which is devoid of any left hand expression. In performance the string player uses an almost continuous vibrato. If the composer wants a passage played without vibrato, he writes *non vibrato* at the beginning of the section. On the other hand, if he wants to assure that a passage will be played with full vibrato, he writes *molto vibrato*. Actually neither term is used very frequently. The excitement of the music—if it is convincingly written—is usually enough to stimulate the players to use *molto vibrato*; so they do not need to be told. *Non vibrato* is a special effect, and no special effect should be over-worked.

CHART SHOWING EXTENDED RANGE USING 5TH POSITION

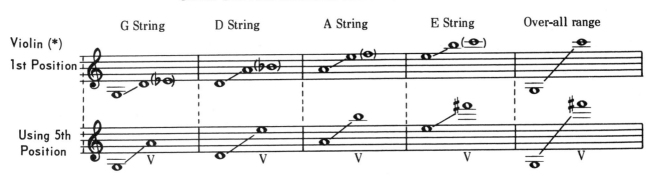

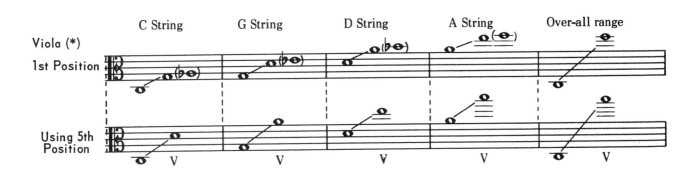

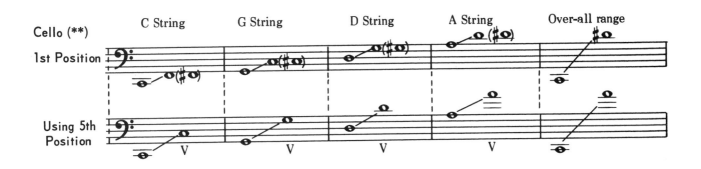

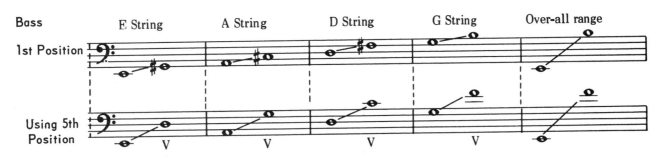

(*) The notes in parentheses are reached by extending the 4th finger.

(**) The notes in parentheses are reached by using the forward hand extension.

OVER-ALL RANGES OF THE INSTRUMENTS AT VARIOUS STAGES

Beginning   Intermediate   Advanced

(Bass sounds *8va* lower than written)

Moving from one position to another is called shifting. Every string method includes an explanation of the positions and how to shift. Many exercises are devoted to acquainting the student with correct shifting techniques, to the orientation of the hand and fingers to the various positions, and to developing facility in getting from one position to another easily and accurately.

A thorough knowledge of the positions, and shifting techniques which are both fluid and accurate are essential equipment for the advanced player. Bass and cello players will begin shifting early of necessity. Violinists will find that they must know at least third and fifth positions if they are to conquer even a small part of the standard repertoire. Violists can get by for a longer period of time without going above third position.

A shift can be made purely for the purpose of getting to the next desired position. When this is the objective, the shift is made as unnoticeably as possible. To accomplish this the fingers move lightly and quickly to the next position. A shift may be made from one position to another using the same finger or a different finger. What precedes and follows the shift determines this, and there are too

many possibilities to cover here. A shift may also be made from any position to any other position.

SULLA CORDA

The aim of the shift may be to play a particular group of notes on one string rather than move to the next higher string, thus avoiding a change in tone quality. When a composer wants to give a player this kind of direction, he uses the term *Sulla* (sul, sull', sulle) *Corda*, or *Sul* followed by the letter name of the string. In the following example the cellist knows that the composer wants the first four measures played on the D string.

A famous example of playing for an extended period on one string is the *Air* by J.S. Bach as arranged for the violin by the great 19th century German violinist, August Wilhelmj. Wilhelmj transposed the *Air* from the D Major Suite to the key of C which meant that the lowest note in the piece would be G. The highest note is B♭, a minor tenth above. He then indicated Sul G at the beginning of the piece. Over the years the piece became a favorite encore known as the "Air for the G String."

The higher positions on one of the three lower strings may be used to achieve a more intense quality

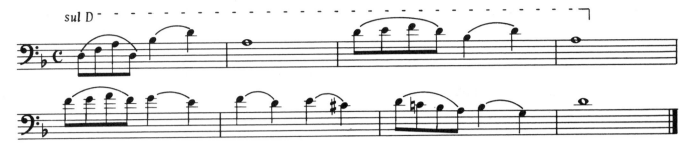

of tone than can be realized by playing the notes in a lower position on a higher string. For example, notes played in fifth position on the violin G string can be far more intense and dramatic than the same tones played on the D string. An excellent example of this is found in the opening section of the Ravel *Tzigane* for violin and piano. Ravel has designed this unaccompanied recitative so that it mounts higher and higher on the G string in both pitch and intensity until it seems that the instrument shrieks with passion.

THE PORTAMENTO

Many times the shift has an ulterior purpose. This purpose is to produce a slide or *portamento* from the note which is being left or to the note which is being approached. This effect gives a poignant stress to the note or sequence of notes and enhances the emotional impact of the interval.

An experienced and competent performer will know when a *portamento* is appropriate and when it is not, without any indication from the composer. If, however, the composer wants to make certain that a *portamento* is executed in a particular spot, he may write the word *portamento* over the interval or use the musical shorthand, which is a slanted line between the two notes in question. This symbol is another example of the exactness of musical notation; for the length of the line is indicative of the scope of the portamento. A short line tells the player to make only a slight slide. A longer line extends the length of the slide.

Example 1 leaves the amount of *portamento* up to the player's discretion. Example 2 tells him that there should be a little *portamento,* but not too much, to the high B. This portamento is executed by placing the second finger on the string below the B with nearly normal pressure and sliding into the B.

Example 3 calls for a heavier, more continuous slide between the two notes than do either of the previous examples. And example 4 could be called either a

portamento or an unarticulated *glissando*. Example 5 is a true chromatic glissando. It is played with one finger which slides down the string, articulating each note.

Example 1

Example 2

Example 3

Example 4

Example 5

The portamento must be used with discretion. It is inappropriate in music preceding the Romantic period. Mechanically the slide must be executed with taste. It must not be too long, too slow, or too heavy, and it must not be over-used. Experience, maturity, good taste, and good examples after which to pattern will create the restraint needed in the use of this device.

INDICATING FINGERINGS AND POSITIONS

Composers who are not string players usually leave the matter of fingering and positions up to an editor or the player; or they collaborate with a performer during the writing process and bring out a fully edited score upon publication. Standard editions of orchestral literature contain a minimum number of fingerings. This is a detail that the composer is often incompetent to execute or one which he chooses not to spend time on. On the other hand, some solo literature is extensively edited with fingerings. There are advantages as well as disadvantages to this. A carefully edited piece of music can convey nearly everything that the composer had in mind. This is helpful, especially to those who feel that they need this kind of assistance. But the artist-performer, and I refer to the majority of highly skilled players, has his own way of doing many things. Ranking foremost among these is fingering. So any piece of music which has been edited is a reflection of the kinds of fingerings preferred by the editor, based, of course, upon what he felt the composer intended. If the edition is cluttered with

fingerings, the better players will look for another edition; for they prefer a relatively clean copy into which they can insert those notations they feel they need. This is not to say that specific wishes of the composer should not be put down; they should. So should fingerings where they are helpful and where they will expedite the player's understanding of the music or speed his ability to execute a difficult passage.

Fingerings and positions can be indicated in two ways. The fingering can be written above or below the notes with Arabic numerals; or the position may be written above or below the notes with Roman numerals. Most editors simply use fingerings. If a misunderstanding is possible, they may use Roman numerals to indicate the string they intend the notes to be played on. I means the top string; II is the second; III the third; IV the fourth. Because the Roman numeral sometimes stands for a string and sometimes a position, confusion is possible. Occasionally the composer's or editor's intentions can be deduced only by drawing conclusions from the use of similar markings elsewhere in the music where the intent is clear.

In the following example, Arabic numerals indicate the fingers which are to play the notes. (Mendelssohn Violin Concerto) The positions utilized in these five measures are written here below the staff only to indicate the shifting which takes place. It is not customary to mark positions in this way except in student literature.

Positions are often indicated by Roman numerals in study materials such as etudes and scales. One reason for using Roman numerals to indicate positions in this type of material is to acquaint the student with the positions he is using. Another is that extended passages or an entire etude may be in one positions; that is, it was written to be played in one position as an aid to learning that position. In such cases there may be a statement at the head of the etude indicating that it is to be played in a particular position; or the Roman numeral symbolizing that position may be used at the start of the etude. Or the etude may be labeled "Etude in 3rd Position." In the examples which follow it is to be assumed that the player will stay in the indicated position until another position is indicated.

Double Stops

The term double stop denotes the technique of playing on two strings simultaneously. The three upper instruments are capable of playing double stops with many combinations of fingering. The bass is less disposed toward double stops because of the difficulty of keeping more than one of its large strings vibrating, and because of the limited number of intervals that the hand can encompass. For these reasons double stops on the bass are generally limited to combinations which utilize an open string. Even this demand is restricted to advanced solos and is virtually never encountered in orchestral works.

The violin and viola are capable of playing double stops ranging from unison to tenths. Larger intervals are possible if an open string is the bottom tone. Advanced instruction on these instruments includes scales in thirds, sixths, octaves, and tenths. The reach is greater on the cello, so fewer combinations are possible; although thirds, sixths, and octaves are not uncommon in solo writing.

Double stops are most effective in the low and middle section of the instrument's register, in the positions which make use of maximum string length. Double stop writing is limited almost exclusively to solos although a composer may occasionally write double stops for one or more of the sections of the strings. Combinations of open strings are not unusual, as well as combinations using one open string while the fingers function on an adjoining string.

Thirds and sixths are the most frequently used double stops because they are the most pleasant and sonorous to hear, and because they are the easiest to manage on the instrument. Fifths are difficult to play in tune. The finger must be pressed flat across the two strings and must be straight across in order to get a perfect fifth.[2] Tenths are difficult but possible on the violin and viola, since they stretch the hand to capacity. Octaves can be played throughout the violin and viola range. Normally the first and fourth fingers are used except when an open string is involved in which case the third finger plays the upper member of the octave. Fingered octaves use a 1-3, 2-4 finger pattern. They are very difficult and are limited to the most advanced players in solo work. In playing octaves and tenths the cellist uses his thumb to play the lower note and his third finger to play the upper note.

Examples of some double stops and their fingerings follow. Needless to say, either note in the following examples may be altered chromatically.

SOME DOUBLE STOPS AND THEIR FINGERINGS
VIOLIN

---

2. This applies only to perfect fifths. A diminished or augmented fifth is played with two fingers as will be seen in the illustrations which follow.

SOME DOUBLE STOPS AND THEIR FINGERINGS
VIOLA

SOME DOUBLE STOPS AND THEIR FINGERINGS
CELLO

Examples

Examples

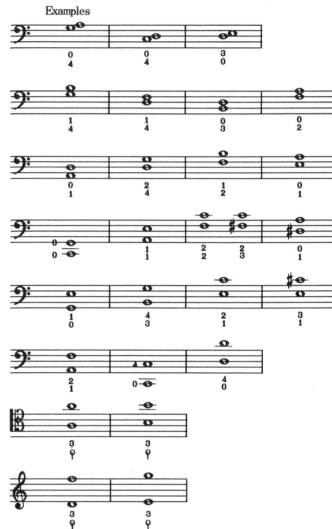

φ is the sign for thumb position.

The examples given above are selective only. Each of the string instruments, except the bass, is capable of playing most major and minor 2nds, 3rds, 6ths, 7ths, perfect, diminished, and augmented 4ths, 5ths, and 8vas throughout the range of the instrument, limited only by the bottom string capabilities and the practicality of the high positions.

DIVISI

In orchestral writing, if a composer or arranger writes two notes and expects both notes to be played by each player, he often indicates his intent with the term *non divisi*. In German the term *nicht geteilt* is used. *Divisi* or *geteilt*, on the other hand, tells the players that they are to play only one note of a two-part divisi. Some conductors have players divide on each stand, the outside player playing the top note while the inside player plays the lower note. Other conductors have the first stand play the top, the second stand the lower notes, etc. When more than three notes are written, special arrangements must be specified by the conductor or the concert master in order to cover all parts. Examples of typical *divisi* and *non-divisi* writing follow.

TILL EULENSPIEGELS LUSTIGE STREICHE

Richard Strauss

Starting with Berlioz, Wagner, and Richard Strauss and continuing through Debussy, Ravel, Sibelius, and into the present, multi-part writing for the strings is commonplace. The opulence created by this kind of scoring seems to answer the need for rich, lush textures of sound. It is not unusual to have each section of the strings divided into two, three, or four parts. This is done by writing the parts on separate staves.

In Ravel's *Daphnis and Chloe Suite* three separate lines are utilized for the viola part. In Sibelius' *The Swan of Tuonela* the first and second violins are each divided into four parts, the violas and cellos into two separate parts, which, in turn, have frequent two-part *divisi*.

Pizzicato

WITH THE RIGHT HAND

Pizzicato is the process of producing tone by plucking the string. Normally pizzicato (abbreviated pizz.) is performed by the right hand. On the violin, viola, and cello the pad of the first finger is used, with the thumb placed against the side of the fingerboard to support the hand and arm. On the bass the first, and sometimes the first and second fingers are used, with the thumb again braced against the side of the fingerboard.[3]

For the playing of extended pizzicato passages the bow is held in the remaining fingers of the right hand or is laid down. If an isolated pizzicato note or chord occurs, with little time for preparation, the bow may be held in its normal manner and the finger (thumb for the cellist) is simply straightened to pluck the string or strings. For an extended passage, the composer will do well to allow time for the player to prepare for the pizzicato, as well as to re-grasp the bow following the pizzicato passage. Without adequate time to get set for the pizzicato, the player must make a mad scramble, hoping to get his finger on the right string in time, a maneuver that does not always meet with total success.

Following a pizzicato note or passage the word *arco*, which is the Italian word for the bow, is placed before the next group of notes to tell the player to again use the bow. This term is used as universally as the term pizzicato. Once in a great while a French edition directs the player to *reprenez l'arche.*

In the proper execution of pizzicato the string is pulled sideways. If pulled vertically, the string slaps against the fingerboard, making an unmusical sound which is only acceptable as a special effect when asked for by the composer. The quality of sound is regulated by the point at which the string is plucked. Toward the bridge the tone will be hard and brittle; well up the fingerboard the tone will be soft and limp.

One, two, three, or four strings may be played pizzicato in one stroke. In playing chords cellists, and sometimes violinists and violists, use the thumb; although the first finger is most often used on violin and viola, in which case it is flattened across the strings involved. In chord playing, more hand and arm action is required than in the playing of single notes; so the thumb is taken away from the fingerboard.

Composers use pizzicato for punctuation, percussive effects, and for relief or change. The music of the early composers made only infrequent use of pizzicato. A charming example is the slow movement from the Haydn F Major Quartet (No. 17 in the Litolff collection of 20 Celebrated Quartets). In this movement the first violin plays a lovely muted melody to the harp-like pizzicato accompaniment of the other three instruments.

Tchaikovsky was enamored of the sound of pizzicato in the orchestra and made frequent use of the technique. The third movement of his Symphony No. 4 in F minor uses the strings exclusively in pizzicato fashion. In a case such as this, where the bow is not used for an extended period, and there is time to pick it up again, it is generally laid on the music stand. Another famous pizzicato passage is found just after the opening woodwind chords in Tchaikovsky's Overture to Romeo and Juliet.

The full string section playing pizzicato has a certain special appeal to most audiences. The reason probably lies in the novelty of seeing and hearing these normally smooth, singing instruments produce percussive sounds which are uncharacteristic of their otherwise sweet and gentle nature, plus the spectacle of these bowed instruments producing sounds without the bow. Leroy Anderson has capitalized upon this special appeal of the pizzicato in his piece for strings called *Jazz Pizzicato*. Composers who write for school groups have also recognized the merits of pizzicato selections and have produced numerous

---

3. In dance music the bass is part of the rhythm section and plays pizzicato exclusively. Because of this, many dance bassists move the right hand and arm rather freely rather than keeping the thumb against the fingerboard. In slow tempi the arm is partially dropped or pulled away from the fingerboard between beats. This serves to keep the arm loose and relaxed, and the motion, which is a rhythmical one occurring on the beats between the notes (beats 2 and 4), can actually help the player to keep a steady beat. When playing a "four beat" figure (a note on each count of a four beat bar), or a fast tempo that puts the notes closer together, the hand is kept closer to the strings.

FIGURE 6.3. Pizzicato on the violin and viola.

FIGURE 6.4. Pizzicato on the cello.

FIGURE 6.5. Pizzicato on the bass (with a French bow).

FIGURE 6.6. Pizzicato on the bass (with a German bow).

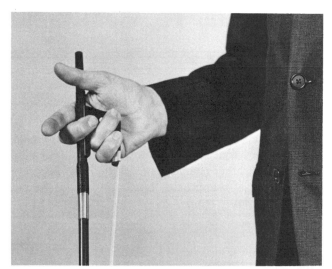

FIGURE 6.7. Holding the German bow for pizzicato.

compositions in various grades of difficulty. They are popular with both young and mature audiences.

LEFT-HAND PIZZICATO

In advanced solo literature for the violin and to a lesser extent the viola and cello, pizzicato is also performed by the left hand. The fingers of the left hand pluck the string in the direction of the palm of the hand. Single notes or groups of notes can be played in this fashion. Considerable strength and control are needed to play left-hand pizzicato; and, at best, not a great amount of tone can be produced. A small plus sign (+) is placed over notes which are to be played pizzicato with the left hand.

Descending scale passages can be played in this manner. The fourth finger plucks the string to produce the note which is stopped by the third finger. The third and second fingers follow suit, and the first finger plucks the open string. The following passage would be played in this way.

Because the little finger is relatively weak and ineffectual in this manner of playing, the notes that it would play in the above passage are often played by striking the string with the bow, as follows:

Patterns in which bowed notes and pizzicato notes alternate are found in the violin solos of Paganini, Sarasate and other composers of virtuoso violin pieces. Such passages are usually brief and are performed at a fairly rapid tempo.

Trill

"A trill consists of the regular and rapid alternation of a given note with the note above."[4] The trill may be a half or a whole step above the lower, or principal, note depending upon the underlying harmonic structure. On the string instruments the finger playing the lower note remains static while the trilling finger moves rapidly onto and off the string.

Trills can be of short or long duration, lasting for as short a time as a 16th note or as long as several measures. Two important qualities in a trill are evenness and clarity. Both are dependent upon strength and control in the fingers of the left hand. Most books of studies have lessons for the development of the trill, all of which have the same purpose, building strength and elasticity in the fingers; for to produce a clear trill the finger must strike the string firmly and leave it instantaneously.

The second finger is generally the strongest; consequently most performers produce their best trill with this finger. The third finger is next in efficiency; the little finger generally ranks from poor to fair. Trills that might involve an open string on the lower note are usually taken in a position; although it is possible to trill with the first finger. The bass is rarely asked to trill because of the slow response of its strings.

In early music the trill is usually started from the higher note. (This is referred to as starting the trill from above.) This produces an *appoggiatura* to the principal note. In most cases the trill lasts for the full duration of the note and is ended with a turn utilizing the note below the principal note. When the trill is in a cadential position it frequently ends with an anticipation of the note of resolution.

Since the Romantic period, practice is to start the trill on the principal note. It may or may not be ended with a turn. Circumstances dictate this matter. Cadential trills are frequently begun slowly; they may be ended in a rhythmical manner with the principal note and the trill note receiving equal amounts of time in a measured fashion.

4. Grove's Dictionary of Music and Musicians.

Played

A series of trills is usually played with no ornamentation.

This is by no means meant to be a treatise on the trill. Grove's Dictionary of Music and Musicians gives three pages to the discussion of the shake or trill, and there is widespread disagreement among the musicologists about the interpretation of the entire field of ornamentation, including trills and their beginning and ending. The important thing to remember here is that a trill that functions well may be adapted to any situation.

Tremolo (Finger)

The word "finger" is added here to differentiate between this tremolo and the more common tremolo which is played with the bow. The finger tremolo is patterned after the piano tremolo wherein two or more notes are played alternately in rapid fashion.

The string instruments are also capable of playing tremolo in double stop combinations.

Or less commonly

In orchestra music the types of tremolo illustrated above would usually be played *divisi*. The single tremolo is encountered quite frequently in orchestra music.

In the slow movement of his violin concerto, Mendelssohn makes very effective use of this device in combination with double stops.

Harmonics

NATURAL HARMONICS

A natural harmonic is a tone produced by placing a finger lightly on a string at one of the string's natural division, or nodal, points. This causes the string to vibrate in segments instead of as a whole. The result is called a harmonic. The harmonic is soft in volume and flute-like in timbre.

The sign usually used for a natural harmonic is a small circle placed over the fundamental note. Diamond shaped notes are also used. By touching the string lightly at that point, the desired harmonic is produced. In the first example below, the finger touches the string at its mid-point. This produces the harmonic one octave above the fundamental open D. By placing the finger lightly at the 1/5 division point, as in the next example, the harmonic produced sounds two octaves above the fundamental open string.

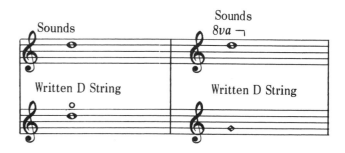

Harmonics which can be produced on the G string of the violin are illustrated below. By simple transposition the harmonics available on the other strings and other instruments can be found readily.

So-called "artificial" harmonics are produced by stopping the string with a finger and then touching the string lightly at the interval of a 3rd, 4th, or 5th above the stopped point. In this way harmonics of the shortened string are produced. Harmonics which are two 8vas, two 8vas and a 3rd, and two 8vas and a 5th above the fundamental can be played. The first of these (two 8vas) is the most common. It is used in playing scale-wise passages and other melodic passages with the flute-like harmonic quality. Some artificial harmonics and the method of writing them are shown below.

Techniques of the Bow

Holding the Bow

The bow is held in the right hand. With the exception of the Butler bass bow, the bows are held in basically the same way. The thumb is placed on the underneath side of the stick, near the frog. The four fingers are placed on top of the stick, curving over the stick to form a grip.

This grip must be relaxed but firm. It must be capable of manipulating the bow with the utmost delicacy at one moment and with fierce roughness the next, with snail-like slowness and tremendous speed. It must be able to make short, staccato notes and then connect notes imperceptibly, to stay on

the string or bounce off, to be at the frog or at the point, or on the top string or the lowest string all in fractions of seconds.

The precise manner of holding the bow is as controversial as the question of how the thumb is placed on the neck, but the bow grip has been regarded as of greater importance. The reason so much importance has been placed upon this matter is due to the difficulty so many players have in achieving a bow grip with which they are satisfied and comfortable in all circumstances. Many diverse demands are made of the bow; it is expected to do many things. If it balks or fails in any of its duties, the performer comes to one of two conclusions—either the bow itself is inadequate to the task, or his grip needs to be adjusted. Once the first question is resolved satisfactorily, the second becomes the center of attention. The search is always for a panacea.

Over the years this search for the perfect way to hold the bow, a grip that would make it possible for any player to execute the most difficult and intricate bowings with ease, has led to the formation of several so-called "schools" of holding the bow. The Russian, the German, and Franco-Belgian Schools of violin bowing are the most prominent. Without going into a lengthy account of each of these schools, it is safe to say that they evolved as did schools of painting. That is, a great artist (who was usually a teacher also), did what was instinctive to him and produced the results he desired. Others observed, copied, or were taught, his techniques, and a "school" was born. Each school has recognizable characteristics which distinguish it. In

NATURAL HARMONICS ON THE VIOLIN G STRING

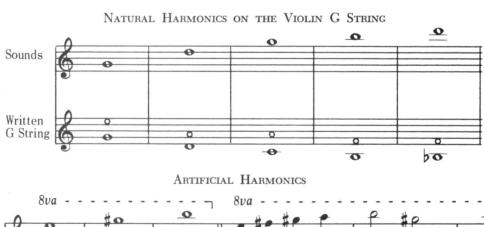

ARTIFICIAL HARMONICS

the case of the schools of bowing the distinguishing characteristics are the placement of the first finger on the stick and the consequent attitude of the wrist and elbow.

The most convincing argument against the position that there is only one correct way to hold the bow is the fact that these several schools of bowing have emerged through the years. If one way of holding the bow were so much better than another, why did not one method become universal? The reason is, of course, that each individual's bone and muscle structure is unique. Being unique, it is therefore impossible for one individual to do something in precisely the same way as another. Modifications to suit individual differences are necessary. No teacher should insist that every pupil adopt his system, his approach, or his mannerisms any more than every one should have to wear size nine shoes and live in a brown house.

Since the onset of the twentieth century and the internationalization of the world through improved transportation and communications systems, the nationalistic aspects of the various schools of bowing have disappeared. In fact, today the terms "German School" or "Russian School" are viewed more with historic interest than as terms having meaningful current applicability. It is not important that the characteristics of these schools be known, but it is a matter of interest; therefore they are described briefly below.

Russian School

The Russian school put the stick at the top of the third joint of the first finger, nearly into the palm, with the hand tilted toward the point. This puts the wrist into a high arch and makes it possible to apply the full weight of the arm with ease. (Figure 6.8)

German School

The German school went in the opposite direction, putting the first joint of the first finger in contact with the wood and maintaining flat fingers and a rather flat wrist. This grip produces a very low wrist position at the point of the bow. (Figure 6.9)

Franco-Belgian School

This was a compromise between the Russian and German positions. The second joint of the first finger was the point of contact, the hand tilted slightly toward the tip, and the wrist in a moderate arch. (Figure 6.10)

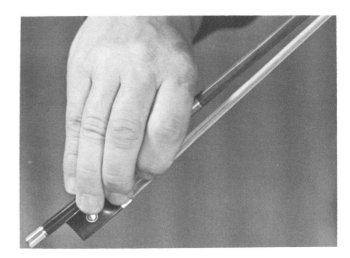

FIGURE 6.8. Holding the violin bow (Russian school).

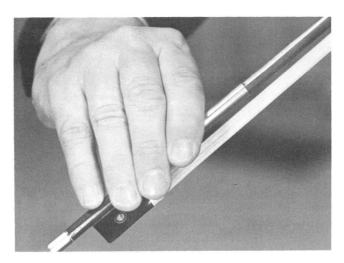

FIGURE 6.9. Holding the violin bow (German school).

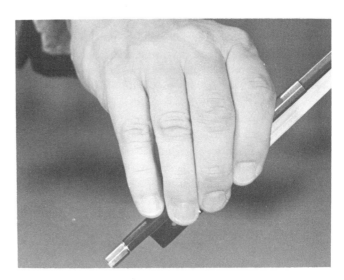

FIGURE 6.10. Holding the violin bow (Franco-Belgian school).

Function of the Bow

The bow's purpose is to draw tone from the instrument. To accomplish this the hair of the bow is placed on the string at right angles and is then moved in a downward or upward direction. The friction produced by the hair and the string cause the string to vibrate. Presto, tone is created. Nothing could be simpler.

There are five basic factors which bear on this very simple principle. They are:

Bow Direction (up or down)
Amount and Speed of Bow
Point of Contact on the String
Amount of Pressure or Weight
Amount of Hair in Contact with the String

All of the infinite number of strokes and subtleties of which the bow is capable are produced by the variables inherent in these five factors. Bow direction stands in a special category because there are only two directions for the bow to travel—up or down. (On the bass and cello this really amounts to left or right, but common practice over the years has been to use the term "up" and "down" in reference to all the strings.) But the remaining factors are capable of a nearly endless number of variations. True, the full bow is the most that can be used. However, skillful manipulation can deceive the listener into believing that the bow has no stopping point. On the other end of the spectrum, as little as 1/16th inch of bow may be used to play a note. So the amount of bow can range from a fraction of an inch to the full bow; and added to this is the factor of speed, which can be from unbelievably slow to incredibly fast.

As to point of contact, the bridge and the fingerboard are considered the reasonable limits. However, it is not uncommon in the music of the Impressionists to be directed to play "over the fingerboard," a technique called *flautato* or *flautando*, which produces a breathy, flute-like quality. The other extreme is behind the bridge, a manner of playing which is required very infrequently and yields a sound which is more a squeak or whistle than a musical tone. Between these extremes lie the infinite number of points of contact from which the player may select to attain the particular volume and quality of tone he wants at a given moment.

Pressure, or weight, is directly related to speed and point of contact. Each influences and is influenced by the other. Pressure of the bow on the string is not increased without moving the point of contact closer to the bridge, and vice versa.

The tilt of the bow governs the amount of hair which is in contact with the string. Tilt changes from frog to point because of the movements of the hand and arm, and because of the need to use more hair and pressure from the middle to the point. It is in this way that the tone and volume throughout the length of the bow is equalized, the heavy lower half using less hair and the upper half using additional hair and pressure as needed.

Tone Production

Learning to "dig in" with the bow and draw a full tone is a long process in most cases. Many students are well into, and some well beyond, the intermediate stage of progress before they acquire this concept. The big string tone is a product of the following factors:

1. Controlled strength in the right arm, hand, and fingers
2. Proper balance between bow-speed and pressure
3. Correct distance of the bow from the bridge in relation to speed and pressure.

The kind of strength referred to in number one is not the bulging-muscle type. However the muscles in the arms and fingers of the string player do need to be steely.

There is a great deal of force and counter-force at work in the bowing process. The first place this happens is between the thumb, which presses up, and the fingers, which press down. The second instance is the pressing down of the bow on the string and the resistance of the string. The thumb and the first finger form a lever action which, if applied to excess, could break the bow. The string and the little finger balance this action. This function of the little finger accounts for the importance of having it on top of the stick.

The arm also plays an important role. From the middle to the point, pressure on the string is exerted through the thumb-first-finger lever with its counter balances. From the middle to the frog the natural weight of the arm comes into play. This weight must be controlled by the shoulder muscles in order to keep the lower-half volume in balance with the volume capability of the upper half.

Tone production is dependent upon all of these factors being in proper balance.

Dynamics

There are several over-all guiding principles in regard to dynamics. They are (1) The softest tone is produced by the least amount of bow pressure,

(2) the loudest tone is produced by the greatest amount of bow pressure and (3) as pressure is increased, the point of contact moves closer to the bridge.

Correlated with this principle is one having to do with the amount, or length, of bow used in regard to dynamics. This principle can be stated as (1) The softest tone is produced by using the least amount of bow, (2) the loudest tone is produced by using the greatest amount of bow.

Of fundamental importance are

1. Point of contact between bow and string
2. Speed of the bow
3. Amount of hair contacting the string.

The question of the amount of hair to use is relatively simple. If more tone is desired, the bow is brought to a more upright position, and more hair is brought in contact with the string. For less tone, reverse the procedure.

Point of contact is a somewhat more complex matter because it is directly related to bow speed. And bow speed is dictated by duration of note, point of contact, pressure, and desired tone quality. If two given notes are of the same duration, and require the use of the full bow, then pressure and point of contact are the factors which will govern the dynamic produced. If something less than a full bow is required to produce the note, then bow speed also enters into the matter, in which case the principle stated above applies.

Bowing directions cannot be given in absolute terms. But it is possible to reduce a few matters to simple terms which will apply in most situations. They are

Forte
    Exert pressure on the bow
    Use as much bow as possible
    Keep the point of contact close to the bridge
Piano
    Exert little or no pressure. Use a light bow
    Limit the amount of bow used
    Keep the point of contact away from the bridge

Bowings

The term "bowings" refers to how the bow functions in relation to the music. It involves whether the bow will go up or down, stay on the string or bounce, start and stop abruptly or smoothly, slur notes or play them separately. The basic orchestral bowings and their symbols will be discussed below, but in order to understand them it is first necessary to become acquainted with the vocabulary of the

bow. Some of these terms have already been presented and should be reviewed. (See Figure 2.3) Others will be new.

Bow Direction

Down Bow

The bow travels in a frog-to-point direction. A down bow may begin at the frog or at any point above the frog. See A in Figure 6.11.

The sign for down bow is almost universally ⊓ . Some old editions use ∧ , which is an inverted up bow sign.

Up Bow

The opposite of down bow. The bow is drawn in point-to-frog direction. See B Figure 6.11. The sign for up bow is ∨ .

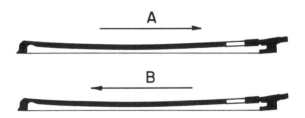

FIGURE 6.11. Line drawing showing bow direction. A. down bow, B. up bow.

Divisions of the Bow

For convenient reference the bow is divided into six playing areas:

Whole Bow	(W. B.)	Upper Half	(U. H.)
Point	(Pt.)	Middle	(M.)
Frog	(Fr.)	Lower Half	(L. H.)

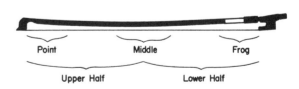

FIGURE 6.12. Divisions of the bow.

These are terms conductors and string players must be familiar with. They constitute the common language of the orchestra. It should be understood that no area of the bow is used exclusive of another.

The upper half includes the point, which is simply the top two to six inches of the upper half. The middle includes portions of both the upper and lower half; and the frog, like the point, is the lowermost part of the lower half.

The area near the frog is the heaviest part of the bow and consequently is used for the heavy bowings. The point is the lightest part. It is in this area that soft tremolo is played. If a conductor's admonition is, "Play at the point" or simply "Point!!", be assured he wants very little volume.

If a conductor orders "on the string," it will be in regard to a passage which could very possibly be interpreted to be played off the string (spiccato) as well. In quiet passages which need special control, such as a staccato passage at a moderate tempo, many conductors prefer to have the bows left on the string. They believe that the string section can achieve increased uniformity and precision in this way.

"In the string" means that the hair is to maintain firm and continuous contact with the string. Increased pressure is usually part of this concept. The sound resulting from this approach is the opposite of the flautato, which is a light, airy sound.

Use of the Bow

It is possible to digest some basic principles of bow use which are based upon the laws of physics, and are influenced by tradition and the need of the player for comfort and security. Immediately following are the various divisions of the bow and the kinds of bowings which are most frequently performed in those divisions.

Down Bow
When the music begins on a strong beat
For heavy accents and chords
For diminuendo on one note or a slur

Up Bow
When the music begins on a weak beat
For pick-up note(s)
For crescendo on one note or a slur

Lower Half
Heavy accents and chords
Heavy repeated staccato notes, on or off the string
Heavy marcato

Middle
Spiccato
Détaché
Staccato
Ricochet

Upper Half
Détaché
Spiccato
Staccato
Marcato
Tremolo
Ricochet

Point
Tremolo
Light détaché and staccato
Ricochet

Full Bow
Long sustained tones
Long slurs
Long, heavy staccato or marcato

Bow Use and Distribution

One of the commonest faults among young string players is failure to distribute the bow intelligently and practically. "Running out of bow" is frequently experienced by the young player. It is caused by the failure to plan ahead. The solution to "running out of bow" is simply to "save the bow." "Saving the bow" is a relatively simple concept to demonstrate and is not difficult to put into practice. All that is needed is a little self-discipline.

"Running out of bow" is a problem which shows up in long notes . . . usually whole notes or longer, in moderate to slow tempi. (The factor involved is not actually the note value but the duration of the note in actual time—seconds.) Any note which must be held for more than 3 to 5 seconds is a long note for a young player. His natural, youthful instinct is to keep moving, get it over with and onto the next thing. So he hurries through the first part of the note with the bow, realizing too late that he does not have enough bow for the balance of the note.

In addition, most young players do not avail themselves of the full bow. They avoid the frog area like the plague, automatically cheating themselves out of usable bow. The most plausible reason for this is that the arm must put out extra lifting effort in this part of the bow; so following the line of least resistance, that area of the bow is avoided. A contributing factor is that it is more difficult to make a smooth change of bow at the frog than three to four inches ahead of the frog. The number of bows on which the hair is black from disuse in this area is adequate substantiation of this statement.

To summarize this point, the student who is unschooled in the art of bowing resists using the portion of the bow just ahead of the frog. If the bow is placed on the string at the frog at the start of a piece, or if something compels the bow to arrive at the frog, the student seems to want to get it away from that area as fast as possible. If the note is to be held for four counts, he will more often than not expend three-fourths of the bow on the first two counts, leaving too little bow for the remaining two counts (Figure 6.13).

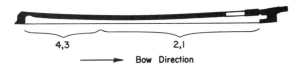

FIGURE 6.13. Poor distribution of the bow.

This use of a disproportionate amount of bow on the first two counts causes the first two counts to be louder than the last two. In addition, there will be no sense of *sostenuto*, and the last two counts will necessarily be "squeezed out." A full string section playing in this manner produces a most unsatisfactory and unschooled sound.

Two things must happen if this very undesirable practice is to be corrected.

First: The student must learn to use the precious inches of bow at the frog. Any kind of inducement or coercion is fair to achieve this end. Mostly it is a question of breaking down resistance.

Second: In playing any long note, the student must begin the note at the extreme point or frog, however it occurs in context. Then, he must consciously allocate a given amount of bow to each count. The simplest rule for the child is to get to the middle of the bow at the middle of the note. This, at least, assures him of an equal division of the bow.

A more advanced approach is to use the bow faster in the upper half where there is less bow and arm weight and more slowly in the lower half where the bow may be moved very slowly without the tone breaking.

Another aspect of bow distribution involves the problems inherent in figures made up of notes or slurs of unequal duration. For example:

These examples are extremely elementary but they clearly demonstrate the point. If the short notes are played with the same amount of bow as the long notes, without compensating for weight and pressure, the short notes will be considerably louder than the long notes. Again in this case the solution is simple—use less bow on the short notes than on the long notes. To illustrate:

Playing the short notes alternatingly at the U. H. and L. H. is good as long as the pattern continues. This technique applies regardless of tempo. Of course, as the speed of the figure increases, less bow is used. At fast tempi very little bow is used; as little as three to five inches on the long note and one inch on each of the short notes. But each long note permits the bow to regain its position.

This principle becomes more difficult to apply when the figure does not allow for natural compensation. For example:

In this case the accent on the first beat is helped by the fast movement of the bow which is necessary if the bow is to reach approximately the same point for each up bow.

Somewhat more difficult to manipulate is a figure such as that above which is to be played softly and without accent.

To achieve the desired results the down bow must be light and quick in the first four bars and the up bow held back. In the next bars this is reversed.

Intelligent use of the various areas of the bow, learning to maneuver the bow to the desired spot for a figure, moving the bow quickly and lightly and having it compensate for a preceding or succeeding slower bow, are skills which must be developed to reach an artistic level of performance. However these skills are of a highly sophisticated nature and would be dealt with more appropriately in a treatise on advanced techniques.

There are some well established practices in bowing orchestra music which are based upon the natural laws of bow direction as they apply to and are governed by the music which motivates them. In her book, *Orchestral Bowings and Routines*, Elizabeth A. H. Green outlines some of the basic principles of orchestral bowings and gives musical examples to illustrate the application of these principles. She enumerates thirteen rules which apply to basic bowings and nine which apply to what she labels "Artistic Bowings." Toward the end of her book, she recapitulates the thirteen basic rules in simple form.

No. 1. The note on the first beat of the measure is down-bow.
No. 2. The note before the bar-line is up-bow.
No. 3. If the note before the bar-line is slurred across the bar-line, play it down-bow.
No. 4. An odd number of notes before a bar-line (without slurs) starts up-bow.
No. 5. An even number of notes before a bar-line (without slurs) starts down-bow.
No. 6. Alternate bowing, down and up, on after-beats. If rhythmic figures between rests have an even number of notes, chance a down-bow on the first note: if an odd number of notes, try an up-bow on the first note.

Note: The teacher must guide herein with his fuller knowledge. These short rules will cover most rhythm found in the easier music.

No. 7. In groups of four notes, starting on the beat, play the first one down-bow.
No. 8. Chords are played down-bow.
No. 9. Link the dotted eighth and sixteenth.
No. 10. Link the quarter and eighth in six-eight time.
No. 11. The dotted eighth and sixteenth is not linked when the execution of the figure is too fast to perform the link feasibly, and the linked bowing is often omitted in soft passages where extreme neatness and clarity are desired. In this case, the dotted eighth is up-bow at the point and the sixteenth is down-bow.
No. 12. If your closing chord has a little, short note before it, play the little note up-bow starting near the frog.
No. 13. In four-four time a half-note on the second beat of the measure is down-bow.[5]

TYPES OF BOWINGS

Détaché

Separate bows. One note per bow alternating up and down bow. Played in the middle or upper half generally. Hair flat on the string. From 1/3 to 1/2 the bow is used.

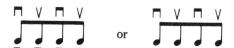

Slur

Two or more notes played in one bow. Any part of the bow may be used.

Portamento Slur (Portato)

This is a type of slur in which each note gets a slight articulation. It is a cross between a slur and a slurred staccato.

5. Reprinted from *Orchestral Bowings and Routines* by permission of the author and copyright (1949, 1957) owner, Elizabeth A. H. Green. Edwards Letter Shop, Ann Arbor, Michigan. It is forbidden to mimeograph or further reproduce this material.

Staccato

A short, quick stroke played with the bow on the string. The stroke begins and ends abruptly. Pressure is applied at the beginning and end of the stroke. Amount of bow and area used depends upon length of note and volume. This can range from one or two inches of bow in the upper half for "pp" to the full bow for "ff."

There is a limit to the speed of the staccato. When the speed of the notes exceeds this limit, they are played spiccato.

Marcato (Martelé)

A heavy staccato stroke, usually played in the middle or upper half. Limited speed. Medium to loud volume.

Spiccato

A stroke in which the bow bounces onto and off of the string. The fingers, wrist, and arm make the stroke. The mid-area of the bow is used, above the middle for a lighter stroke, below the middle for a heavier stroke. The bow bounces onto the string to produce the note, bounces away, and repeats this procedure. Up and down strokes are used. The stroke can be played from medium to fast tempi. The length of the notes depends upon how long the hair is allowed to remain in contact with the string.

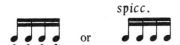

Sautillé

This is a first cousin to the spiccato. In the sautillé the natural spring of the bow is depended upon. It is played very near the middle of the bow and at a rather fast speed. At slower speeds the spiccato is used.

Slurred Staccato

A series of staccato notes played while the bow is moving in one direction. This calls for an

abrupt start and end of each note. Slurred staccato is usually played up bow although down bow staccato is occasionally asked for in virtuoso solos. Up and down bow staccato involving two or three notes at a moderate tempo is not unusual in orchestra playing. If circumstances suggest it, the skilled performer will play the up-bow staccato groups by lifting the bow between notes. When played rapidly, this is referred to as flying staccato.

sul ponticello

This term indicates that the bow is to be drawn deliberately close to the bridge. The effect produced is a shrill, piercing quality. It is employed most frequently with tremolo but occasionally with sustained tones.

sul tasto

The bow is drawn close to or over the fingerboard. The result is a soft, flute-like quality of tone.

col legno

With the wood. This means literally to hit the string with the back, or stick of the bow. The sound is percussive and the pitch only faintly apparent. Only notes of very short duration can be performed since no sostenuto is possible. This is an effect and is never used for an extended period.

Chords

Three and four note chords are effective on violin, viola, and cello, and are not difficult if the notes of the chord are properly arranged. Short three note chords can be played as a unit, that is the three notes can be played simultaneously. This is accomplished by exerting sufficient pressure with the bow upon the middle string of the chord.

If the chord has a duration in excess of a quarter note, it is played as though the lower two notes were grace notes to the top two.

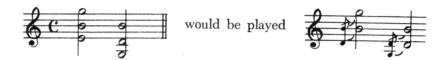

would be played

In this way the effect of the chord is produced and the top notes can be held as long as the bow can reasonably sustain them. This same principle of "breaking" chords pertains to four note chords.

becomes

The length of time the bow remains on the lower notes of the chord before moving to the upper notes is dependent upon the style and period of the music, the tempo, and the context in which the chord is placed.

Chords are played more easily down bow than up bow because of the weight of the bow and arm at the frog, but they can be played either way. If consecutive chords are spaced or separated, they should be played with a series of down bows.

If they should be connected, or played as part of a legato line, they should be played up or down bow as the bowing comes.

When chords appear in the orchestra music of Haydn, Mozart, Beethoven and other composers of that period, they are usually played *divisi*. That is, the notes of the chord are divided between the two players on a stand. In a three note chord, the outside player takes the two upper notes, the inside player the two lower notes. These notes are played as double stops. The reason for doing this is to keep the music rhythmically clear and precise, an impossibility if twenty or thirty players are "breaking" a chord. This practice, obviously, does not apply to solo playing.

The following are some excerpts from the first violin part of the Symphony No. 35 ("Haffner") by Mozart. Chords are shown as they are written by Mozart and as they are played according to common orchestral practice.

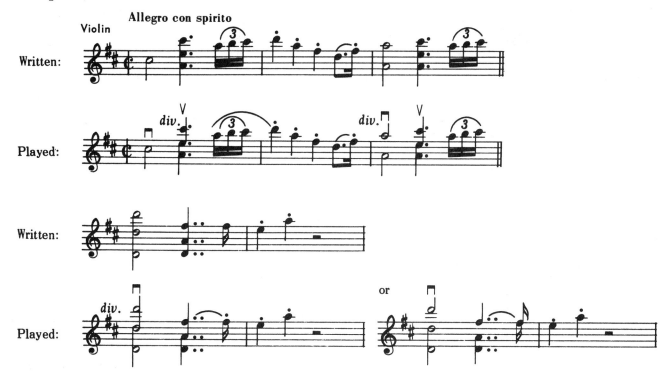

Note that the chords, which are played *divisi*, are played with the bowing as it comes. In cadential situations such as the two which follow, some conductors ask that the chords be divided and played with consecutive up and down bows, as they come. Others prefer the increased punctuation and finality that comes from playing all of the chords down bow. This is purely a matter of personal taste.

The chords at the end of the finale should be played divisi and with up and down bows, with the exception of the last three, which are spaced by rests. The fact that Mozart wrote the consecutive chords in the third and fourth bars from the end without staccato dots makes it important that they be played without unnatural spaces between them.

In the later symphonic works of the Russian and German composers and in Italian opera orchestrations, full chords for the strings are common. The full, rich, dramatic character of this music is enhanced by the strings playing their heavy, sweeping chords.

Part III

Chapters 7, 8, 9, and 10 deal with teaching each of the string instruments. These chapters do not pretend to take the place of a step-by-step method. A good method presents one concept at a time in a logically progressive order and provides well conceived drills to assist in the mastery of each concept. There is no substitute for this complete and sequential approach.

The aim of the following chapters is to present objectives for each of three developmental stages—Beginning, Intermediate, and Advanced—and suggestions which will help to achieve those objectives. These objectives are not often spelled out in method books. So by familiarizing himself thoroughly with the content of these chapters, plus the chapter, Playing the Stringed Instruments, the teacher will be in a position to direct the student to maximum achievement as he makes his way through appropriate material.

CHAPTER 7

Teaching the Violin

The violin is the soprano of the string family. It is the melody instrument. In the orchestra there are more violins than any other instrument. In a symphony orchestra there may be as many as twelve to sixteen first violins and ten to fourteen second violins.

In school string programs the large majority of students begin on the violin. Out of a class of thirty beginners in an elementary string program, there may be two violas, two or three cellos, and one or two basses, the balance violins. This imbalance is not desirable, but it is a fact in most cases. It is no wonder, then, that when we think of school string programs we think first of the violin. It is important, therefore, that the teacher candidate become well acquainted with the violin.

Selecting the Correct Size Violin

The teacher's first responsibility is to see that each student is equipped with an instrument of the correct size. Violins are made in sizes ranging from full (4/4) down to 1/16. There is a size for every size child, and it is important that the right one be selected. Some age-range suggestions are found on page 139. These are admittedly rough; since children grow at varying rates.

The objective is to find an instrument which is neither too long nor too short. If it is too long, the arm will have to stretch out too far to reach the first position; the elbow cannot form an easy angle; the arm will tire quickly; the fingers will be unable to assume the proper attitude on the strings; and the distance between notes will be too great for the child to manage easily. If it is too short, the arm will be constricted; the elbow will be at too acute an angle; the spacing between notes will be too narrow for the width of the child's fingers.

The most common sizes are 1/2, 3/4, and 4/4. Most school-age children can be adequately fitted with one of these sizes. If a child is between 1/2 and 3/4, it is best to give him the 1/2 size. He will be comfortable with it. As he grows, move him to the 3/4.

One way to determine if an instrument is the correct size is shown below. The instrument is held in playing position. The arm is extended so that the fingers touch the scroll. If the fingers easily encircle the scroll with the elbow bent slightly, the violin is the correct size. This is demonstrated in Figure 7.2. Figure 7.3 shows the same procedure being followed with an instrument which is too large.

If school instruments are not available, and the parent must purchase an instrument, the matter of economics enters the picture. Some parents will resist buying a small violin knowing that they will have to arrange for a larger one when the child has grown—in perhaps one or two years. Fortunately many dealers have rental or trade-in plans, giving the purchaser a full, or very liberal, allowance when a small instrument is traded for a larger one. Under such an arrangement, the parent is not jeopardized **financially.**

A Complete Outfit

Every violin outfit should be complete and in good working order. It should include the following:

A well made violin with proper strings, tuners that work, pegs that work properly, strings at proper height and properly spaced, a satisfactory chin rest

A bow full of good hair, properly rosined, a frog that fits properly and slides smoothly, a screw that works easily

A shoulder pad that is fitted to the child

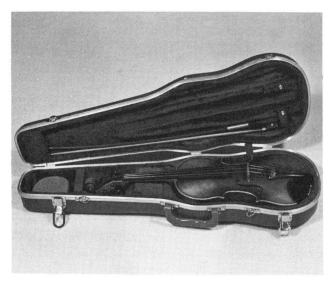

FIGURE 7.1. A complete violin outfit.

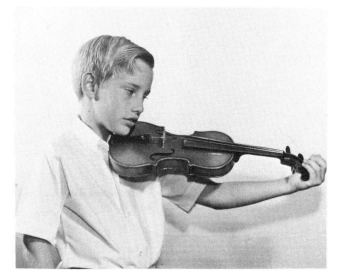

FIGURE 7.2. Tom Peron with correct size violin.

FIGURE 7.3. Tom Peron with too large a violin.

A cake of rosin

A case that fits the violin, has a good bow holder, pockets for rosin, and a place for the shoulder pad, closes securely and has fasteners which work and keep the case closed securely, has a good handle and a carrying strap.

First Steps

The first lessons are extremely important—and the most difficult. The child must begin to learn some of the following:

To take the violin from the case carefully and put the shoulder pad on it

To take the bow from the case, tighten it to the proper tension and rosin it

Hold the violin correctly

Hold the bow correctly

Know the names of the strings

Place the bow on a given string and draw the bow correctly to produce a tone

Recognize the printed notes that correspond to the open strings

Learn the rhythmical value of notes and rests

Learn to keep a pulse and play given notes and rests within that pulse.

The above tasks must be approached in a manner and at a pace which suits the age and maturity of the child. While with one child this may be a slow and uncertain process, with another it may be accomplished with speed and surety.

Because the holding of the violin and the bow are two separate, distinct, and exacting tasks, some

methods postpone these matters so that the child can begin almost immediately to play music. This is, of course, his primary objective, one he feels he should accomplish the minute he takes the violin from the case.

One method has the violin played in guitar-fashion. It is held under the right arm and the strings are plucked with the thumb. The left hand is held in relatively normal position fingering notes which are taught by rote or by numbers.

Several methods modify this approach to the degree that the instrument is held under the chin in normal fashion, but the right hand plucks the strings rather than playing them with the bow. After following this pizzicato approach for a few lessons, the bow is introduced and normal procedure is followed.

Most traditional methods advocate a bow-on-the-strings approach from the beginning. Among these methods there are fundamental differences. These differences can be described as follows:

The whole-note or whole-bow approach
versus
The quarter-note or partial bow approach

The note-reading approach
versus
The rote approach

The whole-note approach is typical of the early methods. The theory was that the use of the full bow should be inculcated in the pupil from the outset. It was reasoned further that if the pupil could draw a full bow properly and with ease, all other bowings would be easier.

The quarter-note approach and the pizzicato approach are examples of much recent educational psychology which contends that the child will learn more quickly and more cheerfully if he can realize success in terms he can measure, in this case play music on the violin. There is no question about the greater difficulty in drawing a full bow in contrast to a short bow, using the middle of the bow. So the pupil learns to control the bow in small amounts, gradually increasing the use to the full bow.

Advocates of the rote approach maintain that note-reading interferes with the important and difficult process of learning to hold the violin and the bow. These two functions are so complex that full attention should be given to them, without the distraction of learning notes and counting. Shinicki Suzuki, the now famous Japanese violin teacher, has had phenomenal success with this approach in Japan. He has had thousands of Japanese children under his instruction and has proved that he can get results. His system includes close parental involvement, private and group instruction.

In the school instruction program there are several drawbacks to the use of the rote method. The first is that individual attention is limited. Secondly, parental involvement is virtually impossible to achieve to the degree it is needed in this kind of an approach. Thirdly, the objective of the school program is to develop orchestra players; therefore reading music is a prime requisite and needs to begin early.

Some teachers have had success using a rote approach for the first few lessons before introducing note-reading. This makes it possible to concentrate fully on the violin and the bow, give the pupil an early sense of achievement, and then present notes as a new and interesting aspect of his progress.

Holding the Violin

The violin is placed on the left shoulder, about 45° to the left of a straight forward position. The end pin button touches the neck. The shoulder should remain in a normal position; it should not be raised to meet the shoulder pad. The shoulder pad rests on the collar bone and the inner part of the shoulder. The fingerboard should be about parallel with the floor.

FIGURE 7.4. Correct position of the violin.

To achieve the proper setting of the violin, have the pupil stand facing you. His stance should be straight but relaxed, his arms hanging normally at his sides, weight balanced on the feet. Place the violin in position on the pupil's shoulder, pushing it lightly but firmly under the chin and against the neck.

At this point, still holding the instrument, ask the pupil to press his chin and jaw down upon the chinrest until he has the feeling that he is holding the instrument himself. His head should be turned so that the sight-line is towards the scroll and tilted so that the side of the jaw touches the chinrest. This process should be repeated several times before having the pupil perform it alone.

When he is ready to do this without help, have him hold the violin by the right side of the lower bout, as shown in Figure 7.5 and place it in position. When it is in position, tug it gently to make sure the grip is firm.

FIGURE 7.5. The violin held by the lower right bout prior to placing it in position on the shoulder.

FIGURE 7.6. Correct position of the thumb and hand on the neck.

Left Arm and Hand Position

With the violin securely in position, the left hand should be raised to the neck of the instrument. The neck is held between the thumb and the base of the first finger as shown in Figure 7.6. *The wrist should be straight.*

The pad of the thumb is held lightly against the side of the neck with the end of the thumb extending slightly above the fingerboard. The amount of thumb that projects above the fingerboard depends upon the length of the fingers and hand. The longer the fingers, the lower the neck will be on the thumb. The shorter the fingers, the lower the thumb will be on the neck, even to the point of being under the neck.

The arm should be swung to the right until it is well under the violin. Its exact position varies depending upon which string is being played on. It moves to the left when the fingers are on the E string and to the right when on the G string.

The hand should be turned in so that the palm is close to and nearly parallel to the neck. This position is necessary so that the fingers can be poised over the strings at all times.

Sitting Position and Rest Position

The violin is held the same whether the player is standing or sitting. A comfortable seated position is attained by sitting straight with the left foot slightly forward. The feet should be on the floor, not wrapped around the chair legs or over the chair rung. Sitting position is illustrated below in Figure 7.7.

During long periods of rest in orchestral music, the violin is put in a position of complete rest by being placed across the lap. This position is shown in Figure 7.8.

If the rest is of long enough duration to warrant taking the instrument down from the shoulder but not long enough to warrant putting it on the lap, it is held vertically on the knee as shown in Figure 7.9. This might also be described as "At the Ready"; for the instrument can be very quickly raised to playing position from there.

Common Faults in Holding the Violin

The violin is held too far to the left or right. Either extreme causes problems for the bow and the left arm.

The angle of the violin is too flat. This makes the bow arm raise excessively to reach the G string and puts the head and neck in a strained position.

The violin is tilted at too much of an angle. This puts the E string at a difficult angle for the bow and repudiates the assistance which gravity lends to the bow.

The violin is held too high or too low. Both positions are detrimental to good bowing, shifting, and to appearance.

The arm is held too far to the left. This puts the fingers in an unsatisfactory position and causes problems in shifting.

FIGURE 7.7. Correct playing position while seated.

FIGURE 7.8. The violin in complete rest position.

FIGURE 7.9. The violin in partial rest position.

The violin is held in the crotch of the hand. This impedes good fingering and makes for excessive motion in the shifting process.

The wrist is bent inward so that the palm of the hand is in contact with the neck. This is a common and extremely bad position since it precludes correct finger action and later on makes shifting nearly impossible.

The wrist is bent outward. This position strains the wrist and arm muscles and is in no way helpful.

Tightening the Bow

At this point the violin should be returned to the case, and the bow removed from the case. Before turning the bow over to the pupil, the teacher should demonstrate how to tighten it and how to loosen it.[1] Determining about the number of turns to the right to tighten the bow and using the same number to the left to loosen it again eliminates the guess work from this procedure, and is generally a satisfactory technique at this stage. The student should be warned about over-tightening the bow and impressed with the need to loosen it before returning it to the case. Reasons for the foregoing are discussed in the section on the Bow.

The teacher should also show the student how to rosin the bow and explain how often and how much the bow should be rosined. This is also covered in the section on the Bow. The student should also be impressed with the need to keep his fingers off the hair.

Holding the Bow

Before having the pupil hold the bow, some teachers establish the position of the thumb and fingers by having the pupil hold a pencil or similar object. The advantage is that the pencil is familiar to the pupil while the bow is unfamiliar. In addition, the pencil is light in weight, and, being short, presents no balance problems. The length and weight of the bow are the first factors that stand in the way of a good bow grip.

Another technique to establish the shape of the hand is to have the pupil hold a ball that fits comfortably into the hand, and attempt to transfer that hand position to the bow.

Teaching the Bow Grip

Next the teacher hands the bow to the pupil who takes it in his left hand, holding it by the screw button with the thumb and first finger. The hair is facing up. The right hand is held with the palm facing upward and the fingers slightly curved.

The pupil places the bow into the right hand, which takes it as follows:

The point of the thumb is placed on the underneath side of the stick with the right part of the thumb touching the grip and the left side touching the lower, inside edge of the frog. The first joint of the thumb is bent outward.

The first three fingers curve over the top of the bow and slant toward the tip. A point just above the second joint of the first finger rests on the grip. The second finger curves over the stick and touches the thumb. The third finger curves over the stick and touches the frog. The tip of the little finger rests on top of the bow just ahead of the screw. The second and third fingers should touch each other. There are small spaces between the first and second and third and fourth fingers. The fingers should neither be spread nor squeezed together, but assume as easy and natural a position as possible.

All of the fingers should be curved. The greatest problem in this regard is with the little finger. In too many cases it is held straight and stiff, a condition which causes problems in acquiring a smooth change of bow at the frog. Also, with many children, the thumb bends *in* instead of *out*. This makes the thumb inflexible and stiffens the hand and wrist, conditions which impair satisfactory bowing.

With the hand still palm-up, check the position of the fingers and thumb. Adjust if needed. Now have the pupil "squeeze" the muscles in these fingers, maintaining the same position on the bow. This should be repeated several times. It firms up the grip and helps to give each finger a sense of where it belongs on the bow.

The arm should now make a half turn to the left so that the hair is pointing down. This is the pupil's first exposure to the playing attitude of the bow. He now senses the need for balance and sees the need for a firm, relaxed grip. Rotating the arm to the right and back again is a good exercise in itself. It also exposes the position of the fingers for easy examination.

Common Faults In Holding the Bow

The thumb is inserted too far through the bow.
The thumb bends *in* instead of *out*.
The thumb is positioned too far from the frog.
The fingers are spread too far apart.
The little finger is flat instead of curved.
The entire hand is too far up the bow.

---

1. In groups the teacher can demonstrate this procedure to the entire class and have them tighten and loosen the bow under his supervision.

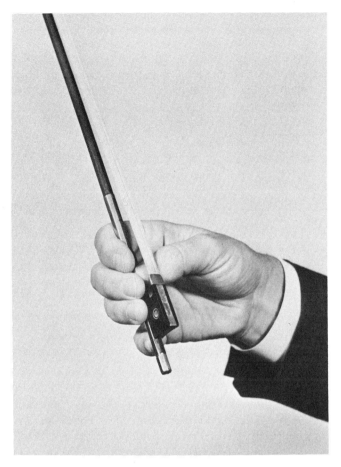

FIGURE 7.10. Correct position of thumb and fingers on the bow from below.

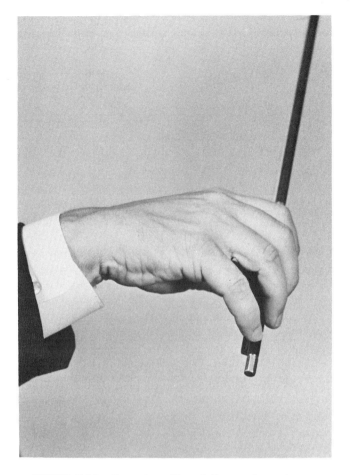

FIGURE 7.11. Correct position of fingers from above.

The Beginning or Open String Stage

The various "stages" used in this book may be related to school levels as follows:

> Beginning—Elementary
> Intermediate—Junior High
> Advanced—High School and beyond

It must be understood that these "stages" do not connote neat, pat compartments into which students can be conveniently placed for the simple prescribing of appropriate materials and procedures. Each student progresses at a different rate; and while one student may excel in reading ability and have poor intonation, another may not read well but have excellent intonation, etc. Students of the same age group may be located in any of the three stages of development, and a given student may be a cross between Beginning and Intermediate or Intermediate and Advanced.

Objectives

To hold the instrument and bow correctly.[2]

To draw the bow parallel to the bridge.

To draw the bow on the proper string.

To draw the bow for the specified duration.

To make satisfactory bow changes from up to down and down to up.

To identify the strings by their letter names.

To know the signs for down bow and up bow and follow these directions.

To be able to identify the following parts: bridge, fingerboard, neck, chinrest, shoulder pad, bow, frog, point, hair, screw, upper half, middle, lower half.

To associate a printed note with the corresponding open string.

To know the names of the notes corresponding to the open strings.

To know how to count quarter notes, half notes, whole notes and their corresponding rests in 2/4 and 4/4 time.

To keep one's place while playing a line of music.

2. During the open string stage it is permissible for the left hand to support the violin by holding it by the upper right bout. This rests the left arm and hand.

Most method books spend several lessons on the open strings; so the pupil must learn their identity on both the instrument and the printed page. To review, they are:

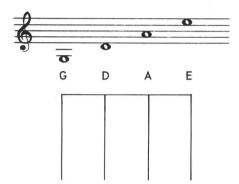

G   D   A   E

Using only open strings allows the pupil to concentrate on how he is holding the instrument and the bow, which is of paramount importance during this formulative period.

At the outset the pupil should not be expected to hold the instrument in position for more than a few minutes. However, his arms will soon become accustomed to the position, and within two to three weeks, it is not unreasonable to expect ten to fifteen minutes of steady practice.

The first lessons will consist of open string notes and rests. The rests allow the pupil to check his position and look ahead to see what is coming. Drawing the bow parallel to the bridge and producing a smooth, even tone are the aims of these first lessons, plus learning to follow the written music and keep a steady beat.

When first using the bow, many children have difficulty staying on one string. They may start the bow on the right string but touch one of the adjoining strings during the progress of the bow. This is not unusual, for it takes some time for the arm and wrist to make the adjustments needed to keep the bow in alignment.

Exercises To Aid Bow Alignment

The following two exercises can help the alignment problem. They help the arm to sense the planes of the various strings as well as the distance the bow moves to get from one string to another.

EXERCISE NO. 1 TO ORIENT THE BOW TO THE STRING PLANES

1. Put the point of the bow on the A string. Press. Hold for four counts.

2. Lift the bow one inch above the string. Move to the middle. Press. Hold for four counts.
3. Repeat

This should be done on each string which is being used in the lessons. Gradually move closer to the frog in step 2. The exercise is done silently.

EXERCISE NO. 2 TO ORIENT THE BOW TO THE STRING PLANES

1. Put the bow on the A string two inches from the point. Press. Hold for four counts.
2. Keeping pressure on the string, elevate the arm until the bow is fully on the D string. Hold for four counts.
3. Move back to the A string for four counts.
4. Lower the arm until the bow is fully on the E string and hold for four counts.
5. Move back to the A string.
6. Repeat

Do the same exercise with the bow at various locations, i.e., middle, frog, and points between. Also use the D as the fulcrum.

Another problem beginners have is keeping the bow parallel to the bridge and at a more or less constant distance from the bridge. To cure a wandering bow, students should draw slow bows, watching the point of contact. To cultivate a straight bow, students should practice Exercise No. 1, above, observing the angle of the bow in a mirror. Also notes on the open strings should be played while observing the bow in a mirror.

It is difficult, at first, for young violinists to know when their bow is not straight, and watching the bow in a mirror is not a fool-proof method of checking its alignment. Another device that is often helpful is to point out that when the middle of the bow is placed on the string, the bow, the forearm, and the upper arm form three sides of a square, and that they should be in the same plane. Using this perspective, it is also relatively easy to tell if the wrist or upper arm are too high or too low.

If the child's arm is too short to draw the bow to the point without pulling the bow out of line, the best solution is to get a shorter bow. If this is not practical, he can be told *not* to draw his bow beyond a given point. This point can be marked with a piece of adhesive tape.

Tilt of the Bow

If the method being used employs quarter notes in the upper half of the bow, the angle, or tilt, of the bow is no concern; since, in the upper half, the hair is kept flat on the string. However, when the

FIGURE 7.12.   A. Correct position of the bow at the point.   B. Correct position of the bow at the frog.

lower half is used, the pupil must become aware of the need to tilt the bow as it approaches the frog.

At the frog the bow should tilt in the direction of the fingerboard at an angle of 15°-25°. The cause of this tilting is the curve of the wrist. The effect is to use less hair, thus balancing the tone with the remainder of the bow and facilitating a smooth bow change at the frog.

Common Faults of the Open String Stage

The instrument is allowed to sag.
The thumb and fingers slide out of place on the bow.
The bow is drawn at an angle to instead of parallel to the bridge.
The distance of the bow from the bridge varies excessively.
The bow touches two strings at the same time.
The pupil loses his place in the course of a line of music.
The pupil fails to count steadily and is unsure in the reading process.
The bow is tightened too tight or is not loosened when returned to the case.

Locating the Notes

After a few weeks of playing only open strings the pupil will be champing at the bit to begin playing "real music." The first step is to use the first finger on the A or D string. Sound the pitch of the desired note and help the pupil locate the correct place for the first finger. On a 4/4 violin the first finger will be located about 1 1/8 to 1 1/4 inches from the nut to produce a B on the A string. The distance will be about 1 inch on a 3/4 violin. Measurements are all relative and are not completely trustworthy. The pupil must now begin to use his sense of pitch. If he has real trouble finding the notes, use one of the devices shown in Figures 6.1 and 6.2.

The same procedure is followed for the second finger. At this point the relationship of one finger to another enters. The distance of the second finger from the first should be discerned visually while the interval is listened to. The first finger should be kept on the string when the second is being used, and the first and second when the third is being used.

Half Steps and Whole Steps

The element of half steps and whole steps enters now. When the second finger is close to the first a half step is produced. In first position this is about 1/2 inch distance from finger contact point to finger contact point. The fingers will be about 1 inch apart for a whole step. If the fingers are broad enough, they may touch each other when forming half steps.

There will be a space between the fingers when forming whole steps. The following are some of the symbols used to indicate half steps and whole steps.

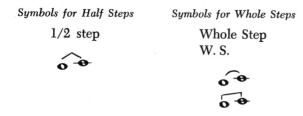

Symbols for Half Steps *Symbols for Whole Steps*

1/2 step   Whole Step
W. S.

When the 2nd finger is a whole step above the 1st, it is sometimes referred to as the "high" 2nd. When it is close to the 1st, it is called "low" 2nd.

During this stage it is important that the hand maintain its location and that the fingers are placed on the strings with the ends of the fingers depressing the strings and the first joint nearly vertical. It is also important that the fingers develop strength in order to stop the strings firmly; for it is the efficacy of this action that determines, to a degree, the clarity of intonation and tone.

Some methods endeavor to simplify matters during this stage by keeping the same fingering pattern on each string. This is accomplished by changing key as needed. The pattern is:

Other methods vary the interval and finger pattern on the premise that the student should acquire flexibility early.

The fourth finger is introduced somewhat later. It should be delayed until the other fingers are fairly well established. When the fourth finger is brought into play, all fingers should be placed on the string and strength applied. This will build the muscles. Since the fourth finger is the weakest, it should, at this point, be given full use and extra exercise. The following exercise will do wonders for the fourth finger if done for a couple of minutes each day. The fourth finger should be raised as high as possible and brought down onto the string with a snap. The exercise is to be done on each string.

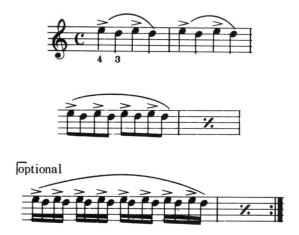

[optional]

Common Faults During This Stage

The pupil is inconsistent in the placement of the fingers. In other words, he plays "out of tune."

The half steps are too wide and/or the whole steps are too narrow.

The first joint of the finger collapses so that it is flat on the string instead of vertical.

The Intermediate Stage

Objectives (All Appropriate Previous Objectives Continue)

To play in tune.

To learn to tune the instrument.

To play with a pleasant tone.

To play with a range of dynamics from pp to ff.

To attain a velocity measured by slurred 16th notes at = 66-76 and bowed 16th notes at = 56-66.

To use the bow skillfully in a variety of bowings, i.e., slurs, staccato, marcato, slow spiccato.

To begin the study of third position.

To begin to develop a vibrato.

Tuning the Violin

Until this time the teacher has, in most cases, been tuning the violin for the pupil. He has done this to save time and to be certain the instrument is in tune. Now it is time for the student to begin trying his own hand, and he should begin whenever he feels inclined. The teacher must bring his judgment to bear in this matter. He should not encourage students whose ability to handle the tuning process he questions. On the other hand, he should give assistance and support to those whom he feels are ready.

At first, tuning strings individually to the piano or a pitch pipe is enough. If the violin has regular pegs, the student should be shown how to turn and set them. At this stage, the violin should be held on the knee for support, and the strings plucked. The right hand works the "A" peg while the left thumb plucks the string. The left hand works the "D" and "G" pegs while the right thumb plucks the strings. This can be done either standing or sitting, but it is easier while sitting. Students whose instruments are equipped with patent pegs will have less trouble; since they do not have to worry about the pegs slipping.

After following the above procedure for awhile, the student will be ready to refine the process somewhat. He should now tune the A string to the piano, or other source, and then tune the other strings by fifths. He should first tune the A-E, then the A-D, then the D-G.

As the student's bowing becomes steadier and more reliable, his fingers stronger, and his ability to tune by the above method improves, he should begin to tune with the bow, using the following procedure:

Tune the A string to the piano, bar, or tuner.
Play the A and E separately and then together, tuning the E to the A. When the 5th is perfect, there will be no "waves" or pulses. If the E is quite sharp or flat, the pulses will be rapid. As it is brought in tune, the pulses slow and finally stop. The pulses are hard for some students to hear at first. The teacher should tune his violin, bringing out the pulses for the student to hear.
Follow the same procedure on the A-D and D-G.

Several things need to be taken into account in regard to tuning. They are:

1. Pegs must be in good working order.
2. Pegs must be correctly oriented so the fingers can grasp them and turn them easily.
3. The upper half of the bow should be used, starting at the point and going up bow.
4. In turning a peg, always turn it towards you first. This reduces the tension on the string and lowers the pitch. Then raise the string to the correct pitch, pushing the peg *in* as it turns. Set the peg firmly.

The pupil should be shown how to hold his hand and fingers in tuning. (See Figs. 7.13, 7.14.) Note the position of the hand while tuning the A peg and

FIGURE 7.13.   Position of hand when tuning left pegs.   **FIGURE 7.14.**   Position of hand when tuning right pegs.

the position while tuning the D and G pegs. The E peg should rarely need to be touched; it changes little, and the tuner can take care of most of the minor adjustments. If, however, the E slips badly, it should not be tuned with the violin on the shoulder. It is much better to put the violin on the knee.

Tone Development

(Refer to pages 76 to 77 for a general discussion of tone production.)

In the early stages it is quite enough to expect the bow to be drawn parallel to the bridge at a point half way between the bridge and the fingerboard. Even this objective is difficult for some children to reach. However, as the pupil gains increased control of the bow, he should be shown that the bow must move closer to the bridge when producing a louder and more intense sound, and should move toward the fingerboard when producing a quieter, more *flautando* sound.

An excellent way to achieve this concept is to draw the bow very slowly from frog to point and

back, making a crescendo and diminuendo in the course of each stroke, as follows:

At the peak of the crescendo, which occurs in the middle of the bow, the bow should be close to the bridge. At the beginning and end of the stroke the bow should be toward the fingerboard. This stroke can be practiced on open strings, scales, arpeggios, or appropriate etudes. The exercise should be done very slowly, counting four or eight. The crescendo should peak at the mid-point, and both the crescendo and the diminuendo must be gradual and even.

The following variations on this exercise will develop even more tone and control and will create increased sensitivity in the bow hand.

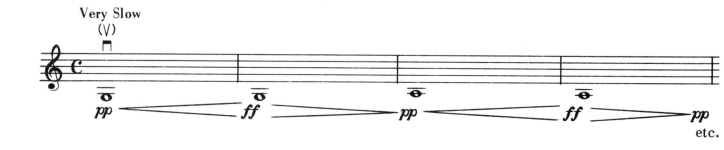

Intonation, Dynamics, Facility

By this time the student should be able to play in tune in a variety of keys, including C, G, D, F, Bb, and Eb. He should be able to move easily from string to string. He should be able to read and perform rhythmic figures and note patterns of intermediate difficulty as well as a variety of bowings.

Intonation will continue to need constant attention, but if the student has ability, is conscientious and has good instruction, his intonation will be acceptable by now and improving all the time.

A true concept of dynamic range is usually difficult to acquire. Most students play neither pp nor ff. The actual possible dynamic range of a violin is not great. A string instrument can play very softly, but it is limited on the loud end of the scale. Frequently students end up playing everything mf, thinking they are achieving a good range of dynamics, and must be coaxed persuasively to hear their dynamics objectively.

Left-hand facility comes from finger strength and resiliency. These are developed through the practice of scales and other technical studies and exercises. Practice with gradually increasing metronome rates is a good method to improve speed.

The bow should be capable of playing sixteenth note runs, dotted-eighth-sixteenth figures, simple double stops and chords, staccato, marcato, and possibly spiccato at a slow tempo using the lower half of the bow.

Third Position

It is time for most students to try their wings now by moving to third position. Third position puts the hand a third higher than first position. The first finger moves up to where the third finger was.

Third position extends the upper range of each string by a third—to a fourth considering the extension to the harmonic—and runs the high range to D or E above the staff.

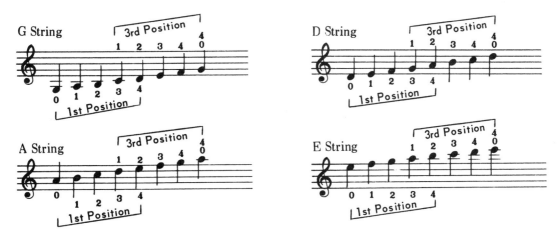

In third position the lower part of the palm comes into contact with the upper left bout. It does not necessarily remain in contact, but this is an excellent guide to third position.

The first finger should be the "guide" in third position. Playing naturalized notes with the first finger on the upper three strings, the 8va of the next lower string is sounded, thus affording a method of checking the placement of the first finger.

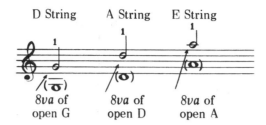

Smooth shifting, both up and down, are the product of careful, slow practice and faithful adherence to the principle that finger pressure must be eased while shifting. In the ascending shift, the hand and finger are relaxed and prepared, and the hand, forearm and upper arm move together. In the descending shift, the thumb moves to first position and is followed by the hand and arm.

Shifting with one finger is accomplished as described above.

Shifting to a different finger uses the same technique. The finger playing the previous note is used as a "guide" finger. In practicing the shift this "guide" note is actually sounded. As the shifting technique improves, the intervening guide note can be eliminated.

FIGURE 7.15. Hand in third position.

Vibrato

The general nature and purpose of the vibrato has been described earlier (See p. 62). On the violin the vibrato is produced by a back and forth rocking or rolling motion of the finger which is generated by the hand moving from the wrist, first toward and then away from the player. This motion causes regular fluctuations of the pitch. Since the end of the finger contacts the string, it stands to reason that the vibrato should be concentrated there. The easy, quiet vibrato is made with the finger, although the hand induces the motion. As the vibrato becomes more intense, the wrist comes increasingly into it; and at extremes the full arm will participate. An ideal vibrato is one that can be varied from softly rolling to very fast, depending upon the nature of the music.

In vibrato the finger must be held firmly on the string in order that no pitch deviation will take place. The vibrato must not be too wide or too narrow, too fast or too slow.

By the time the student is ready to start third position, he is ready to begin the use of vibrato. To some students the vibrato will come easily. To others it will be a struggle.

Vibrato Exercises

The easiest place to get the vibrato started is in third position, with the first or second finger. Here the lower part of the hand can rest against the violin, making a hinge of the wrist. In this position the vibrato usually starts up rather easily. If it starts with the second finger, try the first finger, and then the third. Then move the hand to first position and see if the vibrato will continue.

If the vibrato balks in first position, rest the scroll of the violin on a mantle, dresser, or other object of suitable height. This frees the hand and arm and helps to get the vibrato going. Always work from third position back to first. If the vibrato still refuses to work, try one of the following exercises.

EXERCISE NO. 1 TO BE DONE
WITHOUT THE VIOLIN
Phase 1—Arm lowered to side, palm forward.

1. Raise arm and touch shoulder with fingers.

2. Drop arm to side.

3. Repeat

Phase 2—Arm lowered to side, palm forward (Fig. 7.16A).

1. Bend wrist forward, bringing fingers up as far as possible (Fig. 7.16B).

2. Drop wrist.

3. Repeat

Phase 3—Arm extended to the front with elbow bent Same as Phase 2 (Figs. 7.16C and 7.16D).

Now take the violin.

Phase 4—Hold violin in playing position with the right hand.

1. Put left hand in first position. Do not grip the neck. (Fig. 7.17)

2. With the arm retaining its position, bend the wrist forward until the hand touches the body of the instrument. (Fig. 7.18)

3. Return wrist to first position.

4. Repeat

All of the above should be done in an even rhythm, one motion per count, beginning slowly and gradually increasing the speed.

EXERCISE NO. 2 TO BE DONE WITH THE VIOLIN

1. Put the first finger on note B on A string. First joint should be vertical.

2. With finger keeping point of contact with string, move the hand back slightly toward the scroll, flattening the first joint of the finger.

3. Return to original position.

4. Repeat
This exercise should be done in an even rhythm with gradually increasing speed. It should be done with each finger and on each string. The movement of the hand is modified slightly for the 3rd and 4th fingers.

Additional information and assistance on the vibrato can be found in *The Art of Violin Playing* by Carl Flesch and in *Vibrato Method for Strings* by Gilbert Waller.

Common Faults of the Intermediate Stage

Carelessness in intonation.
Inaccuracy in shifting to third position.
Tone is still small and thin.
Vibrato is too fast or too slow.
Inadequate control of bow.
Limited dynamic range.
Limited reading ability.

A. Arm at side, palm forward.

B. Above, wrist bent.

C. Arm in front.

D. Above, wrist bent.

FIGURE 7.16. Vibrato exercises.

FIGURE 7.17. Hand on neck, first position.

FIGURE 7.18. Hand on neck, wrist bent.

The Advanced Stage

Objectives (All Appropriate
Previous Objectives Continue)

To improve intonation and tone and musicianship
generally, with a more mature concept of style
and interpretation.

To increase and expand technique, including:
Ability to play faster and more clearly both single
note and double stop passages, chords, har-
monics, trills.
Skill in 5th, 2nd, 4th, and higher positions.
Improved spiccato, staccato, ricochet bowings.

To play solo, ensemble, and orchestra literature of
an advanced nature.

The Higher Positions

No single acomplishment typifies the advanced
student more clearly than the ability to play in the
higher positions. Moving from the 3rd position stage
to the 5th position stage is not a huge jump in terms
of difficulty, but it is a big step in terms of the
music which the student can perform. Fifth position
is the threshhold to the great literature for the
violin. Reaching the 5th position stage opens new
vistas and acts as a springboard to the other higher
positions.

FIGURE 7.19. Hand in fifth position.

Fifth position is relatively easy for most students, since the notes in 5th position are played by the same fingers that play those notes in first position. The notes are simply played on the next lower string. For example:

But the glory of 5th position is that it extends the upper range by five notes, a third beyond the top note in 3rd position.

When the student has gained facility in the use of 3rd and 5th position, he should learn 2nd, 4th, and the higher positions. He will then be capable of undertaking more difficult music. Positions 1 through 7 are illustrated below.

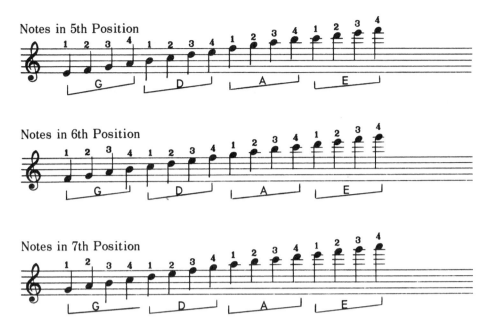

Notes in 5th Position

Notes in 6th Position

Notes in 7th Position

To improve technically, the advanced student should, of course, be studying privately with a good teacher. Each day he should practice scales in three octaves and in various rhythms, plus scales in thirds, sixths, and octaves, and etudes from one of the standard books. Any particular facet of technique that is a problem should be analysed and given special attention. The problem could be shifting, spiccato, trills, double stops, string crossing, bow changes at the frog, or any of a hundred things, any one of which can plague the violinist if not corrected.

The advanced player's diet should include concertos, sonatas, and solo pieces, all of which are available in a great variety of types, styles, and levels of difficulty. Hopefully, experience in small chamber music groups has been part of the string player's development. Playing duets, trios, quartets, and in larger combinations develops ensemble sense, concepts of balance, criticalness of intonation, and general musicianship. The violinist has achieved a very acceptable level of competence when he can participate satisfactorily with a group of matched players in playing the quartets of Haydn, Mozart, and early Beethoven, take part in the local college or community orchestra, and give an acceptable rendition of something from the standard solo literature.

A description of the advanced player must be extremely general; for this is the broadest and most indistinct of categories. It extends from the above average high school student to Oistrakh. And so to understand "advanced" one must know the context in which it is used.

CHAPTER 8

Teaching the Viola

Basically the approach to playing and teaching the viola is identical to that used in teaching the violin, and it is assumed here that all of the material in the previous chapter which pertains to the basic techniques of playing the instrument is applicable to the discussion of the viola. It is left to the student, therefore, to review the previous chapter and to apply the material therein to the present study.

This chapter on the viola, then, will concern itself mainly with the adjustments and modifications which must be made in various aspects of the playing apparatus to compensate for the larger dimensions of the viola. Comparing the viola to the violin is inescapable because, almost without exception, violists are former violinists. Essentially, therefore, this chapter is directed toward the student who is changing from violin to viola, which in no way lessens the applicability of the material to the student who actually begins on the viola. But it should be kept in mind that this chapter and the previous chapter should be studied together.

The viola is the alto of the string family. It plays harmonic and rhythmic accompaniments, counter-melodies, and occasionally the lead. It has a rich, mellow tone quality which complements the upper and lower strings and blends beautifully with french horns and woodwinds. The number of violas in a symphony orchestra ranges from eight to twelve, depending upon the size of the orchestra.

Until recent years a public school student who voluntarily started his string instruction as a violist was practically unheard of. Ninety-nine out of a hundred violists began as violinists. Of those who reach professional status this is also the rule rather than the exception. There has been a little improvement in this situation in the last few years.

Of the hundreds of violinists who begin in elementary school, a few are persuaded by a teacher, dedicated to having a complete string section, to be individualistic and change to the viola. Some of the arguments that are used to bring off this coup are:

Being a member of a smaller section you will occupy a more distinguished position in the orchestra, and can take more personal pride in the achievement of your section.

(If applicable)

There will probably be less competition in the viola section than among the violins; so you should be able to earn a chair close to the front of the section.

The viola has a lovely mellow quality, and composers write interesting and beautiful parts for it.

Outstanding violists are rare. If you work hard, you should be able to earn a handsome scholarship at some college or music school. You will also have less competition in the professional world, if you decide to pursue that goal.

If the teacher-candidate hopes to develop a complete string section, then, he will learn something about alto clef and persuasive diplomacy.

Selecting the Correct Size Viola

Violas come in three basic sizes—Junior, Intermediate, and Standard. Refer to page 13 for the measurements of all of these sizes in inches. The Junior size is 13 1/4 to 14 inches in body length. The smaller is about the size of a 3/4 violin. A student who is playing a 3/4 violin should be transferred to the smallest available viola. If a small viola is not available, a small violin may be strung as a viola. This is not ideal because the small violin does not sound like a viola, and string length and tension are incorrect.

FIGURE 8.1. Viola, playing position.

FIGURE 8.2. Viola, rest position.

When fitting a viola to a child, select the largest instrument possible—within reason. It is not just the fact that a viola is tuned a fifth lower than the violin that makes it sound different from the violin. Chiefly responsible for the distinctive viola tone are the design and dimensions of the body. Therefore a viola that is not much bigger than a violin will have little of the deep, rich tone that typifies the viola. The "real" viola tone can hardly be approximated in an instrument of less than 14½-15½ inches body length. This is not a criticism of the smaller violas. We need them. Just choose the largest one possible.

The same method of fitting child to instrument can be used for the viola as was demonstrated for the violin. (Figures 7.1 and 7.2)

A Complete Outfit

The requirements for the viola are identical with those of the violin. (See Figure 7.3)

First Steps for the Beginner

The procedures detailed for the violin on page 88 would be followed if the student is an absolute beginner.

Holding the Viola

The single point of variance is that the viola should be held slightly flatter than the violin. This can be accomplished by using a lower shoulder pad or by tilting the head a little to the left. The reason for the flatter attitude of the viola is to take maximum advantage of the force of gravity in the bowing process. The viola is larger than the violin; the strings are longer and larger in diameter; the bow is larger and heavier than the violin bow. To pull a big viola tone all the help that can be realized will be needed if fatigue in the bow arm is to be avoided. In all other aspects the viola is held like the violin and the procedures outlined for the violin should be followed.

Learning to Read Alto Clef

The viola student, whether beginner or transfer from the violin, will encounter the alto, or C clef, for probably the first time ever. Classroom instruction usually includes familiarization with the treble clef, and piano students learn to read the bass clef, but seeing the alto clef prior to a musicianship course in junior high school is an extremely rare happening for all but the viola student.

The elementary students may know the syllables, and, if they are bright, the names of the lines and spaces of the treble staff. It is relatively easy for them to transfer what they know to the viola, or alto clef.

The relationship of the alto clef to middle C is the first thing to point out. Using the following visual presentation helps students to see this relationship.

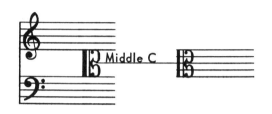

Use of the Janowsky *Viola Note Speller* (See Appendix) will also help the student to learn the notes in this new clef.

Holding the Bow

The similarities which apply to holding the violin and viola apply as well to holding the bow; but again there is a subtle difference. This difference is a matter of degree, and is as much in the "feel" of the bow on the string as it is in the actual grip and use of the bow. Nonetheless, the very fact that the viola bow is slightly larger in diameter, slightly longer, and consequently weighs more than the violin bow, is sufficient evidence that it will require a little huskier grip than the violin bow.

As stated above, the difference between the way the violin bow and the viola bow are held is a matter of degree. In very simple terms, the viola

bow is taken into the hand a little more than the violin bow. The added weight, plus the need to employ more strength than the violin requires, compels the hand and arm to treat the viola bow less delicately than the smaller, slimmer violin bow.

An analysis of the difference described above would show that the thumb is inserted a fraction of an inch farther into the bow, and the first three fingers are extended over the bow a fraction of an inch more than in the violin grip. The little finger still rides on top of the stick, and has to work harder because of the added weight of the viola bow.

Open String Stage

The material on the violin should be referred to again. And again slightly different treatment of the bow is needed. The viola strings are longer and larger in diameter than violin strings. They are heavier. They require more weight and pull than violin strings do. The viola bow is larger and heavier than the violin bow. The frog is wider and the hair-spread is wider. This added weight, length, and width of hair is all intentional, and its intent is to help the violist draw a big tone.

To take advantage of these special characteristics of the viola bow, the bow should be flatter on the string, at less of a tilt than the violin bow. This puts more hair in contact with the string. To achieve this the following things happen:

1. The stick is tilted toward the bridge to a nearly upright position.
2. The wrist is dropped slightly.

Neither of these modifications should be exaggerated. Done in the right amount they will achieve the desired result.

Hopefully the pupil will have begun his orientation to the alto clef and will know the location of the open strings on the staff.

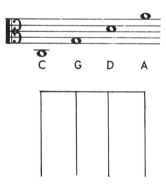

End Pin to Bridge Distance

If the viola is larger than the violin, the distance between the bottom of the instrument and the bridge will be greater than on the violin; since this distance increases proportionately with the size of the instrument. The pupil should be made aware of this factor; for it can be the cause of bowing problems that he cannot account for.

A 3/4 violin measures 5.98 inches from the base of the instrument to the bridge. A 4/4 violin, which is about the same size as a junior viola, (13 1/4-14) measures 6.42 inches. An intermediate size viola measures 6.97.

If the viola is the same size as the violin, the change will present no problem in this respect; for the distance will be the same. If, however, the change is from a 3/4 violin to a junior size viola, or from a 4/4 violin to an intermediate size viola, this increase of distance is considerable. It may appear insignificant in terms of inches, but it requires a definite adjustment in the elbow and upper arm. To reach the greater distance, the elbow will be bent less and the upper arm will be pushed forward. This is not a difficult adjustment and will be made automatically as the pupil puts the bow on the string ahead of the bridge. But as he plays, he will sense a difference, and the bow may ride up on the bridge. If he does not realize what is happening, he could become disturbed. If he understands what has happened, he can consciously correct the setting of the arm as needed.

Locating the Notes

The violinist who transfers to viola has found that the point of contact for the bow is farther away from him than on the violin. This is assuming that the viola is larger than the violin. If it is larger, he will find adjustments of the left arm will be necessary too.

First of all, the left arm will have to extend farther to reach the neck of the viola. This alone can prove tiring for a young person, but adaptation to this difference is usually quick.

A more important difference, and one which most students adapt to more slowly, is the larger spacing between the fingers of the left hand, a consequence of the greater string length on the viola. On a 15″ viola the distance between the fingers to produce whole steps in first position is about 1 3/8 inches— 1/8 inch greater than for a 4/4 violin. This creates a 3/8 inch larger over-all hand-span. On a 16 1/2

FIGURE 8.3. A. Correct position of the bow at the point. B. Correct position of the bow at the frog.

inch viola a distance of 1 1/2 inches between fingers is required to form whole steps in first position.

The reason for documenting the differences in finger spacing is not to indicate specific places to put down the fingers, but simply to dramatize the fact that there is a difference so that the teacher will understand the need to make this difference clear to the student. The bright student with a good ear hardly needs to have the above matter verbalized. His intuition will tell his fingers that they must behave differently, and what they must do, to achieve the results his ear commands. Furthermore, it is never really completely satisfactory to equate pitch with a visually identified place on the string. As pointed out in an earlier chapter, visual or tactile means to locate notes can bring results which are only approximate. The ear is the only completely accurate means to good intonation.

But it cannot be assumed that the majority of pupils are either particularly bright or talented. It behooves the teacher, then, to make the violin-viola transfer a bit simpler and more understandable by pointing out that fingers need to be farther apart on the viola than on the violin. Half steps will, of course, find the fingers close together, but not as close as on the violin.

In playing the viola, the fingers of the left hand contact the string with the fleshier part of the finger tip. Thus, the finger will cover a slightly greater length of the string. This creates a wider vibrato and a somewhat less intense or brilliant tone quality, which is, of course, typical of the viola.

The Intermediate Stage

The intermediate stage on the viola, as the violin, is typified by the study of third position. The techniques of learning and executing the positions are the same on both instruments. During this stage the violist is confronted with two additional tasks that the violinist is spared. The first is half position; the second is reading music which employs a mixture of the alto and treble clefs.

Half Position

Half position is located 1/2 step below first position.

The term "half position" carries to its logical conclusion the practice which has evolved in designating positions, i.e., a position is established not so much by the longitudinal location of the hand on the neck as by the particular finger which is used to play a note occupying a given line or space on the staff,

no matter how the note is altered chromatically. To illustrate:

is considered to be in first position. But the same notes written enharmonically, as follows, are considered to be in second position.

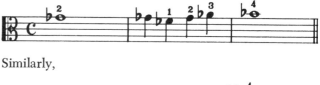

Similarly,

is considered to be

in first position. When written in sharps, but played with the same fingers, it is regarded as half position.

Half position may be as useful to the violinist as to the violist, but traditionally violinists do not study it or commonly regard it as a position in its own right. This is not true of violists, who make extensive use of and frequent references to half position. The reason for this probably has something to do with the fact that the keys of C♯ Major and minor occur more frequently than does G♯ minor. These are the keys that utilize half position on the bottom string of the two instruments. Another factor is that composers and arrangers, in writing for the viola, favor the C string and the lower positions; for this is where the richest viola tone is to be found. And it is in this register that half position occurs most frequently. To the contrary, the high register of the violin is stressed; so positions III through V or higher get frequent use.

On the viola the following passage, for example, would be awkward if it were to be played Sul. C. This would require the third finger to move from the E♯ to the F♯ in measure #1 and a stretch back to C♯ with the first finger in measure #3. If taken in half position, no shifting is necessary.

Simple orchestrations for young players will not require the use of half position. Those orchestrations intended for more advanced school use, which have been carefully edited by a string specialist, will contain half position indications for the violist where they are appropriate.

Reading a Mixture of Alto and Treble Clefs

The *tessitura* of viola parts includes frequent use of the notes which lie several ledger lines above the staff. Traditionally music copyists avoid writing ledger lines when possible, and musicians are just as happy if they do not have to count ledger lines to identify a note. The solution to this problem has been to use the 8va sign or change clefs.

The use of the treble clef is not a factor until the music rises to third position on the A string.

At that time the notes utilizing the third ledger line come into frequent use, and employment of the treble clef becomes a distinct convenience for the writer and for the player—when he gains facility in making the bridge between alto and treble clef.

The switchback to the treble clef would not appear to be a problem for a person who had played violin and knew the treble clef fairly well. But it is surprising how completely oriented to the alto clef one may become in a short time, and how foreign the treble clef can appear to be when it suddenly appears in a line of viola music.

Orientation is the key word in this matter, and the student must learn to change his orientation from one clef to the other in a fraction of a second. There is no short cut or trick to learning to do this. The sequence of notes leading into and out of one clef or the other usually makes for a logical connection. The more thorough the student's musical background, the more readily he will learn to clear the clef-switching hurdle.

A few examples of the mixing of the alto and treble clefs follow. They will illustrate the points made above. These illustrations encompass notes in 5th position; since the treble clef is particularly useful in writing notes in 5th position and higher.

Vibrato

The vibrato is made on the viola precisely as it is on the violin. Differences lie in its speed and width but not in its method. On the viola the vibrato may be wider than on the violin, although this is not always the case, vibrato being such an individual and personal thing. More general is the fact that the viola vibrato will be slower than the violin vibrato. Accounting for this is the lower pitch of the viola and the longer string length, and consequently a slower response to pitch fluctuation.

The vibrato exercises described in the chapter on the violin are applicable to the viola.

The Advanced Stage

Everything that is said in the comparable section of the chapter on the violin applies to the viola. By this stage the student who has transferred from violin has established himself as a bona fide violist. This is surely true of the student who began on the viola. His experience in orchestra and chamber music groups has developed a concept of real viola tone and has taught the player to assume his rightful musical role in these groups.

Through many years of the history of music the viola and the violist served only in a secondary or supportive role. The viola was an instrument to be taken up by second-rate violinists. It was rarely assigned a leadership position, musically speaking. The absence of viola concertos and sonatas by the early composers is ample evidence of the position the viola occupied in the hierarchy of instruments. A concerto by Teleman, the Sinfonia Concertante by

Mozart, a concerto by Stamitz are some of the exceptions. Then Berlioz wrote "Harold In Italy" and a new era for the viola was launched. The viola began to emerge as an instrument capable of a sufficient range of expression and technique to justify a greater literature of its own. Violists such as Lionel Tertis, William Primrose, Emmanuel Vardi, and Walter Trampler, who developed their skill on the instrument to the heights of artistry, have done much to stimulate greater interest in the viola on the part of composers, performers, and listeners.

Largely due to the influence and impact of these artists, the viola has been elevated to a higher status than it had previously enjoyed. This has created new opportunities for the viola and, at the same time, has imposed increased demands and responsibilities upon the violist. No longer can the violist be a converted second-rate violinist. To excel he must be a first-rate violist. This means developing all of the skills and techniques of the instrument to a high level of proficiency. It means mastering a varied and extensive repertoire. It means being prepared to assume a variety of responsibilities including orchestra member, chamber music performer, soloist, teacher.

The road to this level of achievement is built of the same material as the road to violin artistry. The titles may differ but the substance is the same. A balance of scales, studies, and solo literature is necessary. Private instruction and a great deal of hard work are essential.

The following illustrations of notes in positions I-VII on the viola are provided for easy reference.

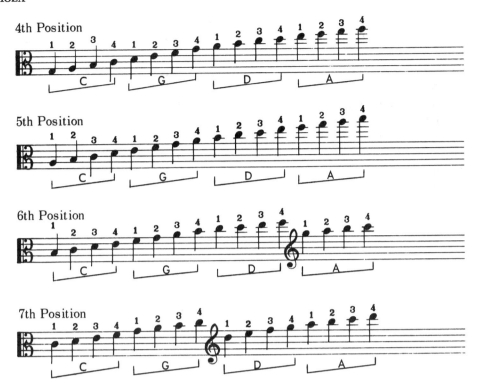

CHAPTER 9

Teaching the Cello

The cello is the tenor of the string section. It has a range in excess of three octaves, has a large and powerful tone, and is capable of a broad range of dynamics. It is a magnificent solo instrument and lends great power and warmth to the string section of the orchestra. A symphony orchestra cello section numbers from six to ten players.

In the music of the Baroque and Classical periods, the cello and bass parts were most often written as one line indicated as Violoncello and Basso. The sections played the same line but sounded an octave apart since the bass sounds an octave lower than written. However, in the Beethoven orchestral works, the cello and bass were treated as separate instruments. True, they frequently played the same line, but their individual capabilities and limitations were considered. When it appeared to be desirable to have the cello without the bass, this was done, or the cello and bass in unison, or the bass entering at a given moment to reinforce a chord or scale passage. Some composers after Beethoven gave the cello even more independence, using its full range in melody and counter-melody.

A broad hand, or long fingers with considerable strength are an advantage on the cello. Just to stop the strings requires strength. But the stretching of the hand, the extensions of the fingers, and the speed and dexterity required of the player are much facilitated if the hand is large and strong. Especially important is the stretch between the second and third fingers, an asset which can be developed by proper exercise.

In first position the hand spans only the interval of a third, in contrast to a fourth on the violin and viola. This means that frequent changes of position are necessary to avoid awkward string changes. So the cellist finds himself shifting constantly. The advantage that the cellist has over the violinist and violist is that the cello is anchored solidly on the floor via the end pin and is braced by the knees and chest. This completely frees the left hand and arm from supporting the instrument and gives the cellist absolute freedom to maneuver up and down the neck of the cello.

Selecting the Correct Size Cello

Cello sizes range from 4/4 down to 1/8. Sizes ordinarily found in schools are 4/4, 3/4, and 1/2. (See page 15 for measurements.) Most elementary school children will require a 1/2 size cello, but one or two 3/4 cellos in each school is a precaution against the extra large sixth grade pupil who shows up occasionally.

The Importance of the Chair

Graduated chair sizes for small cellists is a matter of the utmost importance but is frequently neglected. Most elementary schools have some small chairs in which a child is able to sit comfortably and touch the floor with his feet. The string teacher should have a supply of chairs of various heights from which to choose. For while it is not desirable, the small violinist can get by in a standard chair by putting his feet on the rung; but in the case of the cellist, the knees are part of the holding apparatus, and being able to put the feet on the floor becomes an important item.

The importance of a chair with a straight back and flat seat has been discussed previously (See page 46). It is highly desirable that these features be incorporated into the lower chairs if possible. An end pin holder of some kind is an essential.

The cello is the right size if, when the lower bouts are correctly positioned between the legs, the lower right tuning peg is opposite the left ear.

A Complete Outfit

Every cello outfit should be complete and in good working order. It should include the following:

1. A well made cello with proper strings and tuners that work easily. (All 1/2 size cellos should be equipped with tuners), strings at correct height and correctly spaced, an end pin that is sharp with a good wing-nut set screw and a stop to prevent the end pin from slipping inside the instrument.
2. A bow full of good hair, properly rosined, a frog that fits properly and slides smoothly, a screw that works easily.
3. A satisfactory end pin holder.
4. A cake of rosin.
5. A cloth or hard case that fits the cello, has a bow pocket, a pocket for music and rosin, good zippers, snaps, or clamps, and a good handle.

First Steps for the Beginner

Refer to this section in the chapter on the violin, all of which applies to the cello with the exception, of course, that the cello is never held and played like a guitar. If this technique is used with the violin and viola, the cello is held in a normal position and played pizzicato.

Holding the Cello

The following conditions must be met to achieve a satisfactory basic position for the cello:

1. A flat chair of the proper height, making it possible for the feet to rest flat on the floor. The right foot is forward, the left foot drawn back toward the chair. The body should be erect.
2. An end pin holder that makes it possible to position the end pin so that the cello is at an angle of between 55° and 65°.
3. The end pin should be adjusted so that the corners of the lower bouts are at knee level and the C peg is opposite the left ear.
4. The top of the right side of the back of the cello contacts the body at the chest about at the lower center of the rib cage.
5. The cello should be tilted slightly to the right so that the bow will not hit the knee when playing on the A string.

School teachers from elementary through senior high school will find that girls' tight skirts make holding the cello properly an impossibility. The narrow width of the skirt simply makes it impossible for the girl to straddle the cello. Confronted with this problem, many girls have adopted a side-saddle position in which the legs are placed demurely together on the right side of the cello. This puts the player in an unbalanced position and prevents the knees from lending any assistance in holding the cello. Requiring girls to wear full or pleated skirts will remedy the situation, but fashion trends and peer acceptance are powerful forces to combat. Formal dress for high school performances solves the evening public appearance problem at the high school level.

Left Hand and Arm Position

The left thumb touches the back of the neck about 3 1/2 inches from the top of the neck. The fingers are over the string with the second finger opposite the thumb. The wrist and forearm are in a straight line. The angle of the upper arm varies according to the string which the fingers are functioning on. The fingers are slightly rounded, with the tips pointing down toward the string. The pads press against the string. The position of the thumb depends upon which string the fingers are functioning on. The thumb is under the neck when playing on the A string and moves to the left when on the C.

The following pictures demonstrate the correct playing position and rest position for the cello.

Common Faults In Holding the Cello

The end pin is placed too close to or too far from the player resulting in the cello being too straight or too slanted.

The end pin is set so that it is too long or too short. This places the cello too high or too low in relation to the player.

No end pin holder is provided so the cello slips, making it necessary for the player to hold the cello in place with his legs and knees.

The tilt of the cello is insufficient to prevent the bow from striking the left leg when bowing on the A string or is exaggerated to the point that the bow strikes the right knee when playing on the C string.

The left arm is allowed to drop to the side of the body, putting the fingers, wrist, and forearm in incorrect position.

Tightening the Bow

To tighten the cello bow, hold the frog with the thumb and fingers of the left hand with the hair

FIGURE 9.1. Playing position.

FIGURE 9.2. Rest position.

facing up, as shown in Figure 2.4. The cello bow is thicker and consequently stiffer than the violin and viola bows; so it will be slightly harder to tighten. If the bow has its original camber, the hair, when fully tightened, should be about 1/2 inch (+ or −) from the stick at its nearest point.

As in the case of the violin, the teacher should demonstrate each step for the pupil and then have the pupil repeat them. These steps should include tightening and loosening the bow and applying rosin. How often to rosin the bow and the importance of loosening the hair after each practice or rehearsal session should be stressed.

Holding the Bow

The manner in which the cello bow is held is quite different from the way the violin and viola bow is held. The primary reason for this is that the bow arm is in a lowered position for the cello in contrast to the raised position for the violin and viola. Secondly, on the violin and viola the instru-

ment is directly below the bow, and the weight of the bow, and the hand and arm bear directly down on the string. In the case of the cello, the bow must be pressed into the string and downward toward the bridge. Physically, from the standpoint of the bow itself, this is not as natural as the violin and viola bow position. But this drawback is amply compensated for by the more natural position the bow arm can assume on the cello. Actually the inward pressure of the bow into the string is the only thing that prevents the bow from falling to the floor were it not for the support provided by the thumb and finger of the right hand.

To acquire the correct bow grip, the pupil should take the bow in the left hand, holding it by the screw button. The hair should face upward. Held in this way the placement of each finger can be seen clearly. With the bow held as directed, the following steps should be followed in sequence:

1. With the first joint bent outward, the thumb is inserted into the opening between the frog and the hair. The center of the thumb touches the

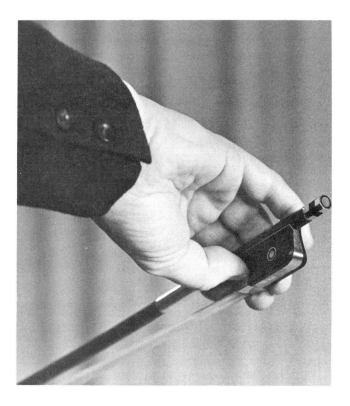

FIGURE 9.3. Correct position of thumb and fingers on the bow.

frog; the right side touches the junction of the stick and the grip.

2. The first finger goes over the bow, the first joint resting on the wrapping.
3. The second finger goes completely over the stick and down the side of the frog. The end of the finger touches the hair.
4. The third finger, like the second, goes over the bow and down the side of the frog. The end of the finger touches the ferrule (the silver mounting).
5. The little finger reaches over the bow about midway on the frog. The tip of the finger reaches down to the pearl eye.

After the position of the fingers is checked by the teacher, the bow may be turned over and laid on the strings.

In playing position the stick is tilted toward the fingerboard. When the bow is on the string at the frog, the wrist will be well arched, providing a flexible hinge for changing bow direction. At the point the wrist will be straight or have a slight break, but it should not be dropped excessively.

Common Faults In Holding the Bow

The thumb is inserted too far through the bow.

The second, third, and fourth fingers wrap around the bottom of the frog, gripping the bow into the palm of the hand.

FIGURE 9.4. A. Correct position of the bow at the point. B. Correct position of the bow at the frog.

The hand slants too much toward the screw button or the tip.

The stick contacts the hand too far up on the first finger.

The thumb bends in instead of out.

The wrist arch is exaggerated, causing the hair to be flat on the string.

The Beginning or Open String Stage

Objectives

To hold the instrument and bow correctly.[1]

To draw the bow parallel to the bridge.

To draw the bow on the proper string.

To draw the bow for the specified duration.

To make satisfactory bow changes from up to down and down to up.

To identify the strings by their letter names.

To know the signs for down bow and up bow and follow these directions.

To be able to identify the following parts: bridge, fingerboard, neck, tailpiece, bow—frog, point, hair, screw, upper half, middle, lower half.

To associate a printed note with the corresponding open string.

To know the names of the notes corresponding to the open strings.

To know how to count quarter notes, half notes, whole notes and their corresponding rests in 2/4 and 4/4 time.

To keep one's place while playing a line of music.

Most method books spend several lessons on the open strings; so the pupils must learn their identity on both the instrument and the printed page. To review, they are:

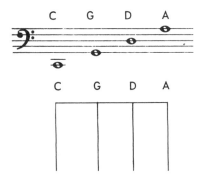

Using only open strings allows the pupil to concentrate on how he is holding the instrument and the bow, which is of paramount importance during this formulative period.

FIGURE 9.5. Cello, left hand.

At the outset the pupil should not be expected to practice more than a few minutes at a time; for his concentration span is short, and the muscles in his bow arm will tire quickly. However, within two to three weeks it is not unreasonable to expect ten to fifteen minutes of steady practice.

Turn back to the section in the chapter, Teaching the Violin, for suggestions and exercises appropriate to the open string stage. Exercises spelled out for the violin are adaptable to the cello by the simple expedient of regarding the second string on the violin as the second string on the cello. In other words, if the violin A string is referred to in the excercise, regard it as the D string on the cello.

Beginning cellists will have the same problems other string players have; namely, they will have trouble keeping the bow on the designated string and parallel to the bridge. The cellist has an advantage over the violinist and violist in that he can sit in front of a full length mirror and observe the alignment of his bow.

1. During the open string stage it is permissible for the left hand to rest on the right shoulder of the cello (left of the neck in playing position.)

Locating the Notes

First attempts at using the fingers on the strings will be on the A or D, depending upon the method being used. On a 4/4 cello the first finger will be about three inches from the nut to produce a note a whole step higher than the open string. On a 3/4 cello this will be about 2 5/8 inches, and on a 1/2 size cello about 2 1/4 inches. As stated before, linear measurements are only approximate and are not completely accurate insofar as pitch is concerned. Only the ear can make a judgment in matters of pitch.

On the cello the left hand is held in such a way that the fingers are slanted toward the nut. The first joint of the first and second fingers are nearly perpendicular to the string, as they are on the violin and viola. The third and fourth fingers assume a somewhat flatter attitude.

The first finger is positioned about three inches from the nut. On the D string this produces an E natural. If the second finger is then placed a little more than an inch above the first, F natural, an interval of a half step is produced. The third finger produces F sharp, and the fourth finger G. The hand itself, from the first to the fourth finger, spans a minor third; from the open string it covers a perfect fourth. Thus, in first position, the cellist's range on each string is one whole step smaller than the range of the violin and viola. Without extensions, the cellist plays these notes in first position:

Whether the second finger is used at the outset depends upon the method being used. If it is a class method utilizing the D major approach, the finger pattern will be:

It is good pedagogy to always play the notes first so that the pupil can hear what he is supposed to produce on his instrument. It is in this way that the pupil begins to listen to and match pitch.

Cellists must be encouraged to press very firmly on the string in order to produce a clear tone and accurate pitch. he rather wobbly fingers of the nine- or ten-year old will gain strength rapidly if each practice period is a finger-strengthening effort. Long tones at full volume will aid this process. Also finger-strengthening exercises such as the following are beneficial.

etc. Note: 16th notes are optional

In doing these exercises the fingers should be raised as high as possible and brought down onto the string with a forceful snap. These exercises should be done on each string.

During this stage the pupil will need to be reminded to keep his left elbow away from the body and at the correct angle. This requires some effort, and it is very easy for the young child to resign himself to the line of least resistance, letting his arm drop to his side. Correct arm position is extremely important in this respect since it controls the position of the fingers on the strings, the amount of strength that can be applied to the fingers, the vibrato, and shifting. The bow hand and the action of the bow must be watched constantly also. Pressure, point of contact, and keeping the bow parallel to the bridge are three important concerns.

Common Faults During this Stage

The pupil is inconsistent in the placement of the fingers. In other words, he plays "out of tune."

The spaces between the fingers are not wide enough. Consequently the intervals are too small.

The fingers do not curve as they come down on the string. The first joint collapses.

The elbow is allowed to drop to the side of the body putting the forearm, wrist, and fingers in a faulty position.

The Intermediate Stage

Objectives (All Appropriate Previous Objectives Continue)

To play in tune.
To learn to tune the instrument.
To play with a pleasant tone.
To play with a range of dynamics from pp to ff.
To gain facility in backward and forward extensions.
To attain a velocity measured by slurred 16th notes at   = 66-76 and bowed 16th notes at   = 56-66.
To use the bow skillfully in a variety of bowings, i.e., slurs, staccato, marcato, slow spiccato.
To begin the study of the positions.
To begin to develop vibrato.

Tuning the Cello

Up until this time the teacher has, for practical reasons, tuned the student's instrument. In the first place, the pupil's ear is not developed sufficiently to do the job, and his muscles are usually inadequate for the job. If the instrument is equipped with tuners, a start may have been made to have the pupil attempt minor adjustments.

The first step is to tune each string individually to a pitch source. The piano is the most satisfactory. If the cello has tuners, show the pupil how to raise and lower the pitch of the string by turning the heads of the tuners to the right or left respectively. If gut-core strings are involved, have the pupil lay down his bow and turn the cello so that the strings are toward him. Of course he is seated. With the cello in this position, he can pluck the A and D strings with the left thumb while the right hand turns the pegs, and pluck the G and C strings with the right thumb while the left hand turns the pegs. The absolute importance of having tuning pegs which work well cannot be stressed enough.

When the A string is plucked, it will continue to vibrate for a short period of time. While the string is vibrating, the left hand should move quickly to the left side of the scroll providing a counter-force to the pushing of the right hand as it turns and sets the A or D pegs. The hands reverse roles as the G and C strings are tuned.

After the pupil has become proficient at tuning each string to an individually given pitch, he should begin to tune one string to the other. This should begin with the A, which is tuned to a piano or pitch pipe. The D is tuned from the A, etc. Since considerable strength is needed to tune the cello, it is advisable to have the pupil continue to tune by plucking, unless the instrument has tuners or patent pegs. In the latter case, he can begin to use the bow.

When the bow is used in the tuning process, only the upper half is used. Begin at the point. Tune the A then the D to the A, playing the two strings together. The phenomenon of the "waves" or pulses is described in the chapter on the violin, page 97. The greater length and sonority of the cello strings make these pulses more pronounced.

In the case of an instrument equipped with tuners, which is being tuned with the bow, the bow hand also adjusts the tuners. With gut-core strings the left hand turns the pegs while the bow functions on the strings. (See Figure 9.6.)

Extensions

Because of the length of cello strings, the fingers must be more than two inches apart to produce a whole step in the first four positions and nearly that far apart in fifth and sixth positions. This distance limits the interval the hand can span, without extending to a minor third. This is, of course, extremely limiting technically and musically. To in-

FIGURE 9.6.   Tuning the cello.

crease the range of the hand and expand the number of notes that can be played on each string, the cellist employs a technique described as "extension."

Extensions can be made in a backward direction and in a forward direction. In both cases the extension is made from the normal setting of the hand. It is very important in the backward extension that only the first finger moves, and in the forward extension that the first finger remains in place.

Backward Extension

The backward extension is accomplished by moving the first finger back one half step. In this position the side of the finger rather than the pad will contact the string. The rest of the hand and the thumb remain in position. This brings within the reach of the hand the note which is one half step above the open string. Example 1, below, illustrates this extension. (Note that the upper three fingers play the same notes they produce normally in first position.)

Half Position

Closely related to the backward extension of the first finger is half position. Half position is realized when the entire hand, including the thumb, is moved backward one half step. In half position the fingers play the notes in Example 2.

This may, of course, be written enharmonically in flats.

Forward Extension

In the forward extension the hand and thumb move down the fingerboard one half step. The first finger pivots in place, becoming nearly straight, and forming a decided angle of divergence from the second finger. The forward extension brings the notes in Example 3 within reach.

Tone Development

The process of tone production is the same on all of the stringed instruments. While it is true that the arm is lower than the bow in the case of the violin and viola and is above the bow in the case of the cello and bass, the same principles are at work. Friction between bow hair and string created by the movement of the hair across the string is still the sound-producing element.

The ideal design of the cello, from the standpoint of string length and acoustical properties, contributes to the large volume of sound the cello is capable of producing. To get the most from the instrument, and to play it in the manner to which it is accustomed, the student must learn to apply strength and force, both of which depend upon the development of the arm and finger muscles along with sensitive balance and control. When called for, the cello can be attacked quite roughly and aggressively. The bow can strike the strings rather savagely without producing an unpleasant sound.

Note: Also refer to pages 76 to 77 for a general discussion of tone production.

Shifting to the Higher Positions

Method books present the positions in varying order. After establishing first position some introduce half position, then second, third, fourth, etc. Others jump from first to fourth. It is difficult to debate the advantage of one over the other. Those who advocate a systematic coverage of the positions in succession feel that there is merit in the orderliness of this approach and that it prevents one position or another being slighted or omitted. The advocates of the quick jump to the fourth position argue that the fourth position extends the range of the player considerably. They feel that the fourth position is an easy position to find and be sure of because the thumb rests in the curve of the neck. It is also an advantageous place to establish the correct position of the left hand.

In shifting positions the hand moves as a whole, with the thumb retaining its position opposite the second finger. The normal setting of the hand pre-

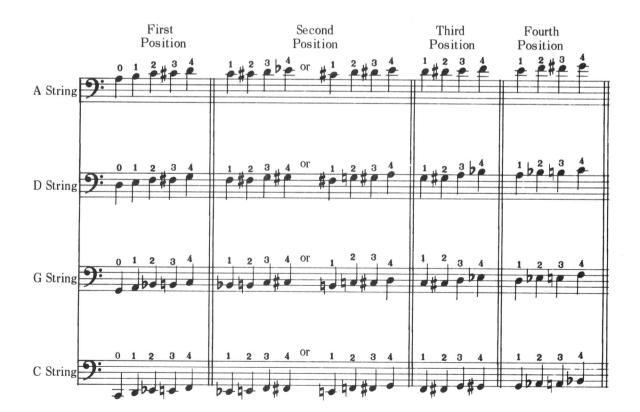

vails, although backward and forward extensions can be made from any position. The simplified chart on page 122 shows the notes in each of the first four positions on each string.

Vibrato

The general nature and purpose of the vibrato has been described earlier. (See page 62) The cello vibrato is produced by a back and forth rolling motion of the forearm. The forearm motion carries the hand and finger with it. It is the movement of the finger on the string which is the cause of the pitch fluctuation, which is the vibrato. It is because the finger is at right angles to the string that it must roll on the string to produce the pitch change, in contrast to the back and forth motion of the finger in producing vibrato on the violin and viola.

In his Vibrato Method, Gilbert Waller advocates initial vibrato practice be done without the cello. The elbow is raised until it is horizontal; the finger tips are placed in the pit of the left shoulder. The wrist is then alternately raised and lowered with the shoulder muscles providing the energy. This routine is followed with a variety of rhythms and at increasing speed. When the finger is placed on the string, the vibrato movement is continued in a mechanical fashion with various rhythms and at increasing speeds.

The hand can be placed at any position on the fingerboard for vibrato practice, but fourth position has some advantage. In fourth position the thumb can rest on the curve of the neck, which provides it with a kind of anchor. The second finger is placed on the D string and the forearm is rocked back and forth rhythmically. This should be done in various rhythms and at gradually increasing tempi.

The cello vibrato must be wide enough to create a genuine feeling of natural vocal-like tone. It must not be so small and quick that it sounds like a nervous tremor nor so wide and slow that it sounds labored. It must assist the bow to bring life to the music. It must project the entire range of emotions inherent in the music. To be fully effective it must be capable of a wide range of speed, width, and intensity. In the final analysis, it must respond to the emotional message of the music and project that message through the cello.

The mechanical exercises described above will not automatically create a vibrato. But they can condition the vibrato mechanism to function more readily than it otherwise might.

Common Faults of the Intermediate Stage

Carelessness in intonation.
Failure to retain basic hand position in extensions.
Inaccuracy in shifting.
Tone is too hard or too soft.
Vibrato is made with hand or fingers rather than the forearm.
Limited dynamic range.
Limited reading ability.

The Advanced Stage

Objectives (All Appropriate Previous Objectives Continue)

To improve intonation, tone, and musicianship generally, with a more mature concept of style and interpretation.

To increase and expand technique, including:

Ability to play faster and more clearly both single note and double stop passages, chords, harmonics, trills.

Skill in 5th, 6th, 7th, and thumb positions.

Improved spiccato, staccato, ricochet bowings.

Ability to read tenor clef.

To play solo and ensemble and orchestra literature of an advanced nature.

Most of the objectives of this stage are common to all the strings. But the thumb position is unique to the cello. Also unique is the need to play music in the bass clef, tenor clef, and occasionally treble clef.

Thumb Position

Thumb position extends the range of the cello and gives the cellist a great deal of facility in the upper register where the notes are close enough together that the cellist can utilize violin-like fingering. A sensible place to begin thumb position is at the octave harmonic on the A and D. The side of the thumb is placed on the two strings simultaneously. It acts as the open strings on the violin, the fingers functioning as they do on the violin— playing either half or whole steps. In thumb position the first finger remains on the string to support the second; the second supports the third, and the third supports the fourth. See Figure 9.7.

The symbol for thumb position is φ. Other fingers such as 1, 2, 3 may follow, but the thumb sign signifies that the notes following it are to be played in thumb position. The following passage is an example:

FIGURE 9.7. Cello, thumb position.

Thumb position also enables the cellist to play octaves.

Tenor Clef

The large range of the cello would, if it were not for the use of the tenor clef, require the use of many ledger lines above the bass staff. As stated earlier, this is an annoyance to both the composer and the cellist. To circumvent the use of ledger lines when the music goes above the bass clef, the tenor clef is used. It brings middle C down to the 4th line of the staff, a third higher than the viola. Thus, notes that would be written several ledger lines above the staff are brought into easy reading range. For example:

becomes

The student must master tenor clef as he did the bass clef. Showing the relationship of the clefs visually can help.

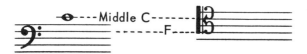

However, by the time the student is ready to play music that uses tenor clef, he should have enough theoretical background to comprehend the new clef fairly quickly. Once introduced to the clef, facility in reading it becomes a matter of repetition and experience.

Treble Clef

The use of treble clef is not unusual in advanced cello music. The reason for using it is to avoid using an excessive number of ledger lines when the music lies in the high register of the instrument. General practice in writing in the treble clef is to have it logically follow the tenor clef. When it occurs in this manner, the notes are written where they are to sound. Early practice, a practice still made use of by some composers, was to jump from the bass clef to the treble clef. When used in this way, the notes in the treble clef were meant to be played an octave lower than they were written. An example of moving from tenor clef to treble clef follows:

The cellist's role in orchestra, chamber music, and solo is every bit as demanding as the violinist's. Consequently, the cellist must develop speed, agility, and accuracy. He must develop great strength in his fingers, hands, and arms, and be capable of moving about very quickly.

The cellist is a key member of any chamber music group. He provides the bass and often has a major responsibility for the rhythmic solidarity of the ensemble. It is extremely important, therefore, that the cellist have a fine sense of rhythm and be sensitive to both the demands of the music and the needs of the ensemble.

Private instruction and a regular and well-balanced practice schedule are essential if the cellist is to reach an advanced stage and continue to progress. His diet should include scales, studies, and music selected from the standard solo literature. His experience should include opportunities to play duets, chamber music, solos, and in orchestra.

CHAPTER 10

Teaching the Bass

The bass is in some respects the most difficult to play of the stringed instruments. It is difficult because it is large and ungainly, with thick strings that are slow to respond. Intervals are far apart on the strings, requiring long reaches of the fingers. The pitchs of its strings are so low it is very hard, at times, to discern the notes that are being played. Composers are aware of the problems and limitations of the instrument and write for it accordingly.

The bass is extremely important in its role as the foundation-stone of the orchestra. In a symphony there may be from six to ten basses. Not only do they furnish the harmonic foundation for the orchestra, but they perform an extremely important function rhythmically. In many instances the bass is primarily a member of the rhythm section, providing the basic beat of the music. However, its ability to move freely to any pitch within its range and to produce a real sostenuto puts it in a special category among the rhythm instruments.

While speaking of the bass as a rhythm instrument, it is appropriate to mention the role it plays in the legitimate instrumental jazz combo. During the entire history of the dance band the bass has been regarded, along with drums and piano, to be one of the essential ingredients of the rhythm section. In this capacity the bass is always played pizzicato, most often supplying the basic beat, but occasionally surfacing to take a chorus.

In the large dance band complex the bass is more often than not lost behind the shining armor of the brasses and saxophones. When a rhythm solo is called for, the drummer usually takes over. But in the emergence of the small combo, the bass has assumed an increasingly important role. First of all it provides the foundation on which the rest of the combo builds its particular individual super-structure, and upon whom the others depend for the harmonic signals which are essential to their ability to function successfully. And in the small combo the bass is often given opportunities to solo. "Taking a chorus" is not something new for the bass, but in the combo it happens with greater frequency. Furthermore, the combo puts the bass more "out-in-front" than it was in the big band. What this adds up to is that the bass player cannot be content with the ability to provide rhythm alone. If he is going to excel, he must be able to improvise; and to improvise well, he must have some technique. True, effective solos are more dependent upon imagination and creativity than upon technical skill, but the technical skill is what makes it possible for the creative bassist to bring his ideas to life.

In the elementary school it is as difficult to find pupils to begin on the bass as it is to find pupils to begin on the viola. It helps if the child who begins on the bass is larger than average and more developed physically. These are not essential qualifications but they do provide an advantage. The small or delicate child, on the other hand, should, generally speaking, be steered away from the bass and toward one of the smaller instruments.

Transportation of the bass is a major problem and is often a serious deterrent to taking up the instrument. Some possible solutions to this problem are

1. Provide practice time at school so the bass does not have to be moved,
2. Persuade the child's parents to provide transportation for the bass,
3. Furnish some kind of wheeled cart to carry the bass,
4. Supply a second instrument for use at home.

It is rather unusual for school systems to purchase 7/8 and 4/4 basses. These sizes are more appropriate to the college and professional levels.

FIGURE 10.1. A satisfactory way to carry a bass.

This discussion will, therefore be limited to 1/2 and 3/4 sizes, the sizes found most frequently in schools. Only the 1/2 size bass should be used in elementary schools. The 3/4 size is too large for elementary children and should be limited to junior and senior high school.

Selecting the Correct Size Bass

All elementary bass pupils should be started on a 1/2 size bass. The height of the bass can be regulated by adjusting the end pin. The bass can sit flush with the floor or it can be raised to about five or six inches above the floor. The end pin should be adjusted so the nut at the top of the fingerboard is slightly above eye level. It is better to have the bass too high than too low so that the right arm does not have to be strained to properly position the bow.

A Complete Outfit

A complete bass outfit includes the following:

A well made bass of the correct size with proper strings and a machine head tuning mechanism in good condition, strings at the correct height above the fingerboard and correctly spaced, an end pin that is sharp, a good wing-nut set screw and a stop to prevent the end pin from slipping inside the instrument.

A bow full of good hair properly rosined, a frog that fits properly and slides smoothly, a screw that works easily.

A satisfactory end pin holder.

A cake of bass rosin.

A cloth case that fits the bass, has a bow pocket, a pocket for music and rosin, with a good zipper or snaps.

A satisfactory and safe way to carry the bass is, in itself, a problem. The bass is large, rather heavy, and is awkward to handle. Small children should not be required to carry a bass any farther than from the storage locker to the middle of the room. The teacher should take responsibility for moving the bass between rooms.

When the student is large enough to be entrusted with the job of carrying a bass, a method such as that shown in Figure 10.1 is recommended.

First Steps for the Beginner

See the statement under Cello.

Holding the Bass

The beginning bass player should not use a stool. This is a luxury reserved for more advanced and mature players. The position of the feet and body are important in attaining a satisfactory playing position. There is considerable difference of opinion regarding the exact setting of the feet; and, as with the other instruments, variations due to individual physical features are not to be frowned upon. The primary objective is to arrive at a position that is comfortable and practical. If the following directions are followed, a satisfactory position can be achieved.

1. Point the left foot straight ahead.
2. Place the right foot 4-6 inches to the right of the left foot, 6-8 inches in back of the left foot, and point the toe to the right at an angle of about 45°-60°. The body will now be facing slightly to the right. The body should be held nearly erect.
3. The bass end pin is positioned 8-10 inches ahead of and slightly to the right of the left foot.
4. The bass leans backward and tilts to the right. The lower right bout rests against the left knee. The upper right bout rests against the left side of the body, just below the rib cage.
5. Adjust end pin so that the first finger will be at eye level when playing "A" on the G string.

FIGURE 10.2. Correct way to hold the bass, standing.

Left Hand and Arm Position

The thumb contacts the back of the neck oppo-site the second finger. The hand should be rounded as though holding a ball. The upper arm is well out from the body, only slightly lower than hori-zontal. The forearm is angled upward, and the wrist is bent a little so that the fingers are just above the plane of the strings.

The open and somewhat elongated position of the hand is important to the development of satis-factory finger action, vibrato, and shifting. A col-lapsed position, with the palm resting against the neck, should positively be avoided. This position looks bad, prevents correct finger action, makes a vibrato virtually impossible, and generally limits tech-nique.

Common Faults In Holding the Bass

The end pin is placed too close or too far from the player resulting in the bass being too straight or too slanted. If the bass is positioned too far ahead of the player, the player will more than likely lean forward. This is to be avoided.

The end pin is incorrectly adjusted resulting in the bass being too high or too low for the player.

No end pin holder is provided so the bass slips and the player feels insecure.

The bass is tilted too far to the left or right.

The arm is allowed to drop to the side of the body, putting the fingers, wrist, and forearm in in-correct position.

The left hand is allowed to collapse against the neck.

Tightening the Bow

To tighten the bass bow, hold the frog with the thumb and fingers as shown in Figure 2.4, page 18. The bass bow is stouter than the other bows and

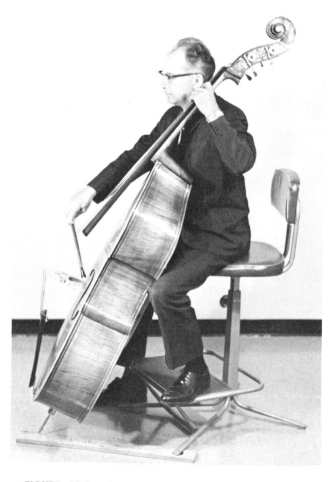

FIGURE 10.3. Correct way to hold the bass, seated.

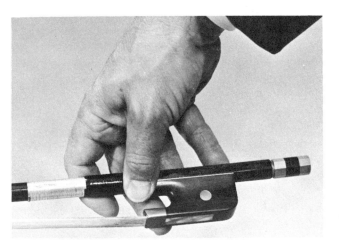

FIGURE 10.4.   Correct way to hold the French bow.

FIGURE 10.5.   Correct way to hold the German bow.

is considerably more rigid. If the bow has its original camber, the hair, when fully tightened, should be from 1/2 to 3/4 inch from the stick at its nearest point. The procedure described and points made on page 18 are applicable to the bass also.

In rosining, the bass bow is always drawn from the frog to the point, never pushed in the opposite direction. The teacher should demonstrate this procedure to the pupil.

Holding the Bow

The French bow is held like the cello bow. The fingers may be slightly more spread.

The German (Butler) bow is placed in the crotch of the thumb, the frog pressing into the thick pad below the thumb. The thumb hooks over the top of the stick. The first and second fingers lie along the right side of the stick, contacting the bow at the leather part of the grip. The third finger is curved back into the frog opening, and the little finger is placed underneath the frog opposite the third finger.

To acquire the correct grip, the bass bow should be taken in the left hand and placed in the right according to the above directions. After the grip has been checked by the teacher, the pupil is ready to use the bow on the strings. In playing position the stick is tilted toward the fingerboard. In the illustrations below notice the attitude of the wrist at the frog and point.

FIGURE 10.6.   Bow at the frog.

FIGURE 10.7.   Bow at the point.

Common Faults in Holding the Bow

French Bow

The thumb is inserted too far through the bow.

The bow is gathered into the palm instead of being held by the fingers.

The hand slants too far forward or backward.

The thumb bends in instead of out.

German Bow

The second, third, and sometimes the fourth fingers are looped through the frog.

The frog is pulled too far into the palm.

The first finger is hooked over the top of the bow instead of lying along the stick.

The Beginning or Open String Stage

Objectives

To hold the instrument and bow correctly.

To draw the bow parallel to the bridge.

To draw the bow on the proper string.

To draw the bow for the specified duration.

To make satisfactory bow changes from up to down and down to up.

To identify the strings by their letter names.

To know the signs for down bow and up bow and follow these directions.

To be able to identify the following parts: bridge, fingerboard, neck, tailpiece, bow—frog, point, hair, screw, upper half, middle, lower half.

To associate a printed note with the corresponding open string.

To know the names of the notes corresponding to the open strings.

To know how to count quarter notes, half notes, whole notes and their corresponding rests in 2/4 and 4/4 time.

To keep one's place while playing a line of music.

Most method books spend several lessons on the open strings; so the pupil must learn their identity on both the instrument and the printed page. To review, they are:

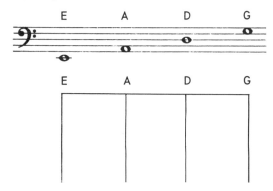

Notice that there is an interval of a 4th between the bass strings.

Turn back to the appropriate sections in the chapters on the violin and cello for suggestions for this stage.

Making the Strings Speak

The size of the strings on the bass presents a rather special problem in inertia. To overcome this inertia the bass player must apply more pressure to the string than is true of the other instruments. The trick is to apply the pressure at the beginning of the stroke, i.e. "bite" into the string with the bow, and then adjust the pressure to produce the desired dynamic level. It is sometimes incorrectly stated that this initial pressure is "released" once the tone is underway. But this is not quite accurate, especially when a f or ff dynamic is desired. The initial pressure may appear to be released for an instant as the bow begins to move, but it is immediately reapplied.

The beginning bass player should be taught to "bite" the string in a moderate dynamic. The "bite" will be achieved by gripping the bow more tightly and pressing down on the string. This should be practiced at the frog first then at the point. Simply make a rote exercise of placing the bow on the D string at the frog and, beginning with a little accent, draw a very short bow. Repeat this until consistency is acquired.

Keeping the Bow Straight

Because the bow functions at considerable distance from the player's eyes, young bass players often are careless about keeping the bow parallel to the bridge. Also, they often fail to exert sufficient effort in the right arm to draw the bow between the bridge and the fingerboard, allowing it, instead, to ride up on the fingerboard, frequently in a see-saw fashion.

The teacher must give special attention to the beginning bass player's bowing if satisfactory results are to be achieved. If the bow functions at an angle, the string will not speak readily and the tone will be unclear. This is an especially acute problem on the bass because of the size of the strings and the difficulty in making them speak.

The exercises to orient the bow to the four string planes, which are described in the chapter on the violin, are adaptable to the bass. The bass bow, as the cello bow, should tilt slightly toward the fingerboard.

Common Faults of the Open String Stage

The bow is drawn over the fingerboard instead of halfway between the bridge and the fingerboard.

The bow is drawn at an angle to instead of parallel to the bridge.

The bow touches two strings at the same time.

The tone is fuzzy and notes are not started with a bite.

Locating the Notes

The difficulty of discerning pitch on the bass has already been mentioned. This problem, and the frequency with which young bass players completely ignore it, results in some appalling standards of intonation among bassists. It may appear to be heretical to say that visual finger placement aids, such as tape, are more practical on the bass than they are on the smaller string instruments. But the length of the bass strings allows a little more latitude in the placement of the finger for a given pitch than is the case with the violin, viola, and cello. Whereas a quarter or eighth of an inch movement of the finger on the violin makes a very apparent difference in pitch, this degree of deviation from "dead center" on the bass may not be intolerable.

In spite of what is said above, it is imperative that the bassist learn to listen to himself as carefully as do the players of the other strings. It must be understood that while measurements and visual aids can and may help, they are not the final answer. The ear is the ultimate authority.

Some methods start the bass player in half position. Others start with first position. Some approxi-mate measurements are given to help in the location of these two positions on the 1/2 and 3/4 size bass.

Finger Placement Measurements

1/2 Size Bass

Distance from nut to 1/2 position	2 inches
Distance from nut to 1st position	3¾ inches

3/4 Size Bass

Distance from nut to 1/2 position	2¾ inches
Distance from nut to 1st position	5 inches

When moving from half position to first position, the whole hand moves, including the thumb. The hand should maintain the same rounded shape. The length of the bass strings, and the consequent distance between notes, limits the span of the hand to a minor third in 1/2 position, including the open string (Example 1).

The third finger is used only to support the fourth finger until the hand reaches sixth position. At this point the third finger is put into active use. In general the first finger should assist the second by remaining on the string.

In first position the notes shown in Example 2 fall within the span of the hand.

The bassist must develop great strength in his left hand. Long tones at full volume on each finger and the finger-strengthening exercises in Example 3 are beneficial.

Example 1

Example 2

Example 3

In doing these exercises the fingers should be raised as high as possible and brought down onto the string with a powerful snap. These exercises should be done on each string.

During this stage the pupil will have to be reminded to keep his left arm out at the correct angle and the wrist curved. There seems to be a strong tendency for most young bass players to allow the arm to drop to the side and the wrist to cave in.

Common Faults During This Stage

The pupil is inconsistent in the placement of the fingers.

The spaces between the fingers are not wide enough; consequently the intervals are too small.

The elbow is allowed to drop to the side of the body putting all parts of the arm in a faulty position. In this position the palm of the hand is usually allowed to lie against the neck and the fingers are used collectively rather than independently. In this position it is impossible to gain any facility with the left hand.

The Intermediate Stage

Objectives (All Appropriate
Previous Objectives Continue)

To play in tune.

To tune the instrument.

To play with a clear tone.

To play with rhythmic precision.

To play with a range of dynamics from pp to ff.

To attain a velocity measured by slurred 16th notes at ♩ = 60 and bowed 16th notes at ♩ = 50.

To play in positions II through V as well as the half positions.

To use the bow skillfully in a variety of bowings including slurs, staccato, and marcato.

Tuning the Bass

As is the case with the other instruments, the teacher will have been doing most of the tuning up until this time. This is particularly true in regard to the bass because of the difficulty in hearing the pitch of the low strings.

The bass strings are tuned to G, D, A, and E on the bass staff. The actual pitch of the strings is one octave below where the notes are written on the staff. There are three ways to tune the bass. The bow is used in each case.

1. One way to tune the bass strings is to use the octave harmonic which is located half way between the nut and the bridge. This produces a pitch one octave higher than the open string.

2. The harmonic located a fourth above the open string may be used also.

This harmonic produces a note two octaves above the pitch of the open string. Each of the strings may be tuned in this manner.

3. Still another method of tuning the bass is to use harmonics which produce unisons on adjoining strings. This is achieved in the following way:

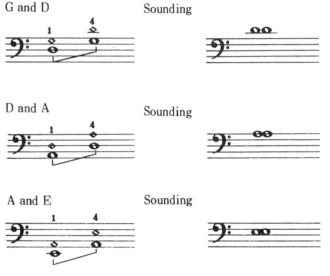

When tuning with harmonics, care must be taken to draw the bow evenly. Changes of speed, pressure, and point of contact may alter the pitch of the harmonic. The playing of harmonics is discussed in Chapter 6 pages 73 and 74.

Tone Production

Good tone production on the bass is achieved as it is on the other string instruments. The bow must be drawn evenly at a point between the bridge and fingerboard, which point will vary according to bow speed and volume. The left hand must depress the string firmly upon the fingerboard in order to completely stop the string. The length and diameter of the bass strings require that considerable strength be exerted by the fingers.

In playing staccato and marcato bowings, scratchy and rough attacks must be guarded against. Good tone quality can be achieved on the bass. It just takes work and care.

The Positions

The bass is tuned in fourths. The span of the hand is only a major second. Consequently the overall range, without shifting, is extremely limited. When working with the bass in a mixed string class, this limitation poses a problem. Unless shifting is introduced early in the course of instruction on the bass, the bass will inevitably be omitted from some of the class exercises. It is for this reason that class methods introduce half position, first position, and third position relatively early. Third position extends the range on the G string to D and provides the flexibility that is needed for the bass to enjoy full participation in the group.

In shifting, the entire hand moves as a unit, the thumb retaining its place opposite the second finger. The following chart shows the notes in positions I through III and the half positions.

Common Faults of the Intermediate Stage

Carelessness about intonation.

Poor left hand and left arm positions.

Bow is allowed to function over the fingerboard producing a muddy, unclear tone.

Beginnings of tones lack precision, or bite.

The Advanced Stage

Objectives (All Appropriate Previous Objectives Continue)

To improve intonation, tone, and musicianship generally, and gain a more mature concept of style and interpretation.

To develop a vibrato.

To increase and expand technique.

To develop skill in the higher positions.

To develop a spiccato.

To play solo and ensemble literature of an advanced nature.

Most of the objectives of this stage are common to all of the strings. Attainment of these objectives

implies the development of a good sense of pitch discrimination, a critical attitude toward tone and other aspects of performance, and a maturation of taste and musicianship in general. Private instruction from a good teacher is essential to the attainment of these objectives.

Vibrato

Bass vibrato, like cello vibrato, is produced by an up and down movement of the entire forearm. To produce a full and pleasant vibrato this movement must be fairly broad and unhurried.

To induce a vibrato, begin by removing the fingers from the strings and the thumb from the neck. With the hand freed, simulate the motion of the vibrato. When the correct action begins to appear, touch the thumb lightly to the neck while continuing the motion. It is possible in this way to develop the vibrato motion in the arm and condition the arm to respond to the vibrato impulse.

Higher Positions

The higher positions on the bass are achieved by moving the hand down the fingerboard toward the bridge. The thumb remains in its position opposite the second finger until reaching V½ position at which time the thumb reaches the curve of the neck. It remains there until advancement down the fingerboard forces it to move.

Solo and ensemble literature for the bass is rather limited. Not very many composers have regarded the bass as a solo instrument, and in only a few cases is it included in small ensembles. Some solos have been transcribed for bass, however; so there is material available for the enterprising bassist.

The bass is extremely important in the orchestra—chamber or symphonic. And to be an asset to these groups the bassist must have good intonation, a good tone, a steely sense of tempo, and an adequate technique. The latter implies good shifting, speed and dexterity with both the left hand and the bow, and the ability to read and play with authority.

CHAPTER 11

The School String Program

History of Instrumental Music Instruction in the Public Schools

As stated in the section dealing with the history of the string instruments, exhaustive historical treatment is not the intent of this book. However, the student should have at least a minimal understanding of the relationship of the development of strings and the string program in the schools to those events in history which he uses as guideposts. The following will provide that perspective.

Music in the Colonies

The early American colonists were too absorbed by the business of growing food and providing clothing and shelter to find time for the pleasures of music and art. Some groups actually opposed music, claiming it was sinful to indulge in the frivolous pastime of singing or playing on an instrument. Only with the arrival of some of the wealthy aristocats did music find a place in society.

Music in America at the Beginning of the 19th Century

At the end of the 18th and beginning of the 19th century, wars and revolutions in Europe caused many people to seek a better way of life in America. It was inevitable that musicians were among those who came to this country. As cities such as New York, Baltimore, Philadelphia, and Boston grew, cultural activities, including concerts, became an accepted part of the social structure.

The middle of the 19th century brought another influx of Europeans to America. A significant group was the Germania Society, a group of professional musicians. This group constituted a professional orchestra which concertized in America for a period of six years. In 1854 it disbanded, its members settling in various cities about the country.

Thomas, Damrosch, Sousa

A man who was extremely influential in shaping the musical history of this country was Theodore Thomas (1835-1905). Thomas organized an orchestra with which he toured the principal cities. He brought good orchestra literature to the people and made a giant step in establishing a place for this kind of music in America. Thomas set the stage for the establishment of the Boston Symphony and the New York Symphony, the latter under the direction of Leopold and Walter Damrosch.

During this same period the concert band movement was making progress under the leadership of such conductors as Patrick Gilmore (1829-1892) and John Philip Sousa (1854-1932).

Music in the Public Schools

At the close of the 19th century, public school music consisted almost entirely of classroom singing. A prime objective was to teach children to read musical notation. But just before the end of the century a few high school orchestras were organized informally. Private instrumental study was becoming more commonplace, and a good many competent instrumentalists were being turned out by colleges and conservatories. These people often set up private studios, and, in turn, produced more instrumentalists. Players gravitated toward each other in schools and inevitably ensembles were formed. Formal instrumental instruction in the schools was slow to develop. But in the early 1900's a few dedicated and persevering musicians began to organize orchestras and instrumental programs in various schools.

It was in the period from 1900 to 1920 that instrumental music began to get a solid foothold in the public schools. Bands and orchestras were a part of the activity programs in many elementary schools and high schools. At first rehearsals were scheduled after regular school hours, but gradually these groups became an accepted part of the curriculum and their needs a part of the school budget.

The demand for formal preparation of teachers brought about appropriate courses in teacher training institutions. Class instruction in the schools became an accepted thing, and the public school instrumental music program was launched.

Subsequent development of school music programs has seen the development of highly structured regional and national contests, and the organization of state-wide and nation-wide bands, orchestras, and choral groups, many of these in conjunction with conferences of the Music Educators National Conference. Standards of instrumentation have been achieved, standards of excellence have risen to amazing heights, and the music program has become an accepted part of the curriculum.

In spite of widespread acceptance of music into the curriculum, when financial troubles occur, music is frequently one of the first subjects to be cut. Because of the important role music can play in fostering emotional health and personal well-being, in other words its therapeutic values, music may very well occupy an increasingly important position in our society in the future. True, it may not be music as we know it today. The sound source may be an oscillator instead of an orchestra; the composer may employ circuits instead of copy paper; and the listener may push a button instead of purchasing a ticket in order to select the kind of music he wants at a given moment.

In the meantime, school programs demand well prepared teachers who are expert in the orchestra, band, or choral fields. These teachers must have a thorough knowledge of literature, techniques of performance, and pedagogy, the ability to demonstrate, analyze, and inspire. They must be academician, musicologist, counselor, leader, press agent, concert manager, repairman, liason between school and public, idealist, and pragmatist.

The teacher who becomes absorbed in music will find teaching a most rewarding and gratifying experience; for nothing can quite equal the thrill of hearing a group you have worked with for tedious hours play "over their heads," inspired by the strides they have made, and individually and collectively determined to do better than their best. Experiences like these keep music teachers going, each year trying to improve upon what was done the year before, searching for better ways of doing things, and never being quite satisfied with what has been

achieved. The truly dedicated music teacher willingly and joyfully gives of his time and energy far beyond the call of duty. The limits of the school day are inadequate for his purposes. He finds himself devoting time to students before and after school and in the evening, all of which increases the pleasure he derives from this role. Music teaching is not a job for a time-clock puncher. The teacher who thinks in terms of his job being finished when the last bell of the day has rung does a disservice to himself and to music education.

How the Instrumental Music Teacher Functions

In most school systems in the United States, instrumental music teachers who function in the elementary segment will be assigned to several schools. The number of schools to which they are assigned will depend upon the size of the schools involved, the number of students enrolled in the instrumental program in each school, the financial status of the school system, and the attitude which the administration and the community as a whole has toward the music program. School enrollment and the financial status of the school system can hardly be affected by the teacher (although the amount of money alloted to music can be), but the other factors can be influenced by the teacher.

Teacher enthusiasm and competence are far more important than buildings, equipment, and materials. There are many examples of thriving programs in small schools and in small communities which are the direct result of an enthusiastic, capable, and dedicated teacher. Such programs can be compared, to prove the point, with small, poorly run programs in schools whose size would justify a much larger program.

Teachers who move from one school to another are often referred to as Traveling Music Teachers. In systems which have junior high schools or intermediate schools, the Traveling Music Teacher is often assigned to the junior high school or intermediate school for a fixed number of periods each day and to elementary schools on a scheduled basis; i.e., two partial days at one elementary school, one partial day at another, etc. to fill out the weekly schedule. A sample of a schedule for a Traveling Instrumental Music Teacher is shown on page 137.

In most systems senior high school music teachers are not assigned on a traveling basis; although exceptions to this practice do exist. The high school performance and activity schedule is generally full enough to keep the music teacher, or teachers, busy

Sample Schedule
Traveling Instrumental Music Teacher

		Monday	Tuesday	Wednesday	Thursday	Friday
A. M.	Jr. High	String Class	Same	Same	Same	Same
		Inter. Orch.				
		Adv. Orch.				
P. M.		Elem. Sch.	Elem. Sch.	Elem. Sch.	Elem. Sch.	Elem. Sch.
		No. 1	No. 2	No. 3	No. 1	No. 2

full time. A high school instrumental position is a demanding one, and dividing a teacher's time between two schools does not produce maximum efficiency in either.

Since many string teachers will be operating on a schedule like that described above, it is appropriate to point out some details of this kind of position that differ from the average teaching position, a knowledge of which may help the new teacher through his first year of teaching.

First of all the traveling teacher must realize that he is working for and is responsible to more than one person; namely, the principal of each school to which he is assigned. This is not always easy; for each principal has the prerogative of determining how certain facets of the program will be handled in his school. The wise traveling teacher maintains an attitude of adjustability and adaptability and retains the philosophy that the ultimate objective is to establish the best possible program of instruction for children. The teacher's desire for uniformity and procedural consistency should be subjugated to the primary goal.

Teaching in more than one school poses problems in establishing rapport with teachers in the various buildings. The traveling teacher's schedule is sometimes so arranged that he is in and out of a school at times when teachers in the building are busy in their own classes. In a situation like this, it is possible for the traveling teacher to remain unknown for months unless he makes a deliberate effort to make his presence known. A speaking acquaintance with the fourth, fifth, and sixth grade teachers is extremely important, and the traveling teacher must go out of his way to know them and become known to them.

The traveling teacher will do well to have a frank discussion with the principal at the beginning of the year about such matters as the teacher's reporting time to the school, leaving time, length of class lessons, method and time of reporting grades, handling of equipment, and programs which he should plan for. The teacher should realize that the purpose of this discussion with the principal is to arrive at a mutual understanding based upon the possible, and that the teacher's responsibilities to other schools must be taken into account when making plans for the year. The importance of a clear understanding on the points listed above cannot be stressed strongly enough; nor can the need for the teacher to carry out his side of the agreement be over-stated. A good and fair administrator is much more prone to support and encourage a program when he knows it is in the hands of a person he can depend upon than he is if he has to make adjustments because of a teacher's poor organization or lack of planning and follow-through.

Recruitment for the String Program

Generally speaking, in most parts of the country, and in most communities, bands have less difficulty recruiting and sustaining membership than do orchestras. Bands have shiny brass instruments, uniforms, parades, and other appealing activities to offer. And membership in a going, successful, accepted organization comes sooner for the brass, reed, and percussion player than it does for the string player. But all of this has been said many times and in far more detail than is necessary here. However, the prospective teacher should be aware, at least, that if he plans to work with strings and orchestras, he is going to have to work harder at recruitment than his fellow band director.

When and Who

The recruitment program can be carried out in the last few weeks of the spring semester if this leads naturally into a summer program; otherwise it should begin in the first few weeks of the fall semester. The advantage of the spring timing is that the classroom teacher is thoroughly acquainted with and able to advise regarding pupil characteristics. The advantage to the fall timing is that everything is starting fresh after the summer vacation and interest in beginning a new activity comes more spontaneously.

Recruitment for the elementary string program should begin by the fourth grade, or the equivalent of the fourth grade in a non-graded school. If age is used as a criteria, nine is a reasonable age for most students to begin. By this time children have adjusted to the school routine, are fairly well established in their study habits, are physically mature enough to meet the demands of a string instrument, and are intellectually and emotionally ready to assume the responsibility which the study of a string instrument imposes.

It must be recognized that all of the assumptions made in the preceding paragraph are generalizations, and that there can and will be exceptions to every one of them. There are the immature nine-year-olds who are not as ready as some seven-year-olds to take on the additional responsibility of the study of a string instrument. And there are those who are physically and intellectually mature enough, but who have emotional problems which an additional task would not benefit. The converse to the latter is just as true, and many students with emotional problems have been helped by the achievement and satisfaction they have been able to realize from instrumental study.

All of this points up the need for the teacher to look carefully at each child who applies for admission to the string program. The teacher must assess the child's physical, mental, and emotional readiness for the program; and these factors should be discussed with the classroom teacher, principal, and parent.

What

DEMONSTRATION OF INSTRUMENTS

There are a number of things which can be done to stimulate the interest of children in the string program. Probably the best and most effective device is to play for them yourself—provided you are a proficient performer—or arrange performances by competent individual students, groups of students, or string players from the community. Caution should be practiced in this approach since a poor demonstration on an instrument, or a good demonstration by a person whose personality or manner might cause an unfavorable reaction among the children,

can do more harm than good. By having men or boys in your demonstration group, the psychological or status barrier that often exists between boys and string instruments can be dissolved. In any case, the demonstration should be short and of interest to the child.

USE OF FILMS, FILM-STRIPS, AND RECORDS

Second to the personal demonstration in effectiveness is the demonstration through the media of film or film-strip and recording, several of which are available from producers of audio-visual materials. In the use of this technique, additional advantage can be achieved by having string instruments in the room to show to the children. Permitting the children to examine and touch the instruments increases their curiosity and interest.

PARENT MEETINGS

In some communities it is possible to arrange an evening meeting of parents and their children at which one of the local music dealers has a display of instruments. If the school does not own instruments, this may be a useful approach. A meeting such as this can be used to discuss the merits of the string program, point out the long-range advantages of learning to play a string instrument, make clear what will be expected of a child who enters the program, and explain the need for parental interest and support of a child who undertakes the study of an instrument.

The music dealer can discuss and display the various grades and qualities of instruments he has for sale and rent. He can explain financial arrangements and answer questions regarding these arrangements. The teacher should avoid becoming involved in the financial phase of this procedure unless it is obvious that his professional judgment is needed to prevent a mistake or a poor decision.

MUSIC APTITUDE TESTS

Another device which can aid in recruiting students is the music aptitude test. This may sound like an odd claim when one considers that the basic purpose of the aptitude test is to assess native musical talent. However, the salutary effect of a good test score is well known, and a number of satisfactory tests are available which are easy to administer and can be completed in twenty to thirty minutes or more. A list of some of these tests and their sources follows:

Name of Test	Source
The Biondo Musical Aptitude Test	Educational Department Scherl and Roth Inc. 1729 Superior Ave. Cleveland, Ohio
Drake Musical Aptitude Tests	Science Research Associates 57 West Grand Ave. Chicago, 10, Ill.
Elementary Musical Achievement Tests	Follett Publishing Company 1010 West Washington Blvd. Chicago, Ill. 60607
Leblanc Musical Talent Quiz	Leblanc Co. Kenosha, Wisconsin
McCreery Rhythm and Pitch Test	Lyons Band Instrument Co. 223 West Lake St. Chicago, 6, Ill.
Music Aptitude Test	Band Instrument Division C. G. Conn Ltd. Elkhart, Ind.
Musical Aptitude Test— Whistler-Thorpe	California Test Bureau 5916 Hollywood Blvd. Hollywood, 28, Cal.
Seashore Measures of Musical Talents	Educational Department Radio Corporation of America Camden, N. J.

These tests can be administered to an entire class, or to several classes, at one time. Children who do well on the test can be encouraged to begin an instrument, and their test score can be a persuasive argument with reluctant or neutral parents. The test can serve the additional purpose of indicating basic strengths and weaknesses in the child's musical make-up, thus making it possible for the teacher to give special attention to these areas in the student's lessons.

Selecting the Instrument to Fit the Child

The availability of 1/2, 3/4, and 4/4 size violins and cellos, small size violas, and 1/2 size basses makes feasible an earlier start for many children than would be possible if these small size instruments did not exist. These fractional-size, or junior-size, instruments are exactly like their larger counterparts in every way; although the quality as well as the quantity of the tone they produce may, in some cases, leave something to be desired. To minimize this drawback, every effort should be made to acquire well-made small size instruments which meet minimum specifications. Acquisition should be from a firm whose reputation for full-size instruments is reliable. Equip these small instruments properly with a well cut bridge and strings of the

correct length. It is impossible to produce from them the amount of sound a full-size instrument will produce. But the small instruments are stepping stones. They are made to accomodate small hands and short arms, and they make it possible for the young child to begin instruction at a time when he is physically and mentally most adaptable and psychologically most eager to begin. The following chart gives the sizes of the various instruments most often needed to fit children at the grade levels indicated. These sizes are based upon children of average height. There will, of course, be exceptions in the case of unusually small and unusually large children.

TABLE 11.1
Recommended String Instrument Sizes
For Various Grade Levels

	Grade 4	Grade 5	Grade 6	Grades 7-9
Violin	1/2, 3/4	1/2, 3/4, 4/4	3/4, 4/4	3/4, 4/4
Viola*	13 1/4″, 14″	13 1/4″, 14″	1/4″, 15″	14″, 15″ +
Cello	1/2, 3/4	1/2, 3/4	3/4, 4/4	3/4, 4/4
Bass	1/2	1/2	1/2	1/2, 3/4

*The 13 1/4 inch viola is referred to as the Junior size. The 14 inch viola is referred to as the Intermediate size. Some schools do not own these small violas. In such cases it is possible to string up a 3/4 violin, viola-style (C-G-D-A) as a substitute.

The size of a child's hands, arms, and his over-all proportions are important factors to consider in choosing among the string instruments. The large, big-boned boy is a better prospect for the bass than for the violin. The small, delicately proportioned child should be steered to the violin. Children of medium build can generally adapt to any of the instruments.

Need to Promote Cello, Bass and Viola

One important aspect of the demonstration not mentioned before should be pointed out here. That is the need to promote each of the strings—violin, viola, cello, and bass—equally. Too often the only instrument which gets a real show is the violin. As a result, violin classes evolve rather than string classes, and the full potential of the strings cannot be realized. The teacher who has responsibility for developing and maintaining an orchestra at a higher segment level will keep in mind the need to foster interest in *all* members of the string family.

There is no magic formula which produces a beginning string class of just the right number of violins, violas, cellos, and basses. In fact, getting any students to show an interest in the cello or bass may be one of those "hardest of all jobs" for the teacher. It may very well call for salesmanship and horse trading. An assisting and controlling factor may be the number and kind of instruments which are owned by the school. Some districts purchase only basses and cellos on the assumption that parents will provide violins. Another practice is for the school to supply the small size violins and cellos as well as basses, on the assumption that parents will provide the full-size instrument when the proper time comes.

The initial opportunity to stimulate interest in the larger string instruments is in the demonstration. It is important, therefore, that the bass and cello be demonstrated as effectively as the violin and viola. The need to develop an interest in the lower strings is stressed here because a balanced instrumentation in the secondary program is completely dependent upon the achievement of a representative instrumentation in the beginning program. Remedial action can be taken, of course, such as bringing in a pianist to play bass (because she can read music), or persuading a souzaphone player to double on string bass. But these measures are usually makeshift at best, and the need for resorting to them can be avoided by careful planning and the diligent use of persuasive techniques in the lower segment program.

A clinching argument in favor of the bass—to the practical minded parent whose thinking takes in this dimension—is that the bass is the first of the string instruments to become a money-earner. With a good ear, the ability to keep a steady beat, and a reasonable amount of practice, the bass player can handle jobs in combos and dance bands by the time he is in senior high school.

The viola probably falls into the "least wanted" category more often than not. In communities which do not benefit from contact with a metropolitan area's cultural resources, and even in some which do, there may be widespread ignorance about this member of the string family. People cannot be expected to want something which they know nothing about; and it follows that the viola falls into sad neglect. Another reason contributing to this neglect of the viola is the relatively unspectacular role it plays in the orchestra. It is like the second violins: not apparent until missing. This lack of built-in salability creates the need for the teacher to point out the advantages and attractive qualities of this instrument—that it has a deep, mellow tone quality;

that it does not have the shrillness sometimes associated with the violin; that its music is generally somewhat less demanding than that of the violin; and that since fewer people take up the viola, there is less competition and more opportunity to excel on it than on its more popular cousin, the violin.

Class Organization

String instruments can be grouped in two ways for class instruction: like instruments (homogeneous), or unlike instruments (heterogenous). Arguments can be made in favor of each of these kinds of grouping, for each has its merits. However it is not always a question of which is best as much as what is possible. An insufficient number of a given instrument to meet an administratively-set class minimum may require the addition of other instruments even though the instructor feels that a homogeneous grouping would be preferable. These two methods of grouping are discussed below.

Homogeneous Grouping

At the beginning stages of instruction homogeneous grouping is desirable for the following reasons:

With just one kind of instrument to deal with, the teacher needs to be conscious of only one set of problems.

Small children will find less to distract them if all the instruments in the class are the same kind.

Children will learn more readily by example if they have only one example to follow.

With only one kind of instrument in the class, everything the instructor does and says, and everything that takes place in the class is pertinent to each child.

Mixed instrument grouping will inevitably result in some lost time for some students while the teacher is giving attention elsewhere. Furthermore, there are few method books which are written in such a way that all instruments receive equally effective treatment at all times.

Heterogeneous Grouping

As students achieve sufficient competence and maturity, heterogeneous grouping becomes not only feasible but desirable. The reasons are:

Heterogeneous grouping relieves the monotony of a single tonal quality and limited range of pitch, which are qualities of like grouping.

There is much more music available for a mixed group than there is for a like group.

In a mixed group bonafide four-part harmony is possible. The addition of harmony to the string sound brings about a new level of interest for the student.

In a heterogeneous group students will begin to listen to other instruments analytically. They begin to hear themselves in proper perspective in the tonal spectrum, and in the relationship they will ultimately assume in the string orchestra.

The greater sonority of the full string section and the fullness of harmony which it is capable of producing will stimulate the development of a fuller tone. At the same time the student will begin to be aware of the need for balance among the instruments. He will begin to know when to subdue and when to predominate, and what he must do to achieve these two results.

Optimum Class Size

An ideal beginning string class should not exceed six to eight students. More than this number makes it difficult for the teacher to give the individual attention which is so necessary during the beginning stages. With more than eight in the class the tuning process absorbs a disproportionate amount of instructional time, and the general progress of the class will be slowed down because of the teacher's inability to get around to each student and to handle all of the details and problems which need to be taken care of.

Physical Arrangements

The Rehearsal Room

Much has been written about the design and arrangement of orchestra and band rehearsal rooms. The reader is referred to the *MENC* publication, *Music Rooms and Equipment,* a book containing a good deal of practical information on the subject. Junior high schools and senior high schools usually are built with special rooms for instrumental and choral music classes. This is rarely done in elementary school construction; since the instrumental teacher is seldom scheduled in an elementary school more than three days a week, and in most cases less frequently than that. As a result, instrumental music classes are superimposed upon the regular daily classroom schedule, and students who take instrumental music are taken from their regular classroom to report to the multipurpose room stage or to a classroom which is available and is designated for instrumental instruction.

Planned rehearsal rooms should receive attention in the following areas:

Lighting

There should be a minimum of 100 foot-candles distributed evenly over the seating area including the teacher's station.

Acoustics

A reverberation time of 1 second per 24,000 cubic feet is recommended for orchestra.

Ventilation

The contemporary trend is the windowless rehearsal room. The argument is that a closed room minimizes both in- and out-transfer of sounds. The problem lies in the failure of architects to understand that a rehearsal room is not like an office building or the administrative wing of the school, or an ordinary classroom, all of which contain normal amounts of activity. The rehearsal room houses an activity in which the students develop an abnormally high quantity of BTU's. Whether bowing or blowing they put out a great deal of energy. To keep the room fresh requires a larger than normal air exchange system.

Arrangement of Stands and Chairs

The way stands and chairs are arranged in the room, or on the stage, will depend upon the size and shape of the room, the number of students in the class, and what instruments they play. Regardless of these factors, however, there are three conditions which should be achieved in the physical setup.

1. Each student must have sufficient room to bow without the threat of hitting another student's music stand, instrument, or bow.
2. The teacher must have a clear and unobstructed view of each student in the class.
3. The teacher must have free access to each student in the class without having to wind through music stands, bows, cellos, or chairs.

Practically, this means that each student must have his own music and his own stand, opposed to having two students reading from a single piece of music. Physical arrangements like those discussed above and shown below are necessary for beginning classes so that the teacher may quickly get to any pupil in the class to adjust the position of his instrument, bow, or fingers, or to point out something in the music. The need for this kind of help from the teacher decreases as the students become more proficient. Two possible seating arrangements are

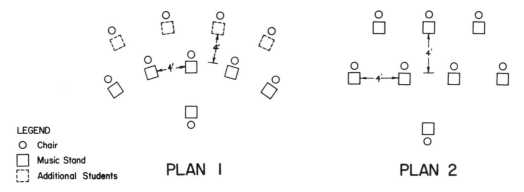

LEGEND
O Chair
☐ Music Stand
⬚ Additional Students

PLAN 1   PLAN 2

FIGURE 11.1. Recommended seating arrangements for string classes.

shown above. Places for the recommended number of students are shown with solid lines. Places for additional students are shown with dotted lines.

A Place for Music Cases and Books

If the room has been specifically designed as an instrumental rehearsal room, provision should have been made for storage of instruments and music, with shelves upon which instrument cases and books may be placed while rehearsals are going on. Without these built-in facilities, movable storage cabinets can be substituted, and chairs or tables may serve as a place to put cases and books. Without the benefit of a planned place for cases and books, the teacher will find that these items are put in the only place remaining for them—the floor, and more often than not on the floor next to the chair which the student occupies. This results in a disorganized classroom which is messy to contemplate and dangerous to navigate.

If permanent instrument storage cabinets are supplied, the floor of each compartment should be covered with a rubber matting or a short-nap carpeting. Without this seeming luxury, case hinges will be damaged. If the cabinets are constructed of metal, the metal to metal abrasion will damage both the case and the cabinet. If the cabinets are constructed of wood, the metal hinges on the cases will soon make splinters of the front lip of the compartment floor at the same time that the instrument case and its hinges are damaged.

Straight Chairs for Cellists

A string rehearsal room must be equipped with straight chairs with flat seats for the cello players. Cellists must sit on the front edge of their chair to play; they cannot comfortably maintain good playing posture on a chair which has a sloping seat.

It was pointed out earlier that in the elementary segment, chairs of varying heights should be available so that the small, short-legged children can touch their feet on the floor.

Cello and Bass End Pin Holders

An end pin holder of some kind is a necessity for each cellist and bassist. Without the benefit of a holding device, cellists and bassists will have a constant problem keeping their instrument in the correct position, and they may become discouraged because of the frustrations that they feel and the insecurity that the situation causes them.

Beginning Steps

The nine-year-old who has passed the music aptitude test, who has shown a desire to start lessons on a string instrument, whose parents have indicated willingness for him to enter the program, enters the room for his first lesson with interest, eagerness, and aspiration. Frankly, his chief desire is to get his hands on an instrument and begin drawing the bow across the strings.

At this point the teacher's forebearance and sense of perspective are put to a critical test. The pupil's eagerness to make sounds on the instrument must not be summarily dampened. But still a sense of respect for the instrument, for the teacher, and for fellow-students, and a realization of the standards of behavior expected of him in the class must be conveyed quickly and clearly.

Most children respond positively to reasonable sets of controls, particularly when the reasons for the controls are apparent to them. Stepping into a new situation such as the instrumental rehearsal room, they will quickly respond to the standards which are set for them. The teacher should explain that string instruments and bows are fragile, that there are certain ways in which they are to be treated and handled, and that anyone who is unable to conform to the rules of the class will have proved that he is not yet ready to assume the responsibility which membership in the string class imposes.

At this point no detail is too trivial or insignificant to cover. Following is a list of some of the procedures and precautions that should be conveyed to the pupil at the first lesson.

How to take the instrument and bow from the case.
How to tighten the bow, and how much.
How to rosin the bow.
How to affix the shoulder pad.
The importance of always returning the instrument and bow to the case and securing the case after each practice session.
The importance of keeping the instrument out of the reach of smaller brothers and sisters.
It goes without saying that as much time as possible should be devoted to holding the instrument and bow.

Elementary children respond more favorably to specific assignments tailored to their attention span than they do to general suggestions. At the outset, lessons assigned should be short. Four to six lines of music is ample. They should be encouraged to practice for about ten minutes twice a day, giving careful attention to the way in which they hold the instrument and the bow.

The amount and kind of material assigned will depend upon the approach used in the class. If a rote approach is used, perhaps the equivalent of only one line of music will be assigned. The background of the children and the kind of music program they have had in the classroom must also be considered.

Most recent string class methods have been prepared with an aim to presenting material which will immediately interest the young pupil. Piano accompaniments are often supplied for open string exercises, and as soon as possible simple tunes are introduced.

Motivation is extremely important. The teacher must give some attention and praise to each student and keep the class, as a whole, progressing at an acceptable rate. The string group needs opportunities to perform for peers, parents, and teachers. Seasonal programs provide an ideal opportunity for the group to appear.

At this point something should be said about the two "key" approaches used in string method books. They are the "C" approach and the "D" approach.

The "C" approach requires the young violinist to adjust his hand to three different settings. On the G string the half-step falls between the 2nd and 3rd fingers.

On the D and A strings the half-step falls between the 1st and 2nd fingers.

And on the E string the first finger must be extended backward to reach the F natural.

Comparable adjustments must be made on the other instruments.

The constant resetting of the finger position is considered by many to be too taxing for the beginning string student considering that he is having to think about how he is holding the instrument and the bow, how he is drawing the bow, and what notes he is supposed to be playing. With a bright student and plenty of individual attention, the added problems inherent in this approach can be overcome.

As school instruction in the strings became more prevalent, teachers searched for ways to reduce methods to the simplest terms, to produce results faster, and to bring the realization of accomplishment to the student at an earlier point in his study. One result of this search was the so-called "D major approach." Literally this method starts the student in the key of D major when he begins using fingers.

First lessons are on the A string, then the D, then the G, where the key is changed to G. When the time comes to move to the E string, the key of A is introduced. This procedure makes the finger setting the same on all four strings, the half step coming between the 2nd and 3rd finger in each case. This is the only finger pattern used for an extended period of time.

This approach has its proponents and opponents. The advantages have been pointed out. The disadvantage is that the student does not learn to adjust his fingers to different settings early enough.

"He does not know the fingers can go any other way" is a complaint often expressed. This method also delays putting the strings together with the winds.

From this point forward in the teaching process the teacher must adapt the suggestions contained in this book on teaching the string instruments to the method book he has chosen to use. He must then apply the best of what he knows about group teaching, control, and motivation. It is important that each student be presented increasingly challenging but achievable goals, and that he realize success and satisfaction as a result of his effort.

CHAPTER 12

Care and Maintenance
of the String Instruments

It has been said that the great artist will play beautifully in spite of any odds. It could also be said that the beginning student would sound no better on a fine Stradivarius than on his $100.00 production-line instrument. Both of these statements may be true; but fine performers are generally very meticulous about the care and condition of their instrument, and the least defect is corrected by a master repairman at the earliest possible moment. This would seem to indicate the high regard the artist-performer has for the condition of his instrument. It follows, then, that if mechanical condition is important to the artist, it must be equally important to the beginner.

Initial responsibility for the condition of the beginner's instrument is the teacher's. (Minimum standards and details of shop adjustment are detailed in the chapter on Selecting Instruments, Bows, and Cases.) Then, in addition to teaching the student to play the instrument, he must be taught to care for it.

Care of the string instruments can be separated into two categories. The first is the kind of thing that the player is responsible for. The second is the kind of repair that should be left to the expert craftsman.

The Player's Responsibilities

1. Do not expose a string instrument to extremes of temperature.
2. Provide a humidifying device in a dry climate. Keep the instrument as dry as possible in a damp climate.
3. Protect the instrument against hard knocks or jolts. Check for openings or cracks.
4. Wipe rosin dust from the strings, instrument, and bow before returning the instrument to its case. Polish the instrument and bow occasionally with a recommended polish such as Hill, Roth, or Lewis.
5. Check the tilt of the bridge periodically. The tuning process tends to pull the top of the bridge forward. It should be vertical or lean backward minutely.
   Also check the position of the bridge feet. They should be opposite the inside notches of the "f" holes, and square across the strings. Release the string tension slightly before moving the bridge.
6. Check strings to see if they are false, frayed, or unravelling.
7. See that the tuning pegs work smoothly. Apply peg dope if needed.
8. Check tailpiece gut. If it is badly frayed it should be replaced.
9. Periodically tighten the nut that secures the tuner(s).
10. Always loosen the bow before returning it to the case. If bow hair is smooth or sparse because of breakage, have bow rehaired. If stick is warped, have it straightened.

Repairs to Be Left to the Expert

1. Adjusting the sound post. (See Figure 12.1.)
   The sound post must be of good wood, correct diameter and length, cut to conform to top and back, properly positioned.
2. Cutting and fitting the bridge.
   The bridge must be of good wood (maple). The feet must be of the proper thickness and conform to the top. The curvature of the top must place the strings at the proper height above the fingerboard. The notches must not be too deep.

FIGURE 12.1. Workman setting sound post. (Courtesy Roth Violins, Cleveland, Ohio.)

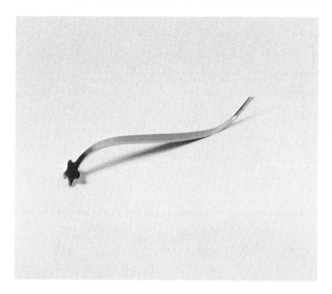

FIGURE 12.2. Sound post setting tool. (Courtesy Roth Violins, Cleveland, Ohio.)

3. Dressing the fingerboard.
The fingerboard becomes pitted and grooved from the pressure of the fingers and the vibration of the strings. It then becomes necessary to plane the fingerboard until it is smooth. A properly dressed fingerboard has a concave dip to provide clearance for the strings to vibrate.

4. Repairing cracks and openings.
Simple openings between the back or top and the ribs are repaired by gluing and clamping. Cracks in the top or back may require that the instrument be opened.

4. Cleaning.
Cleaning of heavy rosin and dirt accumulations is a job for an expert. The varnish on a string instrument is delicate and may be damaged permanently by mistreatment.

6. Reaming peg holes and fitting new pegs. (See Figure 12.3.)
The need for this is rare. If an instrument is originally fitted with good pegs which fit well, it will take years of use to wear them to the point that they need to be replaced. Should it become necessary, it is a job for an expert.

FIGURE 12.3. Workman reaming peg holes. (Courtesy Roth Violins, Cleveland, Ohio.)

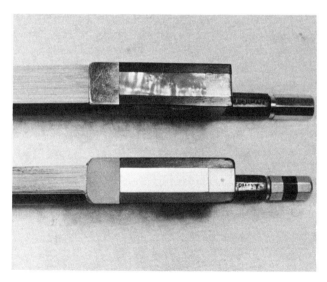

FIGURE 12.4. Top: Rehaired bow. Below: Bow that needs to be rehaired.

7. Replacing a bass bar.
   This is another major job which is rarely necessary. It is sometimes resorted to in an effort to improve the tone or response of an instrument.
8. Rehairing the bow. (See Figure 12.4.)
   The small barbs on the hair wear smooth with playing until the hair no longer grips the string. How soon this happens depends upon the quality of the hair to begin with and the amount of use the bow receives. Some players find it necessary to have their bow rehaired every month, others every two months, or six, or twelve. An annual rehairing is usually adequate for school bows.
   The practice of washing the bow hair has strong proponents and opponents. Those who defend the practice contend that washing gets rid of the accumulated oil and grease and improves the condition of the hair. Opponents of the practice claim that washing the bow hair softens or removes the barbs on the hair, thus reducing its ability to "grab" the string. Those who argue this line also point out the possible danger of swelling and cracking the frog by allowing water to work into it. This danger alone should be enough to divert one from a practice which has doubtful results. Furthermore, by the time a bow is dirty enough to be considered in need of washing, it should be rehaired.

Buzzes and Rattles

Buzzes and rattles originating with the instrument can be a source of great annoyance to the player. Sometimes they are extremely hard to locate and correct. Some of the commonest causes of buzzes or rattles are listed below.

A button or piece of jewelry on the wearing apparel which touches the instrument.
A loose tuner.
Loose chin rest.
Tailpiece contacting the chin rest.
Loose purfling.
Open seam.
Crack.
String too close to fingerboard.

Obviously some of these causes are remedied very easily by the player. Others require the assistance of a repairman. The first four in the above list can be prevented by simple precautionary measures which have been mentioned already. If a crack or open seam is suspected, it can usually be located by tapping with the knuckle around the edges of the top and the back. If the seams are tight, the tapping produces a solid and resonant knock. If a seam is open, the slight flap of wood against wood can be heard.

Whether a crack in the top is tight or open is determined by pressing lightly on either side of the crack. If the wood on either side of the crack can be depressed, the crack is open. All cases of open seams or cracks, nut height, bridge, or fingerboard adjustments should be handled by a qualified repairman.

Bow Problems

Most bow problems and damage should be referred to a repairman. Some of the problems that can occur are discussed below.

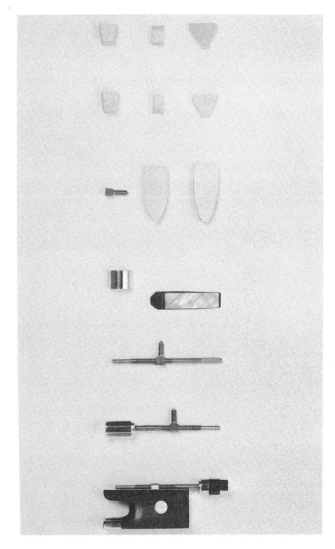

FIGURE 12.5. Wedges and parts of the frog. (Courtesy Roth Violins, Cleveland, Ohio.)

Problem: Hair is so short the bow cannot be loosened or so long the bow cannot be tightened.
Cause: Hair cut too short or too long when placed in the bow.
Solution: Return to dealer or take to repairman for rehairing with correct length hair.

Problem: Entire hank of hair pulls out at tip.
Cause: Loose plug.
Solution: Return bow to repairman.

Problem: A number of individual hairs pull out of tip.
Cause: Poor knot or insufficient bonding of ends of hair.
Solution: Return bow to repairman.

Problem: Bow becomes warped.
Cause: Failure to loosen bow; uneven distribution of hair.
Solution: Repairman will straighten bow over flame. If hair is uneven, bow must be rehaired.

Problem: Tip breaks when bow is first tightened or after some use.
Cause: Faulty grain in wood or tip damaged by blow.
Solution: May or may not be repaired depending upon nature of break.

Problem: Screw turns but hair does not tighten.
Cause: Threads on screw or eyelet are stripped.
Solution: Replace eyelet or screw. Care must be taken to match eyelet and screw since sizes are not standardized.

The preceding lists of problems that can occur to string instruments and bows are purposely detailed in order to make the future teacher aware of the many kinds of things that can happen to this equipment. These lists are not intended to imply that these many kinds of problems will face the teacher frequently and consistently. Most of them need never occur. And chances are that if an instrument is in good condition to start with, and is given normal attention and care, its most serious needs will be new strings periodically. The bow, if kept in good working order, should never require anything more than rehairing.

The string instruments must be handled with care. They cannot be knocked or banged around without being damaged. With consideration for their frailty and the use of common sense, they will remain trouble free for years. A String Instrument Inspection Record will be found in the Appendix. Use of such a form on a regular basis can be an invaluable aid to keeping instruments in good condition.

APPENDIXES

Glossary of Symbols and Terms Used in String Music

Bowing Terms and Symbols

Symbol or Term	Meaning	Explanation or Execution
⊓	Down bow	The bow moves in the direction of frog to point.
V	Up bow	The bow moves in the direction of point to frog.
Fr.	Frog	Frog or heel of the bow.
Pt.	Point	Point or tip of the bow.
♩♩♩♩	Détaché	Played with separate bows; not slurred.
♩♩♩	Slurred	Two or more notes played while the bow moves in one direction.
♩ ♩	Staccato	Notes are played with abrupt beginning and ending. Length of note is shortened.
♩♩♩♩	Slurred Staccato	Two or more notes played in one bow with stops between the notes.
♩ ♩	Martelé	Heavily accented notes, played with staccato qualities.
Spicc. ♩♩♩♩	Spiccato	Played by bouncing the bow off the string.
♫ ♫	Ricochet	The bow strikes the string and rebounds to play successive notes.
col legno	With the Wood	The string is hit with the wood of the bow.
arco	With the bow	Used after a pizzicato passage to indicate that the notes are to be played with the bow.
(musical notation)	spring bow arpeggio	The bow is bounced across the strings striking each string in sequence.
(musical notation)	tremolo	Very rapid up and down bow, usually toward the point.
pont.	ponticello	The bow contacts the string near the bridge producing a hard, shrill tone quality.
sul tasto	on the fingerboard	The bow contacts the string near or over the fingerboard producing a soft tone quality.

149

Other Symbols and Terms

Symbol or Term	Meaning	Explanation or Execution
pizz.	pizzicato	The string is plucked with one of the fingers of the right hand.
(symbol)	left hand pizzicato	The string is plucked with the fingers of the left hand.
(symbol)	natural harmonic	A finger touches the string lightly producing one of the natural overtones.
(symbol)	artificial harmonic	The first finger stops the string and the 4th finger touches the string a 4th above producing a harmonic two 8vas above the fundamental produced by the first finger.
Div.	Divisi	Notes are to be divided among the players.
a^2, non div.	non divisi	Both or all notes are to be played by each player.
sul corda		To remain on a particular string.
restez		To remain in a particular position.
con sord.	con sordino	To be played with the mute.
senza sord.	senza sordino	Remove the mute.
molto vibrato		With much vibrato.
senza vibrato		Without vibrato.

String Instrument Inspection Record

Prepared by Dr. Paul Van Bodegraven, Chairman, Department of Music, New York University

Published by Educational Division of Scherl & Roth, Inc.

To help you determine if your instrument is in best possible playing condition.

	Yes	No
A. PEGS		
1. Do they fit snugly in both peg hole openings?		
2. Do they turn smoothly and silently?		
3. Do they hold in position with slight inward pressure while tuning?		
B. FINGERBOARD NUT		
1. Do all strings clear fingerboard without buzzing when playing open or stopped strings?		
2. Are the string grooves in the fingerboard nut shallow?		
C. FINGERBOARD		
1. Is it smooth with no grooves?		
2. Is it glued securely on to the neck?		
3. Is it free of excess glue along edges?		
4. Is it the proper height?		
D. BRIDGE		
1. Is it the proper height?		
2. Do the feet fit perfectly with the top contour? ...		
3. Is the E string on low side of bridge (violin) A string on viola and cello, G string on bass?		
4. Is it set opposite the inside notches on the F holes?		
5. Are all string grooves shallow?		
6. Is it perfectly straight, not warped?		
7. Does it lean slightly towards the tailpiece?		
8. Is there sufficient arch so the student does not have difficulty playing from one string to the other? ..		
E. TAILPIECE		
1. Is the small end of tailpiece almost even with the outside edge of saddle?		
2. Is there some space between it and top of instrument?		
3. Is there a clearance between tailpiece and chinrest?		
F. STRINGS		
1. Are all perfectly smooth, without kinks?		
2. Is the metal winding tight?		
3. Are the adjusters on all metal strings working smoothly?		
4. Are the strings free of caked rosin?		
5. Do you have an extra set of strings in your case? .		
6. Are your reserve strings sealed from dryness?		
7. If you have any steel strings on your instrument, are they equipped with adjusters?		

	Yes	No
G. INSTRUMENT BODY		
1. Is it free from open cracks?		
2. Is the top clean and free of caked rosin?		
3. Are the front and back thoroughly glued to the ribs?		
H. THE SOUNDPOST		
1. Is it directly behind the right foot of the bridge? ..		
2. Is it perpendicular to top and back?		
3. Is the soundpost setter slot facing the right F hole?		
I. THE BOW		
1. Can it be loosened and tightened freely?		
2. Does it have enough hair?		
3. Does the hair extend the full width of the frog ferrule?		
4. Has it been rehaired in the past year?		
5. Is the bow stick free of caked rosin?		
6. Does it have real wire winding and leather thumb grip?		
7. Is the bow arch noticeable when it is tightened ready to play?		
8. Is there a protective facing, ivory or metal, on the tip?		
J. CHINREST		
1. Is the chinrest securely attached to instrument? ...		
2. Is the chinrest free of broken edges?		
3. Is it of proper height for correct posture and comfortable playing?		
K. ROSIN		
1. Do you have a full size (unbroken) cake of rosin? .		
2. Do you have a clean cake of rosin?		
3. Are you using rosin for the individual bow, i.e. (violin, cello, bass rosin)?		
L. MUTE		
1. Do you have a mute attached to your instrument ready for instant use? (Sihon mute)		
M. CELLO AND BASSES		
1. Is the adjustable endpin in proper working order? ..		
2. Do you have a cello or bass endpin rest that prevents instrument slipping while playing?		

ALL ANSWERS SHOULD BE "YES"

Instructions to correct faults of your instrument are found in repair manual,
"YOU FIX THEM," published by Scherl & Roth Inc.

INSTRUMENT_____ SERIAL NO._____ DATES INSPECTED_____

1st quarter   2nd quarter

_____ _____   TEACHER_____ STUDENT NAME_____

3rd quarter   4th quarter

ADDRESS_____ TELEPHONE NUMBER_____ GRADE_____

SCHOOL_____

APPENDIX III

List of Teaching
Materials for Strings

There is a great deal of string teaching material available. By far the greatest amount is for the violin with the cello coming next. Neither the quantity nor the variety has been written for the viola and bass. A good deal of material has been written for string classes; so the conscientious director should not have difficulty finding material which is suitable for his group. It should not be necessary to stress the importance of using a variety of materials. This keeps up interest and more nearly assures the teacher that none of the important techniques will be omitted.

The best up-to-date sources of information about publications are the publisher's catalogs. These can be seen at most music stores which handle music. The American String Teachers Association publishes a list of string teaching materials. This may be obtained for a small charge by writing School of Music, University of Illinois, Urbana Illinois. Periodically Music Educators National Conference publishes a list of solo and ensemble materials. This may be obtained from MENC, 1201 16th St. Washington 6, D. C. The title of the publication is: Music Lists. (Instrumental and Vocal Solos, Instrumental and Vocal Ensembles).

STRING CLASS METHODS

AUTHOR	TITLE	PUBLISHER	DESCRIPTION OR COMMENTS
Applebaum, Samuel	Belwin String Builder	Belwin	Books 1, 2, 3; piano acc.; teachers manual.
D'Auberge, Alfred	The String Musician	Alfred	A fundamental, illustrative course designed specifically for the beginning string class. Violin, viola, cello, bass, piano conductor score.
Best, George	All-Strings	Varitone Inc.	A basic group method for violins, violas, cellos, basses in any combination. Two books with full score and piano acc.
Bornoff, George	Bornoff's Finger Patterns	C. Fischer	A basic method for strings.
Dasch and Bennett	The Aeolian String Ensemble Method	Fitzsimons	For group or individual instruction. Violin, viola, cello, bass, cond. score. Books I, II, III.
Feldman, Harry	Unison String Class Method	Pro Art	An elementary course for group or individual instruction. Violin-viola, cello-bass, cond.
Fischel, Max and Bennett, Aileen	Gamble's Class Method for Strings	Gamble or Remick	Adapted for separate class instruction of each instrument or any ensemble combination of violin, viola, cello, or bass. Books 1, 2, 3.
Gordon, Beckstead, Stone	Visual Method	Highland Music Co.	For strings, class or private instruction for beginners on all string instruments.
Herman, Helen	Bow and Strings	Belwin	Class or individual instruction. Books I, II, III for each instrument, with piano acc. and teachers manual.
Herfurth, C. Paul	A Tune A Day	Boston Music Co.	Books 1, 2, 3 for violin and viola; 1 and 2 for cello, 1 for bass; piano accompaniments for books 1 and 2; teachers manual. Books 1 and 2 for some wind instruments.
Isaac, Merle	String Class Method	M. M. Cole Pub. Co.	Two books for all strings, piano accompaniment with score.
Jones, Dasch, and Krone	Strings from the Start	C. Fischer	Provides training in solo and ensemble playing for violin, viola, cello and bass. Parts I and II; parent-teacher's manual, score, student's notebook.

AUTHOR	TITLE	PUBLISHER	DESCRIPTION OR COMMENTS
Keller, Marjorie and Taylor, Maurice	Easy Steps to the Orchestra	Mills	A course for beginning string players, suitable for class or individual instruction or any combination of violins, violas, cellos and string basses. Violin, viola, cello or bass Books I and II. Also wind books.
Lesinsky	Rythm Master Method	Gamble Hinged Music Co.	An elementary method designed as the orchestra player's prerequisite. Any combination of strings. Books 1, 2, 3.
Lockhart, Lee M.	The Lockhart String-Class Method	Witmark	Violin, viola, cello, bass, teacher's score, piano score.
Maddy and Giddings	Universal Teacher for Orchestra and Band	Willis Music Co.	A method adapted for class or private lessons containing ensemble pieces for any combination of string or wind instruments or any three instruments of the same kind. Piano accompaniment.
Muller, J. Frederick, Rusch, Harold	Muller-Rusch String Method for Class or Individual Instruction	Kjos	Books for violin, viola, cello, and bass.
Waller, Gilbert	String Class Method	Kjos	For class or private instruction of beginners on all string instruments. Books I and II for violin, viola, cello, bass.
Whistler and Nord	Beginning Strings	C. Fischer	For class or private instruction. Based upon materials and procedures taken from the celebrated violin methods of Hohmann, Wohlfahrt, DeBeriot, Dancla, Alard, and other world masters. Violin, viola, cello, bass, piano accompaniment.
Zwissler, Ruth	First Lessons for Beginning Strings	Highland	Start by rote. Books for all strings.

Most string class methods may be used satisfactorily for individual instruction.

OTHER MATERIALS FOR STRING CLASS INSTRUCTION

AUTHOR	TITLE	PUBLISHER	DESCRIPTION OR COMMENTS
Applebaum, Samuel	Scales for Strings	Belwin	Supplementary studies to develop the string ensemble. Violin, viola, cello, bass, teacher's manual, piano acc.
Applebaum, Samuel	Third and Fifth Position String Builder	Belwin	A continuation of the Belwin String Builder or any other standard string class method.
Bergh, Harris	String Positions	Summy-Birchard	Violin, viola, cello, string bass, full score (and piano acc.)
Best, George	Early String Shifting (5 minutes a day with any method)	Varitone	Violin, viola, cello, bass, full score.
Fussell, Raymond C.	Exercises for Ensemble Drill	Schmitt, Hall, & McCreary Co.	A series of warming up exercises, technical studies and rhythm drill for daily practice by any group—large or small. Arranged for band or orchestra.
Johnson, Harold	The Positions for All Strings	Fitzsimons	A class method for studies in the positions. Violin, viola, cello, bass, conductor's score.
Preston, Herbert	Direct Approach to the Higher Positions for String Classes	Belwin	Violin, viola, cello, string bass, teacher's manual and score with piano acc. for all melodies.
Reese, Wendel	22 Studies for Strings	Belwin	For individual or class instruction. In unison or ensemble. Violin, viola, cello, string bass, piano conductor.
Waller, Gilbert	Waller Vibrato Method	Kjos	A practical approach to vibrato development for all string players.
Whistler and Hummel	Elementary Scales and Bowings for Strings	Rubank	For individual and class instruction, string ensembles, string sections. Violin, viola, cello, string bass, piano accompaniment, full score.
Yaus, Grover	47 Foundation Studies	Belwin	In unison for band or orchestra.

Violin Methods

AUTHOR	TITLE	PUBLISHER	DESCRIPTION OR COMMENTS
Auer, Leopold (Gustav Saenger)	Graded Course of Violin Playing	C. Fischer	A complete outline of violin study ranging from pre-elementary grade to virtuoso accomplishment, with prefatory and incidental text, additional exercises and duets, and systematic grading of all material. Eight books.
Bang, Maia	Violin Method Based on the Teaching Principles of Leopold Auer	C. Fischer	In seven parts. Part I–Elementary Rudiments, Part II–More advanced Studies, Part III–3rd and 2nd Positions, Part IV–4th and 5th Positions, Part V–6th and 7th Positions, Part VI–Higher Art of Bowing, Part VII–Piano Accompaniment.
Barbakoff, Samuel	Fiddling by the Numbers	C. Fischer	A rote method.
Dancla, Chas.	Conservatory Method (Elementary and Progressive Method)	C. Fischer	Two volumes.
Doflein, Erich and Elma	The Doflein Method	Schott	Five volumes. Vol. 1–The beginning, Vol. 2–Development of Technique, Vol. 3–2nd and 3rd Positions, Vol. 4–Further Technique in bowing and fingering, Vol. 5–The Higher Positions.
Fischel, Max	Standard Graded Material for the Violin, Op. 11: Books 1, 2, 3, 4	Gamble Hinged Music Co.	Book 1–Preparatory Violin School for Beginners, Book 2–Graded Material in 1st Position, Book 3–Preparatory Position Studies, Book 4–Advanced Position Studies.
Gardner, Samuel	Violin Method	Boston	Two Volumes. Book 1–Elementary, Book 2–Intermediate.
Hohmann-Wohlfahrt (Whistler)	Beginning Method for Violin	Rubank	Two Volumes. A compilation of two famous methods, entirely revised, re-edited and re-styled to meet the demands of modern education.
Kendall, John	Listen and Play	Summy-Birchard	Based on the Suzuki method.
Laoureux, Nicolas	A Practical Method for Violin	Schirmer	Four Parts. Part I–Elements of Bowing and Left Hand Technique, Part II–Five Positions, Part III–School of Bowing, Part IV–Virtuosity of the Left Hand. With supplements.

Author	Title	Publisher	Description or Comments
Riegger, Wallingford	Begin With Pieces	Schirmer	Elementary method of individual or class instruction using short pieces. Piano accompaniment.
Scheer, Leo	Scheer Violin Method	Belwin	Two Books. Visual aids and tuneful technical studies.
Wohlfahrt	Easiest Elementary Method for Beginners	Schirmer	

OTHER MATERIALS FOR THE VIOLIN
Elementary to Intermediate

AUTHOR	TITLE	PUBLISHER	DESCRIPTION OR COMMENTS
Applebaum, Samuel	Building Technic With Beautiful Music	Belwin	Four Volumes. Progressive through 3rd position.
Johannsen, Anna	Scale Melodies for Violin In The First Position	Birchard	Goes through the keys. Simple scales and pieces with varied rhythms.
Keloeber, Robert	Elementary Scale and Chord Studies	Rubank	Begins simply but progresses rapidly to double-stops, chromatics, scales in thirds, etc.
Sevcik, O.	Exercises in the 1st Position, Op. 1, Part 1	Schirmer	
Sitt	20 Etudes in the 1st Position, Op. 32, Book I	Schirmer	
Whistler	First Etude Album	Rubank	Includes a choice selection of 62 elementary etudes, carefully graded, fingered, and bowed by Whistler and Hummel.
Whistler	Scales in First Position	Rubank	
Wohlfahrt (Blay)	60 Studies in 1st Position, Op. 45, Book I	Schirmer	
Wohlfahrt	40 Elementary Studies, Op. 54	Schirmer	
Wohlfahrt	50 Easy Melodious Studies, Op. 74, Book 1, 1st Position	Schirmer	

Intermediate to Advanced

AUTHOR	TITLE	PUBLISHER	DESCRIPTION OR COMMENTS
Fischel, Max	Scale and Technical Studies, Op. 9	Gamble Hinged Music Co.	
Fischel, Max	Double Stop and Technical Studies, Op. 10, Books 1 & 2	Gamble Hinged Music Co.	
Mazas	40 Selected Studies, Op. 36	Schirmer	Melodious studies.
Paulson, Joseph	Studies in the Positions for Violin	Pro Art	Progressive exercises, melodic etudes. Book I—3rd, 5th, & 7th Positions; Book II—2nd, 4th, 6th, 8th, & 9th Positions.
Schradieck	School of Violin Technics Book 1	Schirmer	Exercises for promoting dexterity in the various positions.
Schradieck	Scale Studies	Schirmer	One octave through three octave scales, single note. Scales in thirds, sixths, octaves, tenths.
Schradieck	School of Violin Technics, Book II	Schirmer	Exercises in Double Stops.
Sevcik, O.	School of Violin Technics, Op. 1, Part II	Schirmer	Exercises in the 2nd to 7th Positions.
Sevcik, O.	School of Violin Technics, Op. 1, Part III	Schirmer	Shifting exercises.
Sitt	20 Etudes with Change of Position, Op. 32, Book III	Schirmer	
Sitt	20 Etudes in the 2nd, 3rd, 4th, & 5th Positions, Op. 32, Book II	Schirmer	
Trott, Josephine	Melodious Double-Stops, Books I and II	Schirmer	Progressive melodious etudes.
Whistler	Introducing the Positions	Rubank	Vol. I—3rd and 5th positions, Vol. II—2nd, 4th, 6th, and higher positions.
Whistler	Developing Double-Stops	Rubank	A complete course in double notes and chords from the first through the fifth and higher positions. Includes etudes in thirds, sixths, octaves, tenths, and chords.

AUTHOR	TITLE	PUBLISHER	DESCRIPTION OR COMMENTS
Whistler	Preparing For Kreutzer	Rubank	An intermediate course of violin study based on the famous works of Kayser, Mazas, Dont, etc. Vol. I–Etudes in first through higher positions, trills, and double stops. Vol. II–Etudes in minor keys, double stops, concert caprices.
Wohlfahrt	50 Easy Melodious Studies, Op. 74, Book II	Schirmer	Studies in 3rd Position.
Wohlfahrt	60 Studies, Op. 45, Book II	Schirmer	Studies in 3rd Position.

Advanced

AUTHOR	TITLE	PUBLISHER	DESCRIPTION OR COMMENTS
Dont	24 Exercises Preparatory to Kreutzer and Rode, Op. 37	Schirmer	
Dont	24 Etudes and Caprices, Op. 35	Schirmer	These studies are extremely demanding in all phases of left hand and bowing techniques.
Dont	Progressive Studies with Accompaniment of 2nd violin, Op. 38	Schirmer	
Fiorillo	36 Studies or Caprices	Schirmer	
Flesch	Scale System	C. Fischer	Scale exercises in all major and minor keys, single notes, 3rds, 6ths, 8vas, tenths, and harmonics.
Gavinies	24 Studies	Schirmer	
Hrimaly	Scale Studies	Schirmer	Single note and double stops.
Kreutzer	42 Studies or Caprices	Schirmer	Probably the most famous of all books of studies for violin. Moderately difficult to very difficult.
Mazas	75 Melodious and Progressive Studies, Op. 36	Schirmer	
Mazas	30 Special Studies, Op. 36, Book I	Schirmer	Excellently written and very musical studies. Used as preparation for Kreutzer.
Mazas	27 Brilliant Studies, Op. 36, Book II	Schirmer	Very difficult.
Mazas	18 Artists' Studies, Op. 36, Book III	Schirmer	Extremely difficult.

AUTHOR	TITLE	PUBLISHER	DESCRIPTION OR COMMENTS
Rode	12 Etudes	Schirmer	Difficult studies which logically follow Kreutzer.
Rode	24 Caprices	Schirmer	Difficult studies which logically follow Kreutzer.
Rovelli	12 Caprices, Op. 3, 5	Schirmer	
Schradieck	Chord Studies	Schirmer	Specific studies designed to improve chord playing.
Wieniawski	8 Etudes-Caprices, Op. 18	Schirmer	Excellent and very musical etudes with 2nd violin accompaniment. Very difficult.

Special Study Materials

AUTHOR	TITLE	PUBLISHER	DESCRIPTION OR COMMENTS
Dounis, D. C.	The Artist's Technique of Violin Playing, Op. 12	C. Fischer	Technical studies designed to improve facility of the left hand and the bow.
Dounis, D. C.	The Higher Development of Thirds and Fingered Octaves, Op. 30	C. Fischer	
Flesch, Carl	Urstudien (Basic Studies)	C. Fischer	A series of scientifically designed exercises for the advanced violinist with limited time to practice.

VIOLA METHODS

AUTHOR	TITLE	PUBLISHER	DESCRIPTION OR COMMENTS
Fischer, Bernard	Modern Viola Fundamentals	Willis Music Co.	Easy progressive material.
Gardner, Samuel	Viola Method	Boston	Two Volumes. Book 1–Elementary, Book 2–Intermediate.
Sitt	Practical Viola Method	C. Fischer	
Ward, Sylvan D.	Rubank Intermediate Method	Rubank	A follow-up course for individual or like-instrument class instruction. Easy to intermediate.

OTHER MATERIALS FOR VIOLA
Elementary to Intermediate

AUTHOR	TITLE	PUBLISHER	DESCRIPTION OR COMMENTS
Bornoff	Finger Patterns	Gordon Thompson	
Bornoff	Patterns in Positions	Gordon Thompson	Double stops, harmonics, shifting.

AUTHOR	TITLE	PUBLISHER	DESCRIPTION OR COMMENTS
Kayser	36 Elementary and Progressive Studies, Op. 20	Schirmer	
Wohlfahrt	Foundation Studies	Schirmer	Two books. Book I—1st position, Book II—30 studies in three positions.
Whistler	From Violin to Viola	Rubank	Easy studies designed to help the violinist make the change from violin to viola.
Whistler	Introducing The Positions	Rubank	Two volumes. Vol. I—3rd and half positions, Vol. II—2nd, 4th, and 5th positions.

Advanced

AUTHOR	TITLE	PUBLISHER	DESCRIPTION OR COMMENTS
Anzoletti	Dodici Studi, Op. 125	Ricordi	Extremely difficult studies and theme and variations.
Bruni	25 Melodies and Characteristic Studies	C. Fischer or Schirmer	Moderately difficult to difficult.
Campagnoli	41 Caprices	Schirmer	Difficult to very difficult.
Dont (Svencenski)	20 Progressive Studies for Viola	Schirmer	With second viola.
Dont (Bailly)	Twenty-four Viola Studies, After Op. 35	Schirmer	Transcribed from the violin etudes. Difficult.
Flesch, Carl (Karman)	Scale System	C. Fischer	Adapted from the violin book.
Gavinies (Spitzner)	24 Etudes	Boosey-Hawkes	Difficult. From the violin book.
Kievman, Louis	Practicing The Viola, Mentally-Physically	Kelton Pub.	Programmed instruction studies for daily reference.
Matz, A.	Intonation Studies	Boosey-Hawkes	Five books.
Primrose, William	The Art and Practice of Scale Playing on the Viola	Mills Music Inc.	Gives special attention to shifting with comment about the use of open strings.
Rode (Blumenau)	24 Caprices	Schirmer	Difficult. From the violin book.
Volmer	Bratschenschule	AMP	

CELLO METHODS

AUTHOR	TITLE	PUBLISHER	DESCRIPTION OR COMMENTS
Bornschein, Franz C.	First Lessons On the Violoncello	Oliver Ditson Co.	Goes through three octave scales.
Deak, Stephen	Modern Method for the Violoncello	Elkan-Vogel Co., Inc.	Two volumes. Vol. 1—through 7th position. Vol. 2—26 studies of medium difficulty.
Dotzauer, J. J. F.	Violoncello Method	C. Fischer	Two volumes. Vol. 1—exercises and pieces in first position. Vol. 2—more advanced material.
Fuchs	Violoncello Method	Schott	3 volumes.
Langey, Otto	Otto Langey's Celebrated Tutors	C. Fischer	Moves rapidly to difficult material in one volume.
Potter, Louis Jr.	The Art of Cello Playing	Summy-Birchard Co.	Considerable explanatory text with pictures. Moves gradually to advanced level.
Schröder, Carl	Violoncello Method	C. Fischer	Three volumes. Part I—through two octave scales. Part II—first four positions and half position. Part III—thumb position, octaves, and double stops.
Stutschevsky, J.	The Art of Playing Violoncello	Schott	Four books.
Werner, Jos.	Practical Method for Violoncello	C. Fischer	Two volumes. Vol. I—through two octave scales. Vol. II—advanced techniques.

OTHER MATERIALS FOR THE CELLO

AUTHOR	TITLE	PUBLISHER	DESCRIPTION OR COMMENTS
Cossman, B.	Cello Studies	Schott	
Dotzauer	62 Select Studies	C. Fischer	Two volumes. Easy to difficult.
Dotzauer, J. J. F.	113 Etudes	Litolff	Three volumes of graded etudes.
Dotzauer	18 Exercises, Op. 120	Boosey-Hawkes	
Duport, Jean Louis	Twenty-one Etudes	Schirmer	
Feuillard, L. R.	Daily Exercises	Schott	
Francesconi, G.	Practical School for Violoncello	Suvini Zerbone	Three volumes. Vol. I—1st position, Vol. II—all positions, Vol. III—advanced exercises.
Franchomme, A. (Becker)	12 Caprices, Op. 7	Schott	With second cello.

Author	Title	Publisher	Description or Comments
Frank, M.	Scales and Arpeggios	Schott	Studies on all four strings, pieces, and scales in thumb position.
Grant, Francis	Basic Thumb Position Studies for the Young Cellist	Concert Music Pub.	Difficult to very advanced.
Guerini-Silva	Thirteen Studies	Ricordi	
Klengel, J.	Daily Exercises	Boosey-Hawkes	Three volumes.
Klengel, J.	Technical Studies	Boosey-Hawkes	Four volumes.
Kummer, F. A.	10 Etudes Melodiques, Op. 57	Peters	Ten etudes of medium difficulty with second cello accompaniment.
Kummer, F. A.	Studien fur Violoncello, Op. 106	Peters	Eight etudes with second cello.
Lebell, L.	The Technique of the Lower Positions, Op. 22	Schott	Two volumes.
Merk (Klengel)	20 Studies, Op. 11	International	Moderately difficult to difficult.
Schroeder, Alwin	170 Foundation Studies Progressively Arranged	C. Fischer	Three volumes. Progresses to very difficult material.
Schroeder, A.	219 Technical Exercises	Leuckart	
Schulz, W.	Technical Studies for the Advanced Cellist	Schott	
Whistler, Harvey S.	Introducing the Positions For Cello	Rubank	Two volumes. Vol. 1–Fourth position; Vol. 2 –2nd through third and a half position.

BASS METHODS

AUTHOR	TITLE	PUBLISHER	DESCRIPTION OR COMMENTS
Bottesini	Metodo Per Contrabbasso	Ricordi	Begins at intermediate level and continues through advanced material.
Marcelli, Nino	Carl Fischer Basic Method for the String Bass	Fischer	Two volumes. Book I–half position through second position, Book II–third position through seventh position.
Simandl, F.	New Method for the Double Bass	Fischer	Two volumes. Book I–all positions and scales. Book II–advanced studies and techniques.

OTHER MATERIALS FOR BASS

AUTHOR	TITLE	PUBLISHER	DESCRIPTION OR COMMENTS
Findeisen	25 Technical Studies	International	Four volumes.
Hrabe	86 Etudes	International	
Kayser (Winsel)	36 Studies, Op. 20	International	
Kreutzer-Simandl	18 Studies	International	
Lee	Studies, Op. 31	International	
Madenski, E.	Double Bass Studies	Universal	Two volumes.
Schwabe	Scale Studies	International	
Simandl	30 Etudes for the String Bass	Fischer	
Simandl	Gradus ad Parnassuma 24 Studies	International	Two volumes. Difficult to very difficult.
Slama, Anton	66 Studies in all Keys	International	
Storch-Hrabe	57 Studies	International	Two volumes.

Special Materials

AUTHOR	TITLE	PUBLISHER	DESCRIPTION OR COMMENTS
Green, Elizabeth A. H.	Musicianship and Repertoire for the High School Orchestra	Presser	Musical and technical problems arranged in a key-sequence.
Janowsky, Edward	Note Speller	Belwin	For violin, viola, cello, and bass. Provides exercises in writing on the staff.

Bibliography

AUER, LEOPOLD, *Violin Playing As I Teach It*, Philadelphia: Lippincott, 1960.

BACHMAN, ALBERTO, *An Encyclopedia of the Violin*, New York: D. Appleton-Century Co., 1937.

BIRGE, EDWARD BAILEY, *History of Public School Music In the United States*, Washington, D. C.: Music Educators National Conference, 1966.

BOYDEN, DAVID, *The History of Violin Playing, From Its Origins to 1761 and Its Relationship to the Violin And Violin Music*, London, New York: Oxford University Press, 1965.

COLWELL, RICHARD J., *The Teaching of Instrumental Music*. New York: Appleton-Century-Crofts, Educational Division, Meredith Corporation, 1969.

COOK, CLIFFORD A., *String Teaching And Some Related Topics*, Urbana, Ill.: American String Teachers Association, 1957.

DOLEJSI, ROBERT, *Modern Viola Technique*, Chicago, Ill.: The University of Chicago Press, 1939.

EDWARDS, ARTHUR C., *String Ensemble Method for Teacher Education*, Dubuque: Wm. C. Brown Company Publishers, 1959.

EISENBERG, MAURICE, *Cello Playing of Today*, London: The Strad., 1957.

FLESCH, CARL, *The Art of Violin Playing*, Books I & II, New York: Carl Fischer, Inc., 1939.

GALAMIAN, IVAN, *Principles of Violin Playing and Teaching*, Englewood Cliffs, N. J.: Prentice-Hall, Inc., 1962.

GREEN, ELIZABETH A. H., *Orchestral Bowings*, Ann Arbor, Michigan: The Edwards Letter Shop, 1949.

GREEN, ELIZABETH A. H., *Teaching Stringed Instruments In Classes*, Englewood Cliffs, N. J.: Prentice-Hall, Inc., 1966.

Grove's Dictionary of Music and Musicians. (10 Volumes) New York: MacMillan and Co., 1954.

HAVAS, KATO, *A New Approach to Violin Playing*, London: Bosworth, 1961.

HERON-ALLEN, EDWARD, *De Fidiculis Bibliographia; Being An Attempt Towards a Bibliography of the Violin and All Other Instruments Played With the Bow In Ancient and Modern Times*, London: Holland Press, 1961.

KENNAN, KENT WHEELER, *The Technique of Orchestration*, Englewood Cliffs, N. J.: Prentice-Hall, Inc., 1952.

KLOTMAN, ROBERT H., *Scheduling Music Classes*, Washington, D. C.: Music Educators National Conference, 1968.

KRAYK, STEFAN, *The Violin Guide (For Performers, Teachers and Students)*, Hollywood, Calif.: Highland Music Co., 1966.

KUHN, WOLFGANG, *The Strings; Performance and Instructional Techniques*, Boston: Allyn and Bacon, 1967.

KUHN, WOLFGANG, *Principles of String Class Teaching*, Rockville Centre, N. Y.: Belwin, 1957.

MATESKY AND RUSH, *Playing and Teaching Stringed Instruments*, Parts I & II, Englewood Cliffs, N. J.: Prentice-Hall, Inc., 1964.

MUSIC EDUCATORS NATIONAL CONFERENCE, *The String Instruction Program In Music Education*, A series of ten reports concerned with string instruction and string program. Washington, D. C. 1957-1959. Book II in this series is a bibliography for string teachers.

MUSIC EDUCATORS NATIONAL CONFERENCE, *Music Buildings, Rooms, and Equipment*, Washington, D. C., 1966.

NORMANN, THEODORE F., *Instrumental Music In the Public Schools*, Philadelphia, Pa.: Oliver Ditson Co., 1939.

POTTER, LOUIS ALEXANDER, *The Art of Cello Playing; A Complete Textbook Method for Private or Class Instruction*, Evanston, Ill.: Summy-Birchard Co., 1964.

RETFORD, WILLIAM CHARLES, *Bows and Bow Makers*, London: Strad., 1964.

RICHTER, CHARLES BOARDMAN, *Teaching Instrumental Music*, New York: Carl Fischer, 1959.

RODA, JOSEPH, *Bows for Musical Instruments of the Violin Family*, Chicago: W. Lewis, 1959.

TANGLEWOOD STRING SYMPOSIA, THE, (Louis Krasner, Chairman.) *String Problems, Players & Paucity*, Berkshire Music Center with the Cooperation of the School of Music, Syracuse University, 1965.

TRZCINSKI, LOUIS C., *Planning the School String Program*, New York: Mills Music Co., 1963.

The American String Teachers Association periodical on string instruments and string teaching, *American String Teacher*, the association's official periodical, is the source of a great deal of current research and practice in the area of string teaching and playing.